Psychoanalytic Approaches to Problems in Living

Psychoanalytic Approaches to Problems in Living examines how psychoanalysts can draw on their training, reading, and clinical experience to help their patients address some of the recurrent challenges of everyday life. Sandra Buechler offers clinicians poetic, psychoanalytic, and experiential approaches to problems, drawing on her personal and clinical experience, as well as ideas from her reading, to confront challenges familiar to us all.

Buechler addresses issues including difficulties of mourning, aging, living with uncertainty, finding meaningful work, transcending pride, bearing helplessness, and forgiving life's hardships. For those contemplating a clinical career, and those in its beginning stages, she suggests ways to prepare to face these quandaries in treatment sessions. More experienced practitioners will find echoes of themes that have run through their own clinical and personal life experiences. The chapters demonstrate that insights from a poem can often guide the clinician as well as concepts garnered from psychoanalytic theory and other sources. Buechler puts her questions to T. S. Eliot, Rainer Maria Rilke, Elizabeth Bishop, W. S. Merwin, Stanley Kunitz and many other poets and fiction writers. She "asks" Sharon Olds how to meet emergencies, Erich Fromm how to live vigorously, and Edith Wharton how to age gracefully, and brings their insights to bear as she addresses challenges that make frequent appearances in clinical sessions, and other walks of life.

With a final section designed to improve training in the light of her practical findings, *Psychoanalytic Approaches to Problems in Living* is an essential book for all practicing psychoanalysts and psychoanalytic psychotherapists.

Sandra Buechler is a training and supervising analyst at the William Alanson White Institute, New York, USA. She is also a supervisor at Columbia Presbyterian Hospital's internship and postdoctoral programs, and a supervisor at the Institute for Contemporary Psychotherapy. Her Routledge publications include *Clinical Values: Emotions that Guide Psychoanalytic Treatment* (2004), *Making a Difference in Patients' Lives: Emotional Experience in the Therapeutic Setting* (2008), *Still Practicing: The Heartaches and Joys of a Clinical Career* (2012) and *Understanding and Treating Patients in Clinical Psychoanalysis: Lessons from Literature* (2014).

Psychoanalytic Approaches to Problems in Living

Addressing Life's Challenges in Clinical Practice

Sandra Buechler

Routledge
Taylor & Francis Group

LONDON AND NEW YORK

First published 2019
by Routledge
2 Park Square, Milton Park, Abingdon, Oxon OX14 4RN

and by Routledge
52 Vanderbilt Avenue, New York, NY 10017

Routledge is an imprint of the Taylor & Francis Group, an informa business

British Library Cataloguing in Publication Data
A catalogue record for this book is available from the British Library

Library of Congress Cataloging in Publication Data
Names: Buechler, Sandra, author.
Title: Psychoanalytic approaches to problems in living : addressing
    life's challenges in clinical practice / Sandra Buechler.
Description: Abingdon, Oxon ; New York, NY : Routledge, [2019] |
    Includes bibliographical references and index.
Identifiers: LCCN 2018047273 (print) | LCCN 2018048571 (ebook)
    | ISBN 9781351204996 (Master) | ISBN 9781351204965
    (Mobipocket) | ISBN 9781351204989 (Pdf) | ISBN
    9781351204972 (ePub 3) | ISBN 9780815383451 (hardback) |
    ISBN 9780815383468 (pbk.)
Subjects: LCSH: Psychoanalysis. | Psychotherapist and patient.
Classification: LCC RC506 (ebook) | LCC RC506 .B8375 2019
    (print) | DDC 616.89/17—dc23
LC record available at https://lccn.loc.gov/2018047273

ISBN: 978-0-8153-8345-1 (hbk)
ISBN: 978-0-8153-8346-8 (pbk)
ISBN: 978-1-351-20499-6 (ebk)

Typeset in Times New Roman
by Swales & Willis Ltd, Exeter, Devon, UK

For Daphne, Phoebe, Isaac, Eva, their parents, and George

Contents

Acknowledgments   viii
List of permissions   ix

Introduction: Problems in living   1

1 Capacity for aloneness and relationship: Love between
   two solitudes   17

2 Mourning   33

3 Healthy aging   50

4 Cognitive, emotional, and interpersonal sources of resilience   73

5 Bearing uncertainty, upholding conviction, and
   maintaining curiosity   92

6 Finding meaningful work and nourishing interests   115

7 Transcending pride, shame, and guilt: Some sources of
   feelings of insufficiency   134

8 Forgiving   149

9 Societal and personal attitudes about suffering:
   Conclusions and speculations   166

10 Training   185

   Index   210

Acknowledgments

As usual, I understand this book better in retrospect than I did while writing it. It continues conversations (with myself and others) from my previous work. All my writing can be read as an extended effort to come to terms with mourning, aging, uncertainty, loneliness, and other fundamental human challenges. I have learned what I could from my own life experience and from my patients, teachers, students, friends, and family. I am grateful to you, for peopling my life.

I owe an enormous debt of gratitude to Kristopher Spring, for his dedicated, patient, thorough assistance. Without him, the book could not have been written. I also want to thank Kate Hawes, Charles Bath, and all those who worked on the manuscript at Routledge. Donnel Stern, our series editor, has been a source of encouragement and support throughout my writing career.

My peer supervision group (better known as the Viceroys), Mark Blechner, Richard Gartner, John O'Leary, Allison Rosen, and Robert Watson, has always sustained me. I am also grateful to the William Alanson White Institute for providing the analytic education that is the substrate of all my work.

Considering the somber subjects of my writing would not be possible for me without the love and joy given to me by Eric and Zoe, their children Daphne and Phoebe, and Michelle and Nick, and their children Isaac and Eva. My late husband, George Hammer, was, and will always be, a source of strength.

List of permissions

Introduction
Problems in living

People often seek treatment for help with one (or more) of life's fundamental dilemmas. Should I try to accept aging gracefully or fight to keep youthful? After a loss, should I force myself to "move on" to another relationship? Am I being selfish, or too greedy, if I want more out of life than I am getting? How much must I object to the outrageous injustices I see being perpetrated in my community, and in the world at large? When is it time to fight, to stand up for what I think is right?

Clinicians frequently face a peculiar bind. We are not sages. We do not know the "right way" to live. We encounter the same quandaries in our own lives, and often feel as bewildered as anyone else. And yet, someone has come to us for help. Many of us find ourselves wishing that our training had better prepared us for the tasks patients present.

When I was in college, one particular joke was very popular. A professor asks a student to explain Einstein's theory. Ignorant of Einstein's theory, the student replies, "Who am I, a mere college sophomore, to explain Einstein's theory? Now as for . . ." In the rest of the sentence, the student answers an easier question.

I am reminded of that joke often, as patients implicitly or explicitly ask me questions I can't answer. Given my analytic training, I wish people would come into treatment asking to understand themselves better. Some do, and then I feel on more solid ground, since what I learned allows me to feel better equipped to face that challenge. In the course of treatment, many eventually become curious about the workings of their psyches. But, in the early phase, most want a more specific kind of help. My basic premise is that the treatment relationship is sustained by a mutual investment in helping patients live more fulfilling lives. For most of the dilemmas patients bring to treatment, there is no simple, direct, obvious approach. While every patient and every session are different, there are recurrent threads that become familiar over the course of a clinical career. This book applies my clinical, literary, and personal experience, and theoretical perspective, to exploring these challenges.

Those of us who trained analytically, and many others, were taught to "educate" patients and, in effect, convince them to want what we have to offer. Subtly interwoven was a hierarchical attitude. Patients who could aim for greater self-understanding and prioritize long-range over short-term goals were more evolved.

In my view, we were quite willing to use persuasion to enlist patients in a treatment consonant with our analytic expertise. But then, armed with some version of the ideal of neutrality, we believed that patients would create their style of life, in a process untainted by our own values. We wanted to think we could function purely to facilitate, not indoctrinate.

But, in my own experience, treatment is never value-free. In sessions, most especially through our selective focus on the material, we inevitably enact our own ways of dealing with fundamental human challenges. This occurs whether or not we consciously intend it. There is a contradiction at the heart of our work. The ideal of neutrality is extremely valuable and should be taught to every aspiring clinician, but it can't and shouldn't mean treatment is value-free. As I have argued elsewhere (Buechler, 2004), the essential human values of the clinician shape our responses to the material, often outside our awareness and certainly outside our conscious control. What we focus on, question, remember, and pass by in silence expresses our priorities. Whether we like it or not, it reveals what we think is important, and what we see as problematic or take for granted as "natural." Our personal cultural upbringing and the assumptions inherent in our training, as well as our individual characters, profoundly affect our behavior in a session. But I would suggest that, aside from the sheer impossibility of conducting a value-free treatment, even if it were achievable, it would not provide the most effective help facing life's greatest challenges. And, whether we like it or not, people will always come to us wanting and, I would argue, needing such help. How can we integrate the enormous benefits of neutrality with an approach that truly augments patients' strengths?

My personal point of view is that analytically trained clinicians (and many others in our culture) have grown wary of making firm statements about living life with emotional strength and, in the process, have forfeited some of our potential to *inspire*. I think that, within the field, many fear the charge of "logical positivism" will be lodged if we express definitive views about any aspect of life. Even mentioning a term like *emotional strength* can raise skeptical eyebrows. This is not a reaction limited to psychoanalysts. In an op-ed piece in the *New York Times*, David Brooks (2016) says it is time to rethink the concept of emotional strength. Basically, he wants to distinguish healthy resilience from a defensive thick skin. He believes that the people whose resilience we most admire are deeply committed to a cause, an ideal, or a relationship. Their determination enables them to bear whatever difficulties they encounter.

Brooks goes on to speculate about sources of what he variously calls grit, resilience, toughness, and emotional strength. He sees these qualities as born of living life with purpose. He voices concern that, in the modern university, in the name of critical thinking, students are encouraged to be detached from purpose. He suggests that human fragility can result from a lack of purpose, or an inability to genuinely commit to other people, or a failure to truly embrace a particular social role for ourselves.

I believe that, in the name of critical thinking, our field has lost its edge. We have become too sophisticated to be inspired or to be inspiring to our patients.

We have become so careful to avoid logical positivism that we have lost some of our passionate conviction in the work we do. In turn, that makes it hard for us to convince insurance to pay for our services, and to influence patients to dedicate themselves to treatment, and to attract and inspire candidates.

Brooks advises that in order for people to become tough, we must evoke their idealism about a cause, or their tenderness for someone else, or their capacity to believe in a hopeful worldview that re-contextualizes our problems. He is critical of current society's notion that only the disenchanted are really sophisticated. On the contrary, he believes that those capable of enchantment can become the real tough customers. We need our candidates to become tough customers, and they will need to be able to inspire their patients to become tough customers, too.

Looked at from another angle, I am asking how our implicit and explicit visions of health affect our clinical work. Adam Phillips (2005) has commented on how hard it is to practice without a clearly formulated notion of healthy functioning.

> Even to consider, as I do in this part, how to rear a sane child, or what a sane sexual life would be like; or, perhaps even more bewilderingly now, what it would be like to have a sane attitude toward money, is to realize just how much sanity—if it is something we aim at—has to be aimed at without a target. Whether, for example, there is such a thing as sane violence has become perhaps our most pressing political concern. Most people don't want to be insane about such important matters, and yet the alternatives to insanity about these issues are not quite clear.
>
> (p. xix)

Thus, it is unrealistic and unproductive to aim to work without a vision of health, but, once we articulate that vision, what happens to our ability to treat rather than indoctrinate? Can we still facilitate a process where the patient freely explores and articulates a personally resonant approach to life?

Much of my writing (Buechler, 2004, 2008, 2012, 2015, 2017) comes from my effort to raise my own consciousness of the "response biases" I bring to my clinical work. How have I been shaped by my background, as a citizen, a reader, born in a particular time and place, growing up in a specific environment, educated and professionally trained in particular schools of thought?

In my previous work, I explored the values I think most clinicians share (2004), the emotions and thought processes we have in common (2008), the professional phases we undergo (2012), and the specific challenges we face working with people who come to treatment with a variety of character styles (2015). In the present book, I ask how we can prepare to face some of the fundamental issues our patients raise. Poets, fiction writers, psychologists, philosophers, sociologists, and many others have contributed thoughts about facing aloneness, loss, aging, uncertainty, suffering, shame, helplessness, and other hardships that are part of the human condition. What can I offer patients struggling with these challenges?

I believe that I can bring my life experience, my clinical experience, and insights drawn from theory. This does not provide (for me or my patients) a how-to manual about life. But it does offer a sense of the frequently occurring questions life brings us all. It provides templates. It helps me conceptualize some fundamental issues, such as the question of when to adapt to circumstances and when to fight for change. Thus, I can hear a particular person's dilemma as, at least on one level, a variant on a theme. This can help me reformulate their question. I believe that, very often, reformulating dilemmas is the clinician's contribution to the patient's struggle toward personally resonant responses to life's predicaments.

It is very hard to write about these subjects without resorting to binaries. Of course, none of us always adapts or always fights for change. More specifically, no one mourns, or ages, or functions in relationships in a clear-cut way that can be captured in a phrase. Yet I have come to believe that there are some fundamental alternatives that recur in many walks of life. In this book, I concentrate on three of these overarching divides:

1   How much is health a matter of graceful adaptation to change or determined resistance to it?
2   Should we aim for the most intense and passionate emotionality or more modulated feelings?
3   Is the most valuable, growth-enhancing human (clinical and non-clinical) experience formulated into words or left unsaid?

In my mind, it is fortunate that these divides also play out in sessions with patients. For example, in a therapeutic relationship, two people may be mainly adapting to each other, to a great degree, and only occasionally fighting for changes in how they operate. Another treatment pair may be negotiating the terms of the relationship on a constant basis. Similarly, one treatment pair may privilege smoothly moving on when painful ruptures occur in the relationship, while another reaches operatic levels of emotional display. For some pairs, living something out is often sufficient, while others feel unsatisfied until the interaction is put into words. In the treatment relationship, as elsewhere, we all tend toward or away from adaptation, intense emotionality, and verbal formulation of our experience. Most often, these inclinations are not the result of conscious choices. They are part of our signature styles of coping with the human condition. Products of our personal and cultural life experiences, they are often reinforced in the professional circles we choose. For example, looking back at my own career, it is not an accident that I trained in an interpersonally oriented analytic institute. Given who I am as a human being, I probably intuited that I would be best suited to a professional environment that privileged the analyst's experience (and sometimes expression) of her emotions.

I see it as fortunate that quandaries about adaptation, emotionality, and formulation play out in treatment, because this gives us an actual opportunity to work on some of life's most pervasive dilemmas. Every time we adapt to the circumstance of being in a relationship with each other, and every time we fight for change, we are saying something about the importance of adapting/fighting. Again, I am using a shorthand, since most interactions are at neither extreme. But, overall, I think it is possible to characterize a relationship (treatment or otherwise) as mainly prioritizing harmonizing or clashing. To the extent that the human condition dictates some challenges as unavoidable, we meet them in sessions, just as we do everywhere else. How we meet them can have great impact on both our lives. Whether or not we are aware of it, clinicians are "more simply human than otherwise" (Sullivan, 1953) and, therefore, inevitably tilted toward or away from adaptation, emotional intensity, and verbal formulation. But how does this affect our ability to offer our patients an open invitation to explore their own inclinations? In other words, what happens to the patient's *self-directed* inquiry if our own attitudes about adaptation, emotional intensity, and verbal formulation inevitably shape the treatment exchange?

The role of neutrality in therapeutic approaches to life's challenges

While neutrality corrects for some untoward influence, it can also neuter us. In my view, in order to help patients fight for health, we can't avoid taking passionate and non-neutral positions. Theoretically, it is certainly possible to be passionate while neutral, but, in practice, it is hard to sustain when patients present the ultimate challenges inherent in being human. For example, a patient struggles to bear the death of her life's partner. What vision of the work of mourning, and of my role in facilitating it, do I bring to the session? If neutrality is its core, how will that affect the implicit (and explicit) interaction? More specifically, if I hold myself to a standard of neutrality, how might this affect my ability to help my elderly patient live with indignities, or my grieving patient bear the loss of her life's partner, or my traumatized patient carve out a future? On the other hand, without some standard of neutrality, how will treatment differ from indoctrination? Are we simply offering our patients ourselves as psychologically adept "models"? Do our theories convince us that we are facilitating the patient's self-directed development, while what they *actually* absorb from us is our own personal way of approaching life? More specifically, while we would like to think we are inviting our patients to fashion their own lives, are we inadvertently influencing them to adopt our attitudes about adaptation, emotional intensity, and the importance of verbally formulated experience?

Each chapter of this book explores how conceptions of our role affect our methods and goals as we try to help our patients at challenging junctures. That is, if I want to see myself as providing a more or less blank screen, how do I approach working with a patient whose child suddenly died? If I place less value on neutrality, how would that affect my methods and goals with the same patient? What am I (perhaps unconsciously) communicating about the value of adapting to circumstances, about healthy emotionality, and about efforts to formulate experience into words? If, as I believe, it is impossible to be completely neutral about these issues, even if the analyst believes it would be best, what stance most helps patients bear aloneness, aging, physical and emotional suffering, helplessness, and other potent trials? More specifically, how will *the implicit*, unformulated interpersonal interaction ready my patient to weather life's ultimate crises? Some might say that it is not our job to "ready" patients for anything, and that I am conceiving of the task in a superficial, non-analytic way. I would argue that many ways to understand our roles can be valid, but, whatever we would like to believe we are doing, we still have to contend with patients who see themselves as coming to treatment to get help coping with what is happening in their lives. In each of the nine chapters that follow this introduction, I describe a clinical example of a human predicament, and provide personal, theoretical, and literary responses. Of course, these are not at all comprehensive literature reviews or definitive practical solutions, but I hope they are evocative enough to stimulate readers' thinking about their own approaches to similar conundrums, as they have encountered them in their personal and professional lives. In a separate chapter, I explore how we might prepare candidates for the difficult task of dealing with these questions in many of the sessions they will conduct for the rest of their careers. Graduates of several training programs have "confessed" how unprepared they feel when confronted by their patients with these issues. While it is not the clinician's job to provide "answers," I think it is helpful if we acquaint candidates with an experienced analyst's thinking process when approached by patients with these quandaries. At the very least, it may help them examine their own, possibly unformulated assumptions. In each chapter, I gather some ideas, lines of poetry, and personal insights that seem to me to be most likely to inspire us as we struggle with problems in living.

My "clinical upbringing": Sources of my attitudes about adaptation, emotionality, and formulation

The issue of adaptation

Two of my most influential clinical forbears represented very different attitudes about adaptation as a way of coping with life. In much of his work, Erich Fromm (1941, 1950, 1955, 1968) championed challenging society's dictates. Overall, he brought a skeptical eye to its expectations, and advised others to do the same. In sharp contrast, H. S. Sullivan (1953, 1956) quite frequently struggled to help his patients develop socially sanctioned styles of dealing with "problems in living." The notable exception to this is his attitude about homosexuality, which is more complex (Wake, 2011). In the present chapter, and throughout this book, I explore the implications of these attitudes as they affect human experience in general, and clinical practice, often outside the clinician's conscious awareness.

In *Psychoanalysis and Religion*, Fromm (1950) is explicit about the issue of adaptation to society. He describes two basic attitudes clinicians can have: "We find that according to one conception adjustment is the aim of analytic cure. By adjustment is meant a person's ability to act like the majority of people in his culture" (p. 73). Fromm goes on to describe a second view, in which "the aim of therapy is not primarily adjustment but optimal development of a person's potentialities and the realization of his individuality" (p. 74). Fromm leaves no doubt that the second attitude describes his point of view about healthy living and about the clinician's task.

My understanding is that Fromm's position stems from his conviction that societies can be unhealthy, as well as his humanistic beliefs about the meaning and purpose of life. Adjusting well to a disturbed society could not be healthy. Of course, this point of view presupposes that there are universal norms for psychologically healthy living, against which a specific society's mores can be measured. On this point, as well, Fromm couldn't be clearer: "Here the psychoanalyst is not an 'adjustment counselor' but, to use Plato's expression, the 'physician of the soul'" (p. 74). This view is based on the premise that there are immutable laws inherent in human nature and human functioning which operate in any given culture. Fromm goes on to name these laws: Human beings must strive to recognize the truth, to become independent and free, to be an end in themselves (rather than a means to the purposes of others), to relate lovingly, to distinguish good from evil, and to listen to the voice of their own conscience. It follows that each human being should strive toward the fulfillment of these goals, and that clinicians should help their patients in this process.

Many (e.g., Burston, 1991; Funk, 2002) have commented on the roots of Fromm's viewpoint in his studies of societies that supported the rise of Hitler, as well as his more general religious, philosophical, historical, and other researches. I feel that Fromm's viewpoint has direct implications for how we live the fundamental challenges that face all human beings. In separate chapters, I suggest how Fromm's thinking might direct us to bear aloneness, mourning, aging, suffering, uncertainty, humiliation, and other aspects of the human condition. While cultures shape meanings that attach to each of these challenges, I believe they exist wherever there are human beings.

Fortunately, these challenges also make appearances in clinical sessions. This allows the clinician to live them with patients, rather than merely discuss them when they arise in the content of the material. I believe that frequently they form a subtext of the work, outside the awareness of both participants. In a sense, they constitute a dialogue about what it means to be a human being and live a human life.

Problems arise when the music is too disparate from the words. For example, if the clinician's words tout the value of free self-expression, but his or her actions pressure patients to adapt, the result is likely to be confused and ineffective. The same holds true for supervision and other forms of communication.

But, while Fromm's voice is probably the strongest in my own "internal chorus" (my phrase for the voices the clinician internalizes), Sullivan's (1954) makes frequent appearances. His is a voice that sometimes privileges adaptation, as a way to avoid the ravages of intense anxiety. Here are his own words:

The brute fact is that man is so extraordinarily adaptive that, given any chance of making a reasonably adequate analysis of the situation, he is quite likely to stumble into a series of experiments which will gradually approximate more successful living.

(p. 239)

In treatment, we facilitate this process, largely by helping the patient become aware of obstacles to fully grasping his interpersonal situation. At some time, these obstacles, or security operations, were instilled in order to avoid anxiety, but now they are standing in the way. Sullivan's optimism about our fundamental drive toward health leads him to believe that clearing away obstacles is often all that is necessary: "work toward uncovering those factors which are concerned in the person's recurrent mistakes, and which lead to his taking ineffective and inappropriate action. There is no necessity to do more" (p. 239). But Sullivan's stated beliefs and clinical approaches were complex, and sometimes contradictory. (As noted above, for a full discussion, see Wake, 2011.)

How much is health a matter of learning to adapt to our circumstances? I see this as a recurrent issue in our lives, and, perhaps, nowhere more evident than in our attitudes about aging.

Do not go gentle into that good night
Old age should burn and rave at close of day;
Rage, rage against the dying of the light.
(Thomas, 2010, p. 19)

Fortunately, the treatment dialogue frequently offers both participants a platform for playing out our inclinations toward or away from adaptation as a goal. Not only does the subject of adaptation often play a role in the explicit dialogue, but, I believe, it plays an even greater part in what remains implicit. A session can resemble a seesaw, in which the participants lean toward or away from adapting. For example, I notice that a patient is using a phrase from our previous sessions. Noting that he tended to dismiss his painful, disappointing experiences, I coined the (ironic) phrase that what happens to him is "no big deal." In a subsequent session, he used that phrase to characterize what happened with his wife. I played with the phrase, exaggerating it, essentially saying that the quality of his life is no big deal. Neither of us may be consciously focused on the ways we are adapting or differing, but, from my perspective, he is implicitly adapting to me by using my words, and explicitly adapting to his wife by going along with what she wants. For my part, by highlighting the long-term costs of adaptation, I am taking a different position. That is, when he said his compromise with his wife was "no big deal," I could have *adapted to him* by saying nothing or by expressing, in some form, the view that adaptations are a necessary part of being in a relationship. When I (somewhat playfully) said that the quality of his life is no big deal, I was, in effect, saying that I would not smoothly, simply, go along with his attitude. I was *enacting with him, as well as explicitly expressing, the value of non-adaptation.*

The issue of emotional intensity

The clinician's values about emotional intensity often get enacted, as well as transparently discussed, in the treatment interchange, especially when the patient presents in crisis. Are we trying to help people fully experience their sorrow, rage, love, joy, loneliness, and other feelings? Or do we see ourselves as helping them modulate, modify, regulate, or even "manage" them? Do we help some patients (for example, those haunted by PTSD) free themselves from their traumatic emotions, while facilitating others to fully inhabit their grief or get in touch with their anger? Do we analyze defenses against desire, implicitly suggesting that fully feeling it is an aspect of health? At what point do we define the *absence of* intensity as a psychological problem (e.g., anhedonia), and at what point is its *presence* considered a disturbance?

Or let us consider shame, guilt, envy, jealousy, hope, and curiosity. What is our attitude when we hear them in the material and when we feel them, ourselves, with our patients? Do we privilege some of these emotions over others, focusing on them as important material, remembering them selectively, spotting them in the patient's dreams? Or are we equally interested in them all? Should we be? Where is the line they must cross in order to be seen as excessive? Do they become a psychological problem only when the patient finds them disturbing? What about how friends and family feel or how the clinician feels in the presence of the patient's intense emotional storm?

What about suffering? Is it always a *sign* of problems, as well as *a problem in itself?* Elsewhere (Buechler, 2010, 2017), I have outlined three basic attitudes toward suffering that clinicians hold, although we are frequently unaware of these values and how they are affecting us in sessions with patients. I suggest that when analyst and patient fundamentally differ in their understanding of the place of suffering in psychic life, potentially treatment-destructive clashes can result. The attitude that pain should be reduced as quickly as possible has a significant impact on the analyst's focus in treatment, most especially on the timing of interpretations of defense. A different orientation is the fundamental attitude that pain is an inevitable part of human experience, best accepted rather than avoided. A third possibility embraces suffering as not only unavoidable, but a primary source of personal identity. Each of these positions will play a role in shaping the analyst's focus during sessions. I think it likely that the analyst who privileges adaptation is apt to respond to intense emotions, including intense suffering, as problematic. With this implicit vision of health, the clinician may lean in the direction of verbal formulation as an important achievement. In other words, the "pro-adaptation" clinician will view intense emotionality as potentially disruptive and verbal formulation as conducive to healthful, controlled equilibrium. On the other hand, clinicians with more ambivalence about adaptation as a measure of health are likely to tolerate, or even implicitly cultivate, the patient's emotional intensity, and experience that remains unformulated.

The importance of verbal formulation

Without necessarily making this explicit, clinicians differ in whether an insight has to be formulated in words in order to be mutative. Is it sometimes enough to live something out together, without either participant naming it? Elsewhere (Buechler, 2008), I have discussed the role of contrast in treatment. I suggested that some experiences that sharply contrast with the patient's unformulated interpersonal expectations can make those expectations more explicit. Whether the explicit, verbalized expression is necessary is a significant question. For example, a patient who expected me (and everyone else) to be competitive suddenly realized I was not behaving that way. This enabled him to become aware of his expectation, which he put into words. Was the verbal formulation essential? Would it have been enough for him to *experience* the contrast between what he expected from me and how I actually behaved?

Clinicians differ in how we would answer that question. Further, even for those who believe verbal formulation is essential, some might view that task as principally the role of the clinician, while others would feel it doesn't matter whether the clinician or patient puts the insight into words, as long as it happens. Some analysts formally differentiate the participants' roles, with the formulating clinician viewed as an "expert." Elsewhere (Buechler, 2008, 2012), I suggest that each of us has to grapple with the question of what we "sell" when we take a fee. Are we "expert" at formulating insights as they are enacted? Is that what we "sell"?

My training was not consistent about whether or not the clinician should be seen as an expert. My analytic forbears expressed differing views on this subject, but I am not sure their legacies differ much, since their clinical and supervisory behavior seems similar. Sullivan was explicit about the "psychiatrist as expert" in interpersonal relating. For example, in *The Psychiatric Interview* (1954), he defined treatment as an expert–client relationship. For Sullivan, an expert is "one who derives his income and status, one or both, from the use of unusually exact or adequate information about his particular field, in the service of others" (p. 11). Later, he says:

> The psychiatric expert is expected to have an unusual grasp on the field of interpersonal relations and, since this problem-area is peculiarly the field of participant observation, the psychiatrist is expected to manifest extraordinary skill in the relationship with his subject-person or patient.
>
> (p. 12)

On the contrary, Fromm (Funk, 2009) explicitly defined treatment as an encounter between the "center" of one person and the "center" of another. It can sound to me as though he is not defining the analyst as an "expert," in Sullivan's sense, although those who worked with him (e.g., Maccoby, 1996) sometimes saw him as passionately convinced of the superiority of his views about how human beings should feel and act.

Whether or not it matters who articulates an experience, I have sometimes felt that finding words for experience *can* change it. I feel most convinced of this when I read poetry. The great poets evoke a vivid experience in the reader on many levels at once. Like a good interpretation, a line of poetry touches our minds and hearts and, in many senses, moves us. That is, we end up in a new place. Poets and psychoanalysts struggle to find words that might incite new experiences. Having found just the right words can feel transformative. When this happens, whether in a poem or in a session, it seems as though verbal formulation has made a difference, although, of course, we can't know whether we could have been equally transformed by the unformulated on a less-than-conscious level. But when, as the analyst or patient, we find just the right word, or when we hear it from the other, it can feel as though something slides into place. It can bring a profound moment of recognizing oneself and/or the other, or being recognized. It is, in itself, fulfilling, and I think it helps to create a shared language, which I think of as a building block of intimacy. Forever after that moment, when either partner mentions the word, it conveys the insight in capsule form, but it also says "I know you."

The poet and critic Edward Hirsch (1999) has described how words gather meaning as they are passed from poet to reader.

> We make meaning together, we wrestle with what we read and talk back to it, we become more fully ourselves in the process. We activate the poem inside us by engaging it as deeply as possible, by bringing our lives to it, our associational memories, our past histories, our vocabularies, by letting its verbal music infiltrate our bodies, its ideas seep into our minds, by discovering its pattern emerging, by entering the echo chamber which is the history of poetry, and, most of all, by listening and paying attention. *Attentiveness is the natural prayer of the soul.*
>
> (p. 260, italics added)

I think what happens in poetry can also happen between analyst and patient. Poetry convinces me that finding just the right words to articulate an experience can electrify it. The right word jumps the track between one person and another. It jolts us into a mutual understanding. Take, for example, Emily Dickinson's (2010) poem about hope, which begins with these lines.

> "Hope" is the thing with feathers –
> That perches in the soul –
> And sings the tune without the words –
> And never stops – at all – . . .
>
> (p. 118)

Dickinson's message about the power of hope is instantly recognizable. Vendler points out that the image Dickinson creates emphasizes hope's aspiring nature. Describing hope as a bird conveys its capacity to (up)lift and lighten, and focusing on its song gives us a sense of its lilt. In the next lines, we hear that hope can be heard in the "chillest land – /And on the strangest Sea" (p. 119). With just a few words, the poet expresses hope that can't be defeated by circumstance. She creates an image that can buoy the reader's spirits. *The words evoke an experience that gives life to thought.* We have all seen a bird take flight. By connecting that image to hope, Dickinson has stirred us and, perhaps, changed us. This is what we aspire to do in an interpretation and, more generally, in treatment.

Words can do many kinds of magic. They sometimes unite the personal with the universal, helping us recognize, at one and the same time, our unique interiority and our shared humanity. Who can read the ending of Robert Hass's (2016) poem "Heroic Simile" without a sigh of recognition?

> A man and a woman walk from the movies
> to the house in the silence of separate fidelities.
> There are limits to imagination.
>
> (p. 50)

I connect at once. The words remind me of my particular experiences of loneliness while in the company of another. Instantly, I recognize and embrace myself. But, at the same time, I am not alone. The poet must also have known such moments to write about them so precisely. Someone is echoing my experience. Hass chose the right words for my feelings. We must have something in common. Similarly, the analyst (often inadvertently) reveals what she has suffered in the words she finds for the patient's suffering. These words simultaneously remind us of our unique life experiences and our common human experiences. While, like Hass, we must remember that "there are limits to imagination," it is also capable of thrilling leaps.

Interestingly, I have elsewhere (Buechler, 2008) described connecting with one's own particularity and connecting with one's common humanity as two sources of feelings of joy. I think glints of joy are possible when an analyst, patient, or poet unearths the words that perfectly fit the listener's experience.

Words can do other magic. When I think of the words from the Bible's declaration that in the beginning was the word, I picture Michelangelo's Sistine Chapel, where God enlivens Adam by touching his fingers. Adam becomes fully human. His eyes register awareness. Unlike the beautiful but lifeless figures that surround the panels, Adam pulses. Some touching moments actually transform us. Hirsch (1999) describes reading poetry as "an adventure in renewal, a creative act, a perpetual beginning, a rebirth of wonder" (p. 2). He goes on to describe the reader's "frame of mind, the playful work and working playfulness, the form of consciousness—the dreamy inattentiveness" (p. 2) that the reader can experience. It is hard for me to imagine a better description of analytic engagement at its best, as I have known it, as patient and as analyst.

But I can't ignore the potential downside of verbal formulation. Words can distort. We may both name the color of a rose "red," but do we really know whether we are having the same experience? Words can also create false dichotomies, making it seem as though we are further apart than we might feel ourselves to be. Wordless understanding can sometimes feel more intimate. Many patients experience words as acts of separation. Some are, in effect, saying that having to name something suggests a lack of trust in the depth of our knowledge of each other. Some also feel they *have* to talk, to participate in the "talking cure," even when they don't want to. I think it is important to ask whether words might distract us from significant nonverbal channels. When might we sense each other more profoundly without them? Perhaps another way to ask the same question is, are there times when putting words to experience brings it prematurely to the conscious level and cuts off preconscious processes?

From my perspective: Adaptation, emotional intensity, and verbal formulation

Each of the nine chapters that follow this introduction considers a human predicament. Bearing aloneness, loss, aging, and other challenges is inherent in life's fabric, although their meanings can differ depending on one's cultural and personal experiences. It is my belief that attitudes about adaptation, emotional intensity, and verbal formulation inform therapeutic efforts to grapple with these fundamental aspects of life.

As I have already suggested, I believe what we enact in sessions tells patients a great deal about our views about coping with life's difficulties. If what we say largely conforms with what we enact, we are more likely to exert a powerful impact. This influence is likely to affect how patients face the recurrent challenges we all face as human beings.

Commonplace moments reveal ways of coping. For example, if the clinician feels annoyed, how does she deal with it? Does it take center stage? Is it subordinated to an effort to adapt to the patient and get along smoothly? Or does the clinician privilege the potentially useful information in it? If the annoyance is intense, is it something to ignore or cover up? Does the clinician make great efforts to find just the right words to convey her annoyance, or does she latch onto any word, however imprecise? All of this tells the patient about the clinician's way of living life. It is inevitable that each participant reveals her characteristic coping style in countless seemingly minor but profoundly meaningful exchanges.

A clinical example, taken from my supervisory experience, comes to mind. One of the patient's presenting problems is difficulty managing his feelings, especially when he gets angry. A few years into the treatment, the clinician gets annoyed when the patient seems to expect an immediate response to an email. Clinicians would probably vary about whether it would be best to:

1   Disclose the clinician's annoyance, or register it without disclosing it.
2   Show his feelings in action rather than words.
3   Consider his annoyance a countertransference reflecting more about the therapist than the patient, and look for its meaning in the therapist's character.
4   Think about what is being projected into the clinician by the patient.

I think most analysts would object to the idea that in this situation the therapeutic task includes *modeling* dealing with the annoyance. For many, this conjures up the disdained "corrective emotional experience," as prescribed by Alexander (1961). If the clinician conducted a deliberate "show" of his or her feelings, I would certainly agree with this criticism. But my contention is that most of the time clinicians express our characteristic styles of emoting *outside* our awareness. Most frequently, it is not a deliberately chosen technique but an inevitable expression of the clinician's attitudes. For example, the annoyed clinician may regard her own annoyance with respect, shame, curiosity, or guilt, and deny it, dissociate from it, project it, rationalize it, associate to it, and so on. I am suggesting that, while training and theoretical allegiance may dictate what we consciously do with our feelings, some of our cultural and personal attitudes and defensive styles are outside our own awareness. Nevertheless, I believe they can have a profound impact on the treatment. They are often the "medium" that becomes the most powerful "message." They "inform" (often outside of the awareness of both participants) both of us about how we cope. Do we privilege getting along over expressing conflict? Do we tone down intense emotionality? Do we struggle to find exact words to express lived experiences? Do we "stand" for different approaches, depending on the major challenges being explored? Do we tend toward different ways of living life when profound loss is the (explicit) subject, as opposed to other life experiences?

Going back to the annoyed clinician, a whole way of living life may be encapsulated in the clinician's (internal) relationship with his or her annoyance. Is it treated as a friend if it is minimal, but an enemy if it towers? Can it ever be amusing? Does it occasion humility? Is it met with compassion for oneself and/or the clinician's burdens and, more generally, the human condition? Is it treated as an unwelcome intruder into an otherwise constructive session? Does the annoyance trigger repentant desire to help the patient? Or is the clinician awash with self-doubt, self-questioning, feelings of fraudulence, and a shame-induced urgency to cover it up? Does the clinician's inner response depend on the annoyance's intensity, accompanying emotions, its duration, the frequency of its recurrence in this treatment, in this session, and/or in this clinician's life? Did the clinician grow up (chronologically and later analytically) in a culture that prizes never showing annoyance? Or is it taken for granted as an eternally present human experience? Is its meaning, to the clinician, solely in terms of whether it can be used to help the patient? Does it carry implications about the clinician's responsibility to the patient? To the profession? To him or herself? Does the clinician feel responsible only for its impact, or for both the impact and the intentions? Does it become an opportunity to put words to feelings, or to know oneself and the other, or to repair, or merely to go on? Does it become a chance to privilege tact over absolutely transparent truth, or the other way around? Does it offer a moment to look for meaning rather than blame, to care for something beyond the clinician's self-esteem? Does it trigger self-care, on the part of the clinician, as well as caring for the patient? Are mysteries about its intentions embraced or feared or both?

This relatively common occurrence has infinite implicit meanings. We may not choose to tell our patients how we feel about our annoyances, our hesitancies, our shining joys. But they show in our faces, our bodies, our pauses, and, most of all, in our focus in the session. Focus is determined, in large part, by what we are able to consider important. I believe our cultural and personal experience in the world, as well as our training and membership in a professional sphere, shape our moment-to-moment focus in a session, largely outside our awareness. Certainly, it would be impossible to register all the other focuses we could have had as we listened to any paragraph of the patient's words.

More generally, both participants can't help *implicitly enacting* how much we prioritize helping, going on with life, experiencing moments, fitting words to experiences, expressing feelings, knowing oneself, acknowledging misdeeds, taking responsibility for one's intentions as well as one's impact, embracing uncertainty, privileging tact, making a good impression, taking positions with conviction, searching for truth, looking for meaning rather than blame, and many other issues. In each chapter, I explore some of these implicit values as they inform the treatment dialogue about some of the essential dilemmas facing us all as human beings.

With every year, my appreciation of the difficulty of the therapeutic endeavor grows. So often, it feels like William James's (1890) "blooming buzzing confusion"! While he was using this phrase to describe the experience of the infant, I think it applies just as well to my clinical experience. Facing life's greatest challenges, patients come to treatment for help. No matter how well-trained and well-meaning we may be, there are times when what we have to offer feels inadequate. We may believe, with all our hearts and minds, that we can help best by working with the patient on their character structure, analytically. I do not disagree, but along the way, the patient is looking for *how to cope now*. The patient, particularly during times of extreme stress, is experiencing the values behind our words (mostly unconsciously). The patient is asking (without being aware of it, most of the time): "What can this interchange tell me about how I might cope with my situation?" The patient reads us, just as much as we read the patient. What are our fundamental assumptions about healthy living?

References

Alexander, F. (1961). *The scope of psychoanalysis, 1921–1961*. New York: Basic Books.
Brooks, D. (2016, 30 August). Making modern toughness. *New York Times*, p. A21.
Buechler, S. (2004). *Clinical values: Emotions that guide psychoanalytic treatment*. Hillsdale, NJ: Analytic Press.

Buechler, S. (2008). *Making a difference in patients' lives*. New York: Routledge.

Buechler, S. (2010). No pain, no gain? Suffering and the analysis of defense. *Contemporary Psychoanalysis*, *46*, 334–354.

Buechler, S. (2012). *Still practicing: The heartaches and joys of a clinical career*. New York: Routledge.

Buechler, S. (2015). *Understanding and treating patients in clinical psychoanalysis: Lessons from literature*. New York: Routledge.

Buechler, S. (2017). *Psychoanalytic reflections: Training and practice*. New York: IPbooks.

Burston, D. (1991). *The legacy of Erich Fromm*. Cambridge, MA: Harvard University Press.

Dickinson, E. (2010). Poem 314. In H. Vendler (Ed.), *Dickinson: Selected poems and commentaries* (p. 118). Cambridge, MA: Harvard University Press.

Fromm, E. (1941). *Escape from freedom*. New York: Farrar & Rinehart.

Fromm, E. (1950). *Psychoanalysis and religion*. New York: Bantam.

Fromm, E. (1955). *The sane society*. New York: Rinehart & Winston.

Fromm, E. (1968). *The revolution of hope*. New York: Harper & Row.

Funk, R. (2002). Psychoanalysis and human values. *International Forum of Psychoanalysis*, *2*, 18–27.

Funk, R. (2009). *The clinical Erich Fromm*. Amsterdam: Rodopi.

Hass, R. (2016). Heroic simile. In H. M. Seiden (Ed.), *The motive for metaphor* (p. 50). London: Karnac.

Hirsch, E. (1999). *How to read a poem and fall in love with poetry*. New York: Harcourt.

James, W. (1890). *The principles of psychology*. New York: Henry Holt.

Maccoby, M. (1996). The two voices of Eric Fromm: The prophetic and the analytic. In M. Cortina & M. Maccoby (Eds.), *A prophetic analyst: Erich Fromm's contributions to psychoanalysis* (pp. 61–93). Northvale, NJ: Jason Aronson.

Phillips, A. (2005). *Going sane: Maps of happiness*. New York: HarperCollins.

Sullivan, H. S. (1953). *The interpersonal theory of psychiatry*. New York: W. W. Norton.

Sullivan, H. S. (1954). *The psychiatric interview*. New York: W. W. Norton.

Sullivan, H. S. (1956). *Clinical studies in psychiatry*. New York: W. W. Norton.

Thomas, D. (2010). Do not go gentle into that good night. In K. Young (Ed.), *The art of losing: Poems of grief and healing* (pp. 19–20). New York: Bloomsbury.

Wake, N. (2011). *Private practices: Harry Stack Sullivan, the science of homosexuality, and American Liberalism*. New Brunswick, NJ: Rutgers University Press.

Chapter 1

Capacity for aloneness and relationship

Love between two solitudes

[T]he love that consists in this, that two solitudes protect and border and salute each other.

Rilke (1934, p. 59)

Rilke's *Letters to a Young Poet* is a wise, compassionate expression of challenges that face all human beings. How do two solitudes extend love to one another? How do those in love adequately retain their solitude? How can we cultivate our own, and others', capacity to live at the border of self and other? In this chapter, I consider the ability to be comfortably alone and the ability to be in a loving relationship as one task, and I discuss some ideas about how it is achieved.

Personally, I have never found a piece of writing that describes the twin challenges of solitude and relationship with greater insight than Rilke's. He advises us not to be confused by our desire to break out of solitude. The fact that aloneness and relating are difficult doesn't make either undesirable; on the contrary, their very difficulty is part of their value. In his own words:

> To love is good, too: love being difficult. For one human being to love another: that is perhaps the most difficult of all our tasks, the ultimate, the last test and proof, the work for which all other work is but preparation . . . Love is at first not anything that means merging, giving over, and uniting with another (for what would a union be of something unclarified and unfinished, still subordinate?), it is a high inducement to the individual to ripen, to become something in himself, to become world, to become world for himself for another's sake, it is a great exacting claim upon him, something that chooses him out and calls him to vast things.

(pp. 53–54)

Rilke goes on to decry the tendency of the young to try to lose themselves in the beloved, which results in perplexity rather than genuine connection. In these passages, Rilke expresses some of our greatest, timeless challenges. In my view, there is no better textbook for the developing clinician (and, more generally, the developing human being) than these ten letters, written by the established poet, Rilke, in answer to an unknown, young, hopeful writer's pleas for guidance.

Rilke's solitude, like his conception of love, requires the individual to be fairly mature. In order to be one of his two loving "solitudes," the individual must be able to distinguish self from other, be able to want to protect the other, and be able to be moved to develop for the sake of the other. This describes someone who is highly individuated. At the other end of the age spectrum, Winnicott's (1965) landmark paper on the capacity to be alone deals with the earliest phase of this process. I think his paper rewards very close rereading.

Winnicott highlights the need for the presence of a mother (or substitute) dedicated to the infant's well-being in the initial stages of the development of the capacity to be alone. The connection with this mother figure provides the benign environment that allows solitude to feel safe. In his words:

> The relationship of the individual to his or her internal objects, along with confidence in regard to internal relationships, provides of itself a sufficiency of living, so that temporarily he or she is able to rest contented even in the absence of external objects and stimuli. Maturity and the capacity to be alone implies that the individual has had the chance through good enough mothering to build up a belief in a benign environment.
>
> (p. 32)

Thus, for Winnicott, the capacity for solitude is born out of the connection with our first relational partner. My way to say this is that the capacities for solitude and relationship are twins, conceived in the benign environment created by our first love. Elsewhere (Buechler, 2012, 2017), I have described the problematic end of the spectrum, where these capacities are not sufficiently achieved and all relationship, including the treatment alliance, is threatened.

It is important to note that Winnicott is writing about the *capacity* to be alone, not the preference or proclivity. Whether one is a loner or highly socially active, the ability to be alone is as essential as the ability to be in a relationship. For both Winnicott and Rilke, each of these capacities is necessary for the other. Another way to describe this is that the person who has had the chance to internalize benign caregivers eventually feels safe enough to be alone *and* to form a relationship with a fully differentiated other. In Rilke's language, "To be a part, that is fulfillment for us: to be integrated with our solitude into a state that can be shared" (Baer, 2005, p. 31).

Looking at both Rilke and Winnicott, it seems to me that the fortunate person, born into good enough caretaking, will (at some point) become able to withstand impulses to merge or flee in order to feel safe. This well-cared-for person will be able to bear difficult passages of solitude *and* relationship. The hard moments inherent in both aloneness and connection will not have the power to persuade her that the inner or outer world is unbearably dangerous. In other words, both difficult aloneness and difficult relating will be non-traumatic challenges. This fortunate child/adult will feel able to navigate these challenges without resorting to drastic measures, such as merging with the other or fleeing.

I think of this fortunate person as capable of object constancy. The inner object's stability allows her to weather fluctuations and absences of the (external) other. Another way to say this is that the intact inner object fills and centers the self. Thus, the fortunate person can continue to love, despite changes in the beloved, and can continue to feel emotionally grounded during periods of aloneness.

In his great sonnet, "Let Me Not to the Marriage of True Minds," Shakespeare (1996) advocated for love that withstands all change.

> Let me not to the marriage of true minds
> Admit impediments. Love is not love
> Which alters when it alteration finds,
> Or bends with the remover to remove:
> O, no! it is an ever-fixed mark,
> That looks on tempests and is never shaken;
> It is the star to every wandering bark,
> Whose worth's unknown, although his height be taken.
> Love's not Time's fool, though rosy lips and cheeks
> Within his bending sickle's compass come;
> Love alters not with his brief hours and weeks,
> But bears it out even to the edge of doom.
>> If this be error, and upon me prov'd
>> I never writ, nor no man ever lov'd.
>
> (p. 332)

Shakespeare tells us what true love can withstand. Neither change in the beloved, nor life's upheavals, nor time, nor implacable fate, alters it. One way to understand this is that not looking outside ourselves for completion of the self, we are able to love no matter what happens and feel that fulfillment is possible even in isolation.

In my language, one of life's greatest challenges is to "love life *anyway*," despite its inevitable pain. Can we achieve "object constancy" toward *life itself* and/or humanity itself, no matter how it "alters"? For me, my relationship with life itself, as well as all my other internal and external relationships, ask this of me. For all of us, how can we love (ourselves, each other, life) anyway? And how can we bring this part of our experience of being human into our work as analysts? An analogy to Oedipus comes to mind. For me, the essential meaning of the Oedipus saga centers on the issue of desire. What happens when we want the (m) other that we can't have? Exquisite regret, eternal shame, unending punishment? We all want what we can't have. We all bear profound disappointments. Yet we need to say "yes" to life, with all its humiliations, indignities, piercing sorrows. If we can forgive life, perhaps our grief can become *just* grief, and not grief potently mixed with rage, guilt, and regret. Whatever life gives, it also takes away. Can we forgive life for that? Can our love for life look on tempests without being shaken? Can we love it anyway? To me, nothing is harder, or more important, than this ultimate test of object constancy.

For me, it is a small step further to think of self-love and love of the other as one and the same. They are just different aspects of an enduring love for humanity as a whole. In his extremely popular book, *The Art of Loving*, Erich Fromm (1956) defined love as "the active concern for the life and growth of that which we love" (p. 24). In my opinion, this does not differ in spirit from Sullivan's (1940) definition: "When the satisfaction or security of another person becomes as significant to one as is one's own satisfaction or security, then the state of love exists" (pp. 42–43). Much later, Harold Davis (1988) defined love as "the relatedness of two selves, which allows each to grow" (p. 163). Unlike early Freudian theory, in which it was assumed that we each have a limited supply of cathexis, so that the quantity of self-love takes away from the quantity of love of another, Fromm, Sullivan, and Davis see love of the self as compatible with love for another. This has enormous clinical implications. For example, as we listen to a patient describing his relationship with his partner, what assumptions guide our focus? When he complains that his selfish wife doesn't love him, I believe that how we understand love will affect what we don't notice, because we take it for granted, and what we question, associate, remember later, and so on. Love is, literally, at the heart of our own lives and our patients' lives, and how we understand it will affect how we hear a session. What do we readily engage as problematic and worthy of clinical exploration? What do we easily see as therapeutic progress? How do we each think about love?

Pathologizing solitude and valorizing relationship

Society at large and our analytic culture often fail to distinguish a preference for solitude from an incapacity for relatedness. All too often, in my opinion, the child who prefers her own company is seen as problematic for that reason. Paul Tillich (1987) once said: "Language has created the word 'loneliness' to express the pain of being alone, and the word 'solitude' to express the glory of being alone" (p. 217).

A textbook used in medical schools, aptly titled *What's Normal?* (Donley & Buckley, 2000), examines assumptions about medical, intellectual, and psychological health. The authors declare: "Too often we convert normal and healthy variabilities into diseases or disorders because they differ from the ideal norm. This reluctance to accept normal variations makes people who are only slightly different from the norm feel unacceptable" (p. 3). Regarding the issues at hand here, I wonder if there can be a "norm" at all.

In this section, I examine some of the values about aloneness and relationship that subtly shape the analyst's views of health and the goals and methods of treatment. I explore the tendency to view inclinations toward relationship more favorably than preferences for solitude. What is a "healthy" capacity for aloneness and relatedness? How do we imagine it is attained, within and outside psychotherapeutic work? How might it affect our theories if we acknowledged the capacity for solitude as sprung from the *same source* as the capacity for relatedness?

Anthony Storr is surely one of solitude's most eloquent spokespersons. In *Solitude: A Return to the Self*, Storr (1988) makes the case for its legitimacy and normality. He criticizes the assumption that human happiness is a product of intimate relationships. Not only does he cite examples to the contrary, but he believes that putting all our eggs in that basket, so to speak, is detrimental to happiness.

> It may be our idealization of interpersonal relationships in the West that causes marriage, supposedly the most intimate tie, to be so unstable. If we did not look to marriage as the principal source of happiness, fewer marriages would end in tears
>
> (p. xiii)

Storr especially decries our tendency to associate the craving for solitude with interpersonal dysfunction. Pointedly, he asks: "[I]s the predilection of the creative person for solitude evidence of some inability to make close relationships?" (p. x). Although this question is raised early in the book, it is already clear that Storr's answer will be a resounding "no."

The "craving for solitude" certainly had another champion in Rilke. Baer (2005) writes of Rilke's belief that:

> Every rite of passage-birth, adolescence, love, commitment, illness, loss, death-marks such an experience where we are faced with our solitude. But this is not a melancholic thought for Rilke. He revalorizes solitude as the occasion to reconsider our decisions and experiences, and to understand ourselves more accurately—and his words can serve as uncannily apt guides for such reflection.
>
> (pp. xi–xii)

Later in the book, Baer quotes Rilke as feeling a need to inhabit his loneliness in order to regain his creativity after a fallow period. In Rilke's words:

> This is the way I would gradually like to become again, but in order to do so I have to remain as alone as I am now; my loneliness first has to be firm and secure again like a forest where no one ever set foot and which has no fear of steps. It must lose all emphasis, exceptionality, and obligation. It must become routine, completely natural and quotidian. The thoughts that enter, even the most fleeting ones, must find me all alone; then they will decide to trust me again.
>
> (p. 87)

As I understand this, Rilke felt he had to bear aloneness in order to make enough room for his relationship with ideas to be truly fruitful. What (societal, psychoanalytic, personal) attitudes toward this way of valorizing loneliness do we each bring when we consider our patients' experience and our own?

Storr (1988) holds late Freudian and post-Freudian analysis responsible for much of society's negative attitude toward the preference for solitude. These analytic theories assume that "salvation is to be attained by purging the individual of the emotional blocks or blind spots which prevent him from achieving fulfilling interpersonal relationships" (p. 2). Although the wording of this statement is somewhat tongue in cheek, it is not far off. For example, in the *Handbook of Interpersonal Psychoanalysis*, Schlesinger (1995), summarizing the Interpersonal point of view, suggests that "[f]or Interpersonalists, disconnection from others is the ground of human malaise, and the search for connection is life's project" (p. 2). I do not disagree with the premise that the search for connection is a crucial aspect of life's project, but I think it is important to consider whether we have neglected to focus on other aspects sufficiently.

I suggest that our emphasis on relating may stem, in part, from *our own loneliness*. Elsewhere (Buechler, 1998, 2017), I have explored the loneliness that can be a significant aspect of the analyst's experience. Briefly, the analyst is not alone, but may, nevertheless, feel intense loneliness during sessions. At times, we may feel permanently unable to communicate to anyone the experience we are having with some patients. Depending on our own character and development, this may trigger acute loneliness. If we have put aside focusing on our own feelings to prioritize the patient's, we may inadvertently exacerbate our loneliness by losing touch with ourselves. I think several consequences are likely. The lonely analyst may rationalize an overly active stance, justifying it as in the *patient's* best interests. Of course, sometimes that is true, but it can also be used to grant ourselves permission for intrusive, disruptive pursuit of contact with the patient.

Nina Coltart (1993) counted loneliness as one of the hardships of life as an analyst:

> The problems are loneliness of a certain sort, and the emotional strains of continually and voluntarily offering oneself to the inner suffering of other people in the hope-or faith-that there is something in the way this self-exposure is offered which may be of therapeutic aid to the other person.
>
> (p. 1)

Aside from tilting us toward over-activity, I suggest that our own loneliness may color our attitudes about patients who share themselves sparingly.

In an extremely significant, forthright, and evocative paper, Joyce Slochower (2017) examines some of the implicit assumptions about health that are inherent in relational theory. In my judgment, many are equally applicable to the Interpersonal orientation. Slochower reflects on several values built into a relational treatment paradigm and their intended and unintended effects. Here I examine Slochower's paper at length, because I think it provides an acute investigation of what current relationally oriented theories privilege, and the significant aspects of human experience that are insufficiently recognized.

According to Slochower, relationally oriented theories emphasize the following values:

1   The value of "asymmetrical mutuality and uncertainty" (p. 283). The analyst is a participant in the co-creation of meaning, rather than an oracle delivering absolute truths to the patient. Neither can claim total objectivity. This accords with much of the writing from the Interpersonal school, though different terms were used. For example, Wolstein (1975) asserts that "the patient is responding to something real, here and now, and in that measure his response cannot be judged as being simply distorted. The psychoanalyst, whatever else he would do about it, has to treat it at least as such" (p. 53)

2   The value of enactments. Lived relational experience during the session can be mutative, *even* if it is not fully verbally formulated. This point of view reflects the privileging of relationship over the patient's solitary self-reflection and the movement away from interpretation as the central mutative element in treatment. Interpersonalists have differed some on this point. Greenberg (1981) describes both Sullivan and Fairbairn as understanding the mutative factor in treatment as "a result of the analyst's use of himself as a new person to break into the closed inner world of the patient" (p. 143). Levenson (1978) describes analysis as a semiotic process "in the sense that it encompasses more than spoken language. It includes also sign systems, non-verbal cueings, distances, dispersions, the whole repertoire of interpersonal language" (p. 82). For him, the mutative force in treatment stems from the dialectic interaction between the content of what is said and how it is enacted as it is said.

3   The importance of helping the patient connect with early experiences of dissociated-self states and trauma. While some recent Interpersonalists agree with this as a priority, most of the early literature emphasizes *avoiding* any technique that might induce the patient to regress. The here-and-now relationship between the two adults in the treatment is highlighted. It is assumed that the most significant interpersonal patterns emerge very early in the treatment, *without* the need for regression to early life. Greenberg (1981) emphasized this point in his effort to distinguish Interpersonal from British object relational theory: "This is not to say that regression cannot be encompassed within an interpersonal model—Bromberg (1979) has suggested that it can be—but I do think that the approach of the British school forces regression on the observer in a way that interpersonal theory does not" (p. 147). As Stern (2017) suggests, for the Interpersonalists, "unconscious is understood to be built into present-day relatedness" (p. 17). For example, in supervision with several adherents of Interpersonalism, I was taught that the surface ripples reflect the depths, that is, that most of what is significant about the patient's interpersonal life is revealed, in some form, in the first sessions, without any need for regression.

4   The analyst's psychological accessibility and self-disclosure can be powerfully mutative. Relational theory moved away from the idealization of neutrality and

abstinence, believing that, often, the self-disclosing analyst can best help the patient repair early interpersonal damage. I would suggest that Interpersonalists have moved in a similar direction, but with a slightly different belief system. From a relational perspective, the analyst's self-disclosures allow analyst and patient to unpack enactments, taking into account both of their subjectivities. While the Interpersonal analyst might similarly disclose, it is not mainly for the purpose of understanding a *repetition* of an (object) relationship from the patient's past. For the Interpersonalist (at least in my experience), the treatment relationship, in that it is shaped by *both* participants, is a *new* experience for both. What is highlighted is the reparative potential in that new experience. For example, Singer (1977) suggests that "the patient's profound and realistic knowledge of the analyst as a representative of his fellow men-past, present, and future-enables him to live authentically, in mutuality, in solidarity, and in communion" (p. 71). Let me emphasize that these are only differences of degree. Neither school focuses exclusively on old or new interpersonal experiences, but the Interpersonalist focuses less on internalized object relationships and more on the reparative potential in new experience.

Writing of relationalists, Slochower (2017) states: "We pathologized those patients who evaded or resisted a focus on our subjectivity and the reenactments occurring between us" (p. 285). I think it is in the spirit of Slochower's paper to say that *all* analytic models pathologize resistance to their primary methods. This means to me that both Interpersonal and relational analysts are likely to pathologize an individual's preference for solitude and valorize the relational dimension. Since, as suggested above, I see the capacity for solitude and the capacity for relationship as two aspects of the same strength, this seems problematic to me. I do think it is important to distinguish a capacity for solitude from a preference for it. But I think if our models pathologize the preference, they may also give short shrift to the capacity.

In contrast, Slochower makes more room for the analyst's and the patient's needs for private, alone experience (as did Wolstein, 1975, 1983, in his efforts to include private experience in an interpersonal perspective). Slochower cites Winnicott when she describes non-anxious aloneness as an achievement, and she tells her colleagues, "we do need to further theorize the clinical meaning and value of aloneness and privacy if we are to avoid pathologizing it" (p. 289). I definitely agree, and this chapter is my attempt to respond to her point.

This issue seems especially significant to me because our analytic bias resonates with society's negative evaluation of those who prefer solitude. It is likely that patients who have grown up in a culture that responded to their preferences for solitude as needing to change, may fail to register that they are getting similar signals from their analyst. These messages may be so familiar that they go without notice. Or, perhaps, the patient will (consciously or less consciously) agree and censor expressions of the need for solitude, within and outside treatment. It is not hard to imagine that those who have craved solitude all their lives have childhood feelings of social insufficiency ready to be recruited in analysis.

It seems clear to me that for both, regardless of the differences between Interpersonal and relational analytic theories, their application to treatment relies on a willingness for analyst and patient to relate and examine their interaction. Whether we emphasize curative factors in the understanding of the patient's past, the verbalized formulation of that understanding, or the repetition of old patterns with new outcomes, the process requires relationship. Within these paradigms, how does the analyst respond to a yearning for solitude on the part of the patient?

Once again, it seems vital to distinguish the capacity for aloneness from the preference for it, and to locate *both* within our models of health. As suggested above, the capacity comes from the same experiences as does the ability to relate interpersonally. Both were conceived in the presence of a relatively benign early caregiver. The preference for solitude is a point on a continuum, not an absolute difference, from the preference for company. Each is a way to express a fundamental belief in safety. I would be more likely to "diagnose" an inability to find *any* resting place on the continuum, rather than a proclivity for one side versus the other. It is the person who didn't experience a relatively benign caregiver, who can find no comfort in solitude *or* relationship, that is bound for an anxious and troubled existence.

Nurturing the capacity for both solitude and relationship in treatment

Mohacsy (1990) cites Winnicott's thinking on the capacity to be alone, as it is normally developed through experiences of playing alone while near the mother. She suggests that the holding environment we provide for patients

> mimics this childhood process and may compensate for it when it has been inadequate. This is not a 'corrective experience' in the more primitive sense of Alexander and Ferenczi. However the analyst can possibly supply the good introject when the mother has failed in this respect.
>
> (p. 363)

Winnicott's seminal work on the capacity to be alone was cited in the first pages of this chapter. Another way to express his insight, using the language of attachment theory (Bowlby, 1973), is that the capacity to be alone depends on the experience of a secure attachment.

I view the patient playing with ideas, lying on the couch, near but not in sight of the analyst as quite literally analogous to the situation provided by Winnicott's good enough mother, who offers proximity without intrusion. Elsewhere (Buechler, 1998), I have suggested that an optimal level of loneliness in treatment may be an experience, when digested, that contributes to the patient's growing capacity to be alone.

Writing of the experience of a World War II prisoner kept in solitary confinement, Fromm-Reichmann (1959) explains how he survived his ordeal.

I believe that his unquestioning, matter-of-fact belief in the spiritual validity of the political convictions which were the cause of his imprisonment may have been an additional factor which helped him to survive his ordeal without becoming mentally ill . . . The delinquent prisoner is not likely to have the determination and devotion to a cause which helped Burney to stay mentally sound, even though he was deprived of the opportunity to work or to receive stimulation through reading, which for many others seem to have been the two most effective antidotes or remedies for the humiliation of confinement and the rise of disintegrating loneliness.

(p. 324)

Fromm-Reichmann is emphasizing the conviction (or what I [Buechler, 2004] have called the "sense of purpose") that can buoy the isolated person. It is worth thinking about just how this works. One perspective is that the sense of self is bolstered by convictions. For example, I imagine that Burney (cited above) did not see himself as any less worthwhile, as a human being, because of his incarceration. He was able to maintain a *self-love* that (to quote, again, from Shakespeare's sonnet) "looks on tempests and is never shaken . . ." Shakespeare is referring to true love of the other, but I think firm conviction can nurture true self-love.

This suggests to me that nurturing the capacity for solitude requires us to pay attention to all the feelings, including, perhaps, shame, that the person experiences when alone. We tend to selectively focus on anxiety and loneliness, but we might look further afield. In addition, we might ask whether feelings that are missing (such as curiosity) play a role in making solitude difficult.

Winnicott referred (above) to the possibility that the analyst might supply a "good introject" when the mother did not fulfill this function adequately. According to this thinking, a new good internal object can create a benign atmosphere, making aloneness less fraught with anxiety. To quote again from Winnicott (1965): "In negative terms: there must be a relative freedom from persecutory anxiety. In positive terms: the good internal objects are in the individual's personal inner world, and are available for projection at a suitable moment" (p. 32).

As any clinician knows, persecutory anxiety takes many forms. It can be expressed in frankly paranoid ideation, or in an addiction, in which much of life is dedicated to distracting oneself from a fundamental sense of life as dangerous. It can take shape as an avoidance of being alone, or an avoidance of other people, or of intimate relationships.

Just how does this "relative freedom from persecutory anxiety" come about, in the treatment of adults? As I read the literature, and from my own clinical experience, I would suggest that the internalization of the analyst is just the first step, though an extremely important one. But, at least in some patients, the internalized "good object" has to contend with powerful "bad objects" that have long dominated, creating a malignant, and far from benign, atmosphere. In several cases (described below), I have felt that the *internalized "good object" has as its task to disarm the bad objects. Mere presence is not enough.* For a fundamentally malignant internal environment to become a prevailingly benign environment, the newly internalized object has to have significant, ultimately decisive power.

While, of course, each treatment is different, my clinical experience tells me that, most often, this kind of power requires the analyst's passionate commitment and integrity. By integrity, I mean consistency of word and deed. If the messages at various levels of communication don't match, the analyst may mystify the patient, and, when internalized, she won't have a moderating impact on the internal environment. If, for example, the analyst's words promote the patient's freedom and autonomy but the analyst's behavior is autocratic, the message is ineffective, or worse.

I believe that each clinician develops a personally resonant treatment style that helps some patients more than others. Some believe that patients need to confront their own aggression to feel safer. Others work differently, relying on more direct or less direct approaches. Those who follow Fromm engage directly, unapologetically, in a fight on behalf of "biophilia." Others believe that creating a safe, receptive space, where anything can be expressed, is most effective. There is no one "royal road" to having an ameliorating impact on the patient's internal world.

What I do think is required, regardless of our theoretical leanings, is that the patient feels partnered by someone whose message is powerful partially because of its passionate conviction and absolute integrity. My first book (Buechler, 2004) was dedicated to some of the values that can make the analyst a powerful presence in the patient's external and internal worlds. These include curiosity, kindness, and courage. If, for example, we talk of courage but fail to meet difficult moments courageously, we limit (or, perhaps, nullify) any positive impact we might have had.

But, if we approach the patient with integrity, passionate purpose, and compassionate love, I think we have a chance to improve internal space. In turn, this can promote the capacity to be alone and the capacity to be in relationships. Both are predicated on an adequate sense of safety.

A moving example of passionate commitment and integrity is Frieda Fromm-Reichmann's treatment of Hannah Green, a version of which became the bestselling book, *I Never Promised You a Rose Garden* (Greenberg, 1954). If there ever was a patient in need of a change in the atmosphere of her internal objects, it was this patient. While *I Never Promised You a Rose Garden* was billed as fiction, it surely captured the essence of their work, so a careful reading of it can give us insight into the spirit of Frieda's treatment style. I see the treatment described by Greenberg as a vivid depiction of Frieda's beliefs about technique, as explicitly articulated in *Principles of Intensive Psychotherapy* (1950) and *Psychoanalysis and Psychotherapy: Selected Papers* (1959). I discuss Greenberg's depiction in detail because, at least for me, it is one of the clearest examples of a thoroughly committed analyst changing both the outer and inner worlds of a patient who could find no peace in either solitude or connection.

At many points in Greenberg's book, "Dr. Fried" (who represents Frieda) clearly asserts that she can bear whatever Deborah (who stands in for the patient, Joanna) thinks and feels. As I read it, this frees Deborah to speak without worrying about her impact. For example, at one point, Dr. Fried tells Deborah to declare to her inner demons that this therapist won't be cowed by them. Their work will continue, no matter what. Since Deborah thinks of herself as poison, Dr. Fried must convince Deborah that she has the capacity to withstand her patient's rages, terror, binges of self-destruction, and scathing contempt. In other words, the doctor has to do more than just become part of the patient's inner world. She has to *triumph over* the powerfully malignant introjects in the patient's world. Throughout the book, Dr. Fried clearly expresses her anger at Deborah's tormentors, from the anti-Semitic children and adults who shunned her, to the unfeeling doctors who lied to her about the unbearable pain their medical procedures would cause. Dr. Fried shows she is a sensitive, yet sturdy human being, who becomes a powerful protector when she is internalized.

It is fair to say that both Dr. Fried and Deborah have met their match. In this treatment, two women, capable of unswerving, devoted, steadfast effort, dedicate themselves to their task. While there are many moments that it looks as though Deborah might not be able to bear the pain, it never seems like Dr. Fried will waver. There can be no doubt that she will not give up. About that, she is quietly fierce. Many times, she assures Deborah that they will keep working together until they have faced everything there is to face. As I read it, Dr. Fried, an interpersonal force to be reckoned with, became an implacable advocate when finally internalized by her patient. As a new internal "object," Dr. Fried takes on the sadistic voices from Deborah's past, tipping the scales toward a more benign inner world.

There is one scene that demonstrates Dr. Fried's brand of tough love more clearly than any other, in my opinion. Deborah has declared that she doesn't want to think any more. Why should she keep working so hard, when it doesn't seem to be getting her anywhere? What is the treatment's purpose? As I read Dr. Fried's reply, I hear frustration and exasperation, as well as profound empathy and dedication. Dr. Fried raises her voice and says that the treatment is for getting Deborah out of the hospital. Deborah balks, and declares that she won't tell Dr. Fried anything more. The doctor grows quieter but not any less determined. They engage in a real battle. Dr. Fried mobilizes her own aggression in order to actively counter Deborah's stubborn self-destructiveness. Essentially, in a provocative way, she gives her patient a stark choice. Deborah has to decide whether or not she wants to stay in mental hospitals for the rest of her life. Dr. Fried's tone is not soft. It is challenging and, at moments, sarcastic. She implies that Deborah can feel sorry for herself and try to evoke the world's pity, or help Dr. Fried fight to save her patient's life. The doctor does not promise her exhausted, demoralized patient any comfortable rose gardens. But she also doesn't let up on the pressure. She meets aggression with a kind of steely aggression of her own. I believe that, more than anything else, it is this fierceness that makes Dr. Fried the ideal advocate *once she is internalized*. Even with much less compromised patients, I think we have to be palpably steadfast to become powerful allies when we (finally) gain entry into the patient's inner world. Of course, this runs counter to the traditional notions of neutrality and abstinence. Advocating any particular change, siding for or against behaviors, allying with some of the patient's internal objects against others, directly contradicts the prescriptions and proscriptions of Anna Freud (1936), among many others. I have discussed this issue at some length (Buechler, 2017), but, briefly, I believe sometimes we have to err on the side of supporting forces in the patient that favor living over dying.

A patient of mine entered treatment frequently depressed, obsessed with images of suicide. She had been abandoned to strangers frequently as a very young child. Hazy memories suggest that she was the observer, if not also the victim, of abuse. As an adult, she was terrified whenever her husband left, even for a brief business trip.

One way I have tried to explore her experience is to ask her who she is alone with, when she is alone. Who takes part in her inner dialogue? My belief is that, as Winnicott suggests, she hadn't internalized a secure attachment sufficiently to make being alone feel safe. Self-critical and aggressive inner objects taunted her with images of ways to die. When she could reflect on these episodes, she was sad that so much of her energy went into fighting these voices.

But the same dynamics were at play when this patient was not alone. Her relationships with others were just as marred. She was intensely jealous and openly suspicious of her husband's motives. The unmediated cruelty of her inner objects colored her relational life just as much as it affected her loneliest hours.

It is easy (and, maybe, useful) to think in terms of paranoid dynamics. Her own aggression was available to project onto her husband and strangers who might break into her house when she was alone. In other words, her inner world shaped her every experience, alone and in company. People at work were waiting for her to make a mistake. Neighbors were watching for her to commit a shameful faux pas. Strangers were ready to invade her house when she was unprotected. Her husband was having a secret affair when he said he was going to the hardware store. Let me emphasize that this patient was an extremely well-functioning member of society, all the while these fantasies went on. She could even challenge them herself and feel sad that her inner life was taken up with them. But, in the grip of one, she felt helpless. In a very profound sense, she was lonely. One of Fromm-Reichmann's (1959) ways of differentiating aloneness from loneliness is that there is a lack of hope of human connection in the profoundly lonely person. Applying this to my patient, I think she felt unlovable, and that the abandonment she expected was a just punishment for her gross inadequacies and badness. Somehow, life would take away all comfort, leaving her as unprotected, exposed as she deserves to be.

I have given you only the briefest of outlines, and there are countless ways to understand what her treatment needed to provide. From my point of view, only the internalization of a strong, protective figure could have enough impact to change the quality of her experience of *both* terrifying aloneness and fraught relationship. That is, only a *real* experience, in the present, with someone who was trusted enough, important enough to her, consistent enough, emotionally expressive enough, and strong enough, could be internalized and change the *internal* balance. This approach relies on new experience, rather than repetition and interpretation of transference.

Hoffman (2009) has provided vivid and compelling examples of the mutative effect of the analyst as an internalized ally. My own assumption is that, once internalized, the relatively benign analyst fosters the development of capacities for both comfortable solitude and relationship. In effect, with this new interpersonal experience, both the patient's outer and their inner world become less threatening.

I know I am coming perilously close to advocating what has been derided as the "corrective emotional experience" (mentioned above). What I am suggesting *is* corrective and an emotional experience. But it is not a show, put on deliberately to achieve an effect. In order to be helpful, it must be a real expression of who I am and what I feel. What Alexander (1961) advocated was a staged response that deliberately varied from the patient's parents' behavior. As I have suggested elsewhere (Buechler, 2008), this lacks the integrity that is an absolutely essential component of the analyst's conduct.

I think what I am suggesting is not unlike Sullivan's (1953) concept of a "chum." This pre-adolescent relationship is crucial for the establishment of relative health. For Sullivan, even the child who did not receive adequate parenting may be saved by the experience of having a chum. With this friendship, the feel of interpersonal relating changes for the better. Regardless of one's age, the world is a different place when a secure relationship exists in it. In a way, there is no difference between how being alone and being with another are altered by this positive experience. I reprint my statement from earlier in this chapter, in order to examine it again. Looking at both Rilke and Winnicott, it seems to me that the fortunate person, born into good enough caretaking, will (at some point) become able to withstand impulses to merge or flee in order to feel safe. This well-cared-for person will be able to bear difficult passages of solitude and interaction. The hard moments inherent in both aloneness and relationship will not have the power to persuade her that the world is dangerous. In other words, both difficult aloneness and difficult relating will be non-traumatic challenges. This fortunate child/adult will feel able to navigate these challenges without resorting to drastic measures, such as merging with the other or fleeing.

My belief is that, for those who were not born into good enough caretaking, only a powerful and good internalized object can enable them to withstand impulses to merge in relationships or flee from them. And only a powerful internalized good object can make the world feel safe enough when one is alone. While revisiting and revising old (transferential) objects may well be of benefit, I think there are times when it doesn't sufficiently alter the current landscape. The person who has not internalized a sufficiently powerful, continuously present protector can't ride through difficult passages of both solitude and interaction. For the more fortunate, these are temporary glitches, however challenging. Each might be difficult, but not nightmarish. For the less fortunate, they are calamitous triggers of trauma responses. Since terrified aloneness and terrified relating express the same insecurity, the same imbalance, the therapeutic task is one and the same. To tip the balance, we need to become meaningful enough to take inside, and, once internalized, powerful and reliable enough to change how life feels.

References

Alexander, F. (1961). *The scope of psychoanalysis, 1921–1961*. New York: Basic Books.

Baer, U. (2005). *The poet's guide to the wisdom of Rilke*. New York: Modern Library.

Bowlby, J. (1973). *Attachment and loss, volume 2: Separation: Anxiety and anger*. New York: Basic Books.

Buechler, S. (1998). The analyst's experience of loneliness. *Contemporary Psychoanalysis*, *34*, 91–115.

Buechler, S. (2004). *Clinical values: Emotions that guide psychoanalytic treatment*. Hillsdale, NJ: Analytic Press.

Buechler, S. (2012). *Still practicing: The heartaches and joys of a clinical career*. New York: Routledge.

Buechler, S. (2017). *Psychoanalytic reflections: Training and practice*. New York: IPbooks.

Coltart, N. (1993). *How to survive as a psychotherapist*. London: Sheldon Press.

Davis, H. B. (1988). The self and loving. In J. F. Lasky & H. W. Silverman (Eds.), *Love* (pp. 159–172). New York: New York University Press.

Donley, C., & Buckley, S. (Eds.) (2000). *What's normal?* Kent, OH: Kent State University Press.

Freud, A. (1936). *The ego and the mechanisms of defense*. New York: International Universities Press.

Fromm, E. (1956). *The art of loving*. New York: Harper & Row.

Fromm-Reichmann, F. (1950). *Principles of intensive psychotherapy*. Chicago, IL: University of Chicago Press.

Fromm-Reichmann, F. (1959). On loneliness. In D. Bullard (Ed.), *Psychoanalysis and psychotherapy: Selected papers of Frieda Fromm-Reichmann* (pp. 325–336). Chicago, IL: University of Chicago Press.

Greenberg, J. (1954). *I never promised you a rose garden*. New York: New American Library.

Greenberg, J. R. (1981). Prescription or description: The therapeutic action of psychoanalysis. In D. B. Stern & I. Hirsch (Eds.), *The interpersonal perspective in psychoanalysis, 1960s–1990s* (pp. 132–152). New York: Routledge.

Hoffman, I. Z. (2009). Therapeutic passion in the countertransference. *Psychoanalytic Dialogues*, *19*, 617–637.

Levenson, E. A. (1978). Psychoanalysis: Cure or persuasion? In D. B. Stern & I. Hirsch (Eds.), *The interpersonal perspective in psychoanalysis, 1960s–1990s* (pp. 75–94). New York: Routledge.

Mohacsy, I. (1990). Solitude in a changing society: A discussion of Fromm-Reichmann's "loneliness." *Contemporary Psychoanalysis*, *26*, 360–364.

Rilke, R. M. (1934). *Letters to a young poet*. New York: W. W. Norton.

Schlesinger, G. (1995). Attachment, relationship, and love. In M. Lionells, J. Fiscalini, C. H. Mann, & D. B. Stern (Eds.), *Handbook of interpersonal psychoanalysis* (pp. 63–79). Hillsdale, NJ: Analytic Press.

Shakespeare, W. (1996). Let me not to the marriage of true minds. In S. A. Stuart (Ed.), *A treasury of poems* (p. 332). New York: BBS Publishing Co.

Singer, E. (1977/2017). The fiction of analytic anonymity. In D. B. Stern & I. Hirsch (Eds.), *The interpersonal perspective in psychoanalysis, 1960s–1990s* (pp. 60–75). New York: Routledge.

Slochower, J. (2017). Going too far: Relational heroines and relational excess. *Psychoanalytic Dialogues, 27*, 282–300.

Stern, D. B. (2017). Introduction: Interpersonal psychoanalysis: History and current status. In D. B. Stern & I. Hirsch (Eds.), *The interpersonal perspective in psychoanalysis, 1960s–1990s* (pp. 1–28). New York: Routledge.

Storr, A. (1988). *Solitude: A return to the self.* New York: Ballantine Books.

Sullivan, H. S. (1940). *Conceptions of modern psychiatry.* New York: Norton.

Sullivan, H. S. (1953). *The interpersonal theory of psychiatry.* New York: W. W. Norton.

Tillich, P. (1987). In R. I. Fitzhenry (Ed.), *Barnes and Noble book of quotations* (p. 217). New York: Harper & Row.

Winnicott, D. W. (1965). *The maturational process and the facilitating environment.* London: Hogarth Press.

Wolstein, B. (1975). Countertransference: The psychoanalyst's shared experience and inquiry with the patient. In D. B. Stern & I. Hirsch (Eds.), *The interpersonal perspective in psychoanalysis, 1960s–1990s* (pp. 45–60). New York: Routledge.

Wolstein, B. (1983). The first person in interpersonal relations. *Contemporary Psychoanalysis, 19*, 522–535.

Chapter 2

Mourning

How can we help someone mourn? What do we know about the process of bearing loss? This chapter explores mourning and suggests some of the ways people find to deal with sorrow. Poets, painters, fiction writers, ecclesiastics, psychoanalysts, and others have contributed thoughts about bearing life's inevitable losses. How can their insights inform the clinician?

While, of course, each death is as different as each human being, what can we learn from the experiences of others? More specifically, how might fighting for someone's every breath, before they die, affect subsequent mourning? Not every death allows us this option, but, even when fighting is possible, we still have the psychological "choice" about the level of our conscious awareness of its meaning to us. Along with Freud (1917), we used to believe that adaptation to loss, letting go, was the best approach, allowing us to heal as quickly as possible and invest in new relationships. Do we still ascribe to this belief, even though most of us no longer accept the drive model on which it was based? That is, we no longer think a human being has a finite amount of "cathexis" to invest, so that "de-cathecting" the dead allows room for new relationships. But, even though most have given up this model, do we still believe in its conclusion that a quicker mourning process is, in some sense, better?

What about other aspects of mourning, such as its intensity and the degree to which the feelings are expressed verbally? If we believe finding words for sorrow helps, why would that be? Does it matter if the words are heard by another person, or does finding them suffice?

I have no doubt that each of these is a very personal question with no generally applicable answer. But there are those who have vividly and evocatively plumbed their own sorrows. I think examining some of their insights might help us each access our own resources.

Fighting death

Elsewhere (Buechler, 2008, 2015), I have explored the idea that a sorrow uncomplicated by regret may be easier to bear. That is, just as Freud (1917) suggested that mourning preceded by an ambivalent relationship is more likely to lead to depression, I have broadened this idea, to include regret, shame, guilt, and envy as potentially encumbering subsequent sorrow.

I have explored several ways to understand this. One (Buechler, 2015) is that emotions such as regret, shame, guilt, and envy empty the self of strengths that are needed to bear loss. The "work" of mourning is a heavy burden and draws on all our coping capacities. Any feeling that diminishes our sense of self will decrease our ability to bear loss.

Another way to see this follows from the emotion theory (Buechler, 2004, 2008) that has informed much of my own thinking. According to this theory, an emotion, such as sorrow, is modulated by all the other feelings occurring at the same time. Just as, in color theory, my experience of yellow depends some on whether it is surrounded by black or white, similarly, sorrow in the context of guilt is not exactly the same as sorrow in the midst of rage. How, then, might sorrow be affected by fierce efforts to forestall accompanying regret?

I know no more forthright expression of the will to keep someone alive than *Death Be Not Proud* by John Gunther (1949). It is the story of two parents' dedication to the treatment of their son, Johnny, through the process of his illness and death. I think it has a great deal to say about fighting death with every resource available, and its effect on subsequent regret and sorrow.

Johnny Gunther was 17 years old when he died of a brain tumor. The son of Frances and John Gunther, Johnny endured heroic medical interventions for 15 harrowing months before he succumbed. In 1949, John Gunther wrote the unforgettable *Death Be Not Proud* to chronicle his son's valiant struggle. The father argues with himself, as he looks back at the decisions he, Frances, and the doctors made, to fight for time, no matter what Johnny had to go through in the process.

> People may ask if it would not have been better if we had had fewer doctors and less treatment. Perhaps we tried to do too much. But Johnny loved life desperately and we loved him desperately and it was our duty to try absolutely everything and keep him alive as long as possible.
>
> (p. 125)

Like so many others, John and Frances Gunther bore, along with their wrenching sorrow, the terrible burden of making a series of decisions about how hard to fight for the smallest shred of a chance for their son's recovery. A few sentences later, John goes on to justify their approach.

> Always we thought that, if only we could maintain life somehow, some extraordinary new cure might be discovered. We thought of boys who died of streptococcus infections just before sulfa came into use. Our decisions were almost always dictated by successive emergencies, with one delicate consideration poised against another, and they were not taken lightly, I can assure you.
>
> (p. 125)

At the same time as John and Frances dealt with these judgment calls, they also had to titrate how much to tell Johnny. At times, he seemed to know his death was near, but sometimes he held onto hope. Just weeks before he died, he was determined to graduate from high school and receive his diploma with his class. Sitting in the audience at the church ceremony, Johnny's parents were anxious about whether Johnny could physically withstand the graduation march. Johnny's name was called and, head bandaged, he very slowly made his way up the aisle.

> The applause began and then rose and the applause became a storm, as every single person in the old church became whipped up, tight and tense, to see if he would make it. The applause became a thunder, it rose and soared and banged, when Johnny finally reached the pulpit.
>
> (p. 122)

John Gunther believed that

> Everything that Johnny suffered was in a sense repaid by the few heroic moments of that walk down the center aisle of that church. This was his triumph and indomitable summation. Nobody who saw it will ever forget it or be able to forget the sublime strength of will and character it took.
>
> (p. 123)

Just weeks later, the tumor eroded a blood vessel, and he died of a cerebral hemorrhage.

Frances Gunther wrote an afterword, in which she described her grief. She remains dry-eyed when she thinks abstractly about death, but what tears at her heart is the "sunny fast wind along the Sound, good sailing weather, a new light boat . . . Johnny would have loved these things, and he is no longer here to enjoy them" (p. 190). She lists her regrets: the pleasures she wishes she had provided for Johnny while she could. Though she clearly loved Johnny with all her heart, still she wishes she had loved him more.

For me, this poignant story epitomizes sorrow that feeds the fight for life. John, Frances, and Johnny did not adapt. They made agonizing choices to endure anything for a ray of hope. Yielding had no place in their hearts. After Johnny died, one of the doctors (Wilder Penfield) wrote to the parents: "You two, by your restless effort, kept him alive a year longer than should be expected. You could have done no more. It was worthwhile" (p. 141). I think that fighting for Johnny's life became an end in itself, in a way. It was not just the scraps of hope that a cure could be found, if they just held out. It was also that they wanted to go down fighting. It was the only way the three of them could bear the tragedy of Johnny's loss of the Sound, good sailing weather, and a new light boat.

I can only speculate that their valiant efforts to keep Johnny alive helped his parents bear his death, in that it eliminated one regret. At the end of the memoir,

John Gunther wrote of another. One of the doctors told him that, had Johnny lived longer, he probably would have gone blind and lost some of his capacity to relate. Gunther believed that "Even Johnny's gallantry could not have stood up under that" (p. 142). When there was absolutely no more hope, sparing Johnny more suffering and loss became his parents' sole priority.

The cerebral hemorrhage ended decision-making, in a sense. Was that, too, a relief? John and Frances didn't have to articulate the words, "Let's stop trying to keep him alive." I can only wonder how this affected their mourning. When we try to understand grief, I think it is important to look at the regrets accompanying it, whether or not they seem rational to an outsider. Frances' wish she had loved Johnny more did not make logical sense to me, given how moved I was by her articulation of her bond with her son. But, of course, it is her feelings that matter, and not a logical argument.

We can speculate how refusing to yield to loss, until there is no more hope, affects the sorrow that follows. If John and Frances had "pulled the plug" a year earlier, would their anguish have been any different? In "Mourning and Melancholia," Freud (1917) highlighted ambivalence as grief's greatest complication. If we ambivalently love someone, we are more likely to suffer melancholia, rather than simple mourning, when we lose them. So, if we fight for their lives with all our might, have we proven to ourselves (and them) that our love for them is pure?

Of course, every sorrow is its own country. What spares unrelieved grief for one person might not have that impact for another. And it is impossible to measure, or compare, one person's fight for life with another's. We are left with more questions than answers. But reading this incredibly moving memoir made me think that the course of grief might be affected by whether (to the extent it is possible) the dying was consistent with the life as it was lived. From all Johnny's diary entries and his parents' anecdotes, it is very clear that Johnny loved life. Helping him fight for it for 15 months may have given his parents a way for him to die as he lived. He was Johnny in his death, as he was in his life.

Johnny wrote a poem, "Unbeliever's Prayer," the year before he died. Here is how it ended.

> And O!
> if Thou art truly in the heavens,
> accept my gratitude
> for all Thy gifts
> and I shall try
> to fight the good fight. Amen.
>   (Gunther, 1947, p. 197)

His father ended the memoir with this poem. As for Frances, her last lines were, "I hope we can love Johnny more and more till we too die, and leave behind us, as he did, the love of love, the love of life" (p. 195).

I am suggesting that, at least for some, maintaining one's identity through the end of life, and maintaining consistency in how we relate, may affect our "adaptation" to loss. John and Frances lost Johnny's body, but his spirit, and their support of it, were uncompromised. It is true that their healthy son was "replaced" by a dying child, but Johnny remained resolutely Johnny, and they remained his unfaltering spiritual parents.

Refusing to register loss

Can it sometimes help to pit our will against awareness of loss? More generally, as our field accepts the idea that dissociation can be adaptive in some circumstances (Bromberg, 1998), do we also accept that denial helps us bear sorrow? If that is so, how should it affect our clinical approach? Should we avoid disturbing denial in those suffering loss? For how long?

I think sometimes we rebel against loss by defensively failing to register it. This omission may come in the form of denial, dissociation, or other defensive patterns. For example, consider a poem by Sherman Alexie (2016), "Grief Calls Us to the Things of This World." In it, Alexie wakes in a hotel room and sees a blue telephone in the bathroom. He wants to tell someone about it, and decides to call his father. He dials home, and his mother answers.

Alexie asks to speak to his father, momentarily forgetting that his father has been dead for nearly a year. He starts to apologize, but his mother quite understands. In fact, she, too, has had a similar experience. She made her husband his usual cup of coffee in the morning, only to realize her mistake hours later. Then Alexie refers to the angels who wait for us to praise our forgetfulness, so that they can slap us with the cold, painful reality we desperately wanted to avoid.

For me, these lines reflect the triumph and failure of defense. We are grateful for temporary reprieves when we "forget" our pain. But then memory, that cold angel, slaps our souls with the truth, and we suffer the loss all over again. In my reading of this poem, I hear a conflict between our willful forgetting of the loss and emissaries from the cold, cruel world. They lurk until they see an opportunity to pounce. Opportunity comes in the form of a detail that trips us up. We ask to speak to the father that (oops!) has been dead for a year. We rejoiced in our forgetfulness until we were caught short by undeniable reality. Then we apologize. But, for what? It seems to me that, in the poem, the son apologizes to his mother as though, by forgetting his father is dead, he has been inconsiderate. He has unnecessarily put her through the pain of explaining her husband's absence. But, for me, the lines have yet another meaning. I think we can feel shame about willfully refusing to acknowledge death. It is as though we have been caught being childish. Metaphorically, unconsciously, we stamped our foot. In effect, our behavior said, "No! He is not dead. I won't have it." Because it is too awful, it can't be true.

I think the mother's forgetting expresses the same sequence. An unconscious, willful, defensive refusal, slapped by reality, becomes shame. The mother laughs at herself. Look at silly me, she seems to say. Fooled by the wishful fantasy that what has happened for 27 years will happen again today. Naive. Wanting to believe, I laid myself open, readied myself to be slapped down by those cruel, truthful, vengeful angels. I thought I could go on with life as usual, thought I could escape the pain, which brought it down upon me even harder than before.

The last lines of the poem make the conflict even more vicious. Those vengeful angels punish us for our blessed moments of forgetting. With ruthless zeal, they bring us to our knees.

Like Alexie's mother, we make ourselves easy prey for avenging angels of reality. Our passionate prayers accompany us as we fall into their grasp. Like the figures in a Brueghel "Last Judgment," our own willful behavior determines our fall.

But, is it sometimes worth it? Does a vacation from the truth, however brief, allow us to bear the ultimately inescapable facts? I can only surmise that the frequency with which loss is denied means that, sometimes, psychic survival depends on a temporary suspension of facing reality.

That moment of unconscious, determined forgetting is beautifully portrayed in John Bayley's (1999) memoir, *Elegy for Iris*. Bayley was married to the brilliant author and philosopher Iris Murdoch. Murdoch developed Alzheimer's disease, and Bayley spent years caring for her as she became less and less able to care for herself. When she died, Bayley closed and opened her eyes, as though they could still play games. For the first time in days, Bayley felt really seen by Iris, as if he had forgotten she was dead.

In this case (and perhaps in others), I think the forgetting is not so much a refusal to steadily maintain awareness of the loss. Rather, I think it is a reflection of Bayley's ongoing relationship with his wife, which changes only in some respects after her death. Bayley tells us that he doesn't miss Iris or remember her as he would remember things and people who are truly gone. His experience is of sleeping quietly at night, with his wife quiet beside him.

A similar phenomenon is recounted by Joan Didion (2005) in *The Year of Magical Thinking*, her memoir about the death of her husband. Didion explains that, after her husband's death, she was unable to give away his shoes, since she believed he was about to return and might still need them. It seems that, quite frequently, we say no to death by refusing to take it in. This response always reminds me of the movement of an amoeba away from a potential threat. It doesn't fight the enemy, but, rather, it just glides away.

The poet Sherman Alexie wrote of the "slap" of the cold truth when he had to realize that his father is dead. A very similar moment is described with great simplicity by Marquez (1985) in his lyrical book, *Love in the Time of Cholera*. Marquez tells of a sleeping woman, recently widowed, searching for a comfortable position in her bed and finding her husband's place empty. For her, this was the moment he died.

W. H. Auden wrote two poems that explore another kind of "slap of cold truth." For the bereaved, it can seem bizarre, and peculiarly unfeeling, that the world goes on about its business as though the tragedy hadn't happened. In his poem, "Musée des Beaux Arts" (Auden, 2010), he says that the "old master" painters were never wrong about suffering. They understood it well enough to situate it in the midst of ordinary life. One person is enduring the most devastating loss, while others, perhaps nearby, simply carry on in total oblivion.

It can seem equally hard to believe that the world simply goes on, and that, for the bereaved, nothing will ever be the same. Perhaps someone opening a window strikes us as strange because we so deeply wish we could ever open one again, trusting life as we did only yesterday. Part of us wants to shake the person walking dully along, perhaps to awaken them to mourning. Auden expresses this in another great elegy, "Funeral Blues" (Auden, 2017). In this poem, he orders all clocks to stop and all telephones, pianos, and dogs to be silent. Only the sights and sounds of mourning should be allowed on this day, which is full of grief. The poet has lost his beloved, who meant everything. "Normal" life would be out of place today. Every particle of earth, sea, and sky should reflect only sorrow. Auden counted on his love to last forever. Now, along with his lover, he has lost the hope that anything good can happen to him.

It might be comforting if, at least, the outer world would mirror our inner desolation.

In James Agee's (1957) *A Death in the Family*, Mary first hears of her husband's car accident from a man who phones but tells her no details. Mary reasons that this means one of three things: Either Jay is badly hurt but will live, or he is terribly hurt and will die of it, or he is already dead and the man on the phone did not want to be the one to break the news. It has to be one of these alternatives, but no matter which it is, there is nothing she can do about it. All Mary can do is try to be ready for whatever comes. For Mary, at this moment, being strong is all that matters, because it is all that is possible.

Mary wonders why she hadn't asked any questions when the man telephoned. Her aunt, Hannah, reassures her that it was not because she didn't care. As Hannah listens to Mary's resolution, she remembers her own awakening to life's sorrows, almost 30 years earlier. Hannah reflects on the crosses we all have to bear, and how she learned to endure her own burdens and accept them. She feels sorry for Mary, whose real suffering has just started and whose soul has just begun the painful process of maturation.

Mary's brother, Andrew, brings her the grim news, that in the crash her husband was killed instantly by a concussion. Andrew says he is sure Jay didn't have time to know he was about to die, and that is something to be glad about. She asks for a whiskey, and tells Andrew that she thanks God that Jay hadn't known what was about to happen. Mary's father warns her not to carry on like some do when they lose a husband. Mary assures him that he need not worry about that, and her father says he knows she will control herself, because she is not a fool. Her father goes on to say that Mary will have to go through her pain alone, because no one can help her. All anyone can offer is a primal kind of sympathy. He exhorts her to bear up, to remember that millions of others have gone through this, and that there is no use carrying on about it. Her father further advises her to get comfort from religion but not to hide in it. To end their conversation, he says that this crisis is a test that a good person would be able to bear. He tells her he has confidence in her, and she thanks him.

Mary seems to acquiesce to her father, just as she tries to accept her beloved husband's sudden death. Then, when she is told the details of the accident, she cries for mercy but quickly asks for forgiveness for her outburst. Andrew apologizes for telling her too much at once, but Mary says it is better to get all the details at once. Andrew proceeds by telling Mary all that could have happened and would have been worse. Jay could have lived but been feeble-minded for the rest of his life. Or he could have been crushed, mangled, and died slowly, agonizingly. Or lived but been a hopeless cripple. Andrew assures Mary that he couldn't have suffered, because death came too fast. Mary takes comfort from the picture of Jay dying with bravery and confidence. She feels she knows Jay must have died just as he lived—with forthright strength and courage. She is sure that in his last moments Jay looked death directly in the face. She wants the words on his gravestone to reflect this. Another family member muses that people try to feel we have some control over death, simply by choosing particular words to describe it or wanting to know exactly how it happened.

Mary's self-control and yielding to fate don't last. Briefly, she feels Jay's presence, but it fades. She prays to truly comprehend that Jay is really gone. She does, at last, on the day of the funeral. The description of her pain breaking through her composure, and her comprehension of the finality of Jay's absence, is one of the most powerful expressions of grief I have ever encountered. It has beauty as well as profound insight about Mary's willful determination to realize her loss, as it became stronger than her determination to adapt in silence. As she tries to leave the bedroom she had shared with Jay to go to his funeral, she begins to understand how her life would never be the same.

Mary rocks backward, forward, and side to side. Her sobs come from deep inside her body, like the groans of a fatally hurt animal. As Mary rocks and groans, she gradually becomes aware of every aspect of her loss, every feeling, thought, and image connected to it. Like slowly emerging countryside in morning light, Mary grasps her new reality.

Initially, Mary defends against the enormity of her loss and all that it entails. And then she begins to understand that this one event will make every tomorrow different from every yesterday. Her future takes a shape, like the subject of a painting by J. M. Turner that is just beginning to emerge from fog. She can no longer numb herself. If she will be able to "adapt," it will be a more active process than the passive yielding we saw in the immediate aftermath of hearing about Jay's death.

The next passages are as remarkable as any of the previous ones. We listen to Rufus, the loving and beloved son of Mary and Jay, go through his own efforts to make his loss real, to *realize* that his father won't come home any more. He tries to listen as the priest explains that he and his sister must now consider God as their father, but all he can do is concentrate on the blue and yellow tiles of the hearth. But, like his mother, Rufus struggles with his own denial. He keeps repeating to himself the word *dead*. He is taken to see his father's body. Then, overwhelmed by the throng of friends and family that descended on their home, he watches as two men screw shut the box with his father's body inside.

When Rufus and his younger sister, Catherine, see their mother again, she has changed, and her touch is no longer tender. The book ends with Catherine wondering where her father is. Other men have come back to their homes on their block. Where is he? Catherine can no longer bear being alone but doesn't know who she can approach. Through a door, she hears her mother and aunt praying. Her mother is choking but refuses to stop praying, even though her aunt pleads with her. Catherine escapes to another room and stares at the carpet until her mother finds her, and she cries and urinates without being aware of it. She, too, has kept control by staring into space until the awful reality is too vivid to deny, and then grief is absolutely overwhelming.

Details define this topography of grief. Some of them can anchor a wavering focus, allowing Mary, Rufus, and Catherine to temporarily lose themselves in the carpet or the hearth. But there are other details, tiny moments or images, that burn through the haze, commanding awareness. Knowing, in the abstract, that her father is "dead" can be kept at arm's length, but seeing that her father doesn't come home at night with the others eventually penetrates Catherine, as it must eventually break through to everyone else.

In just a few lines, Shakespeare (1972) captured Lear's protest and effort to comprehend the senseless death of his beloved young daughter, Cordelia.

> Why should a dog, a horse, a rat, have life,
> And thou no breath at all? Thou'lt come no more,
> Never, never, never, never, never.
> > (Act 5, scene 3, lines 305–307)

Even after this seeming recognition, Lear tries to alter his literally unbearable perception.

> Pray, you undo this button: thank you, Sir.
> Do you see this? Look on her, look, her lips,
> Look there! Look there!
> (Dies.)
> > (Lines 308–310)

Sometimes, we try to refuse to let the facts register. We won't "go along" with what is happening. We "punish" outer reality by abandoning it and turning inward. But, like a child running away, eventually we have to come home. And then we are flooded with all the pain that has been collecting. Suffering pools.

Dwelling on details

As was true for many in the aftermath of 9/11, and in contrast to the denial discussed above, people often comb every detail of a loss, as though a vivid, blow-by-blow account of how it happened will contribute to healing. I sometimes think of someone moving their tongue over a sore tooth, rubbing in the pain. Perhaps (for some) this is a depressive form of fury. We are willing ourselves to face every last drop, to etch in every detail. Do we do this in hope of catharsis? Exorcism? Penance? As a way to counter the defensive denial of the death (see previous section)?

Dwelling on details can take various forms. We can imagine the exact sequence of events leading up to a death. Or we can vividly call to mind every aspect of the person we have lost, every precious quality we miss. We can use memories of times spent with that person to paint the picture of exactly what we will never again experience. It is as though we are etching the pain into our psyches, detail by detail.

Is there something healing about squarely facing every nook and cranny? I think of a poem by Marie Howe (2016), titled "What the Living Do." The poem reads like a letter to her brother Johnnie, who died a slow, agonizing death from AIDS.

> Johnnie, the kitchen sink has been clogged for days,
>   some utensil probably fell down there.
> And the Drano won't work but smells dangerous, and
>   the crusty dishes have piled up.
> Waiting for the plumber I still haven't called. This is
>   the evening we spoke of.
> It's winter again: the sky's a deep headstrong blue
>   and the sunlight pours through
> the open living room windows because the heat's on
>   too high in here, and I can't turn it off.
> For weeks now, driving, or dropping a bag of groceries
>   in the street, the bag breaking,
> I've been thinking: This is what the living do. And,
>   yesterday, hurrying along those
> wobbly bricks in the Cambridge sidewalk, spilling my
>   coffee down my wrist and sleeve,
> I thought it again, and again later, when buying a
>   hairbrush: This is it.
> Parking. Slamming the car door shut in the cold. What
>   you called that yearning.
> What you finally gave up. We want the spring to come
>   and the winter to pass. We want
> whoever to call, or not call, a letter, a kiss-we want
>   more, and more, and then more of it.
> But there are moments, walking, when I catch
>   a glimpse of myself in the window glass,
> say, the window of the corner video store, and I'm
>   gripped by a cherishing so deep
> for my own blowing hair, chapped face, and
>   unbuttoned coat that I'm speechless:
> I am living, I remember you.

(pp. 63–64)

The poet cascades details until we, too, are surrounded by ramshackle. She doesn't tell us *about* anything. She brings us to a place where feeling happens inside us. Brushstroke by brushstroke, Howe portrays the brother she misses. She goes over her store of "Johnnie" moments. Separately, she misses the Johnnie who knew something about plumbing and the Johnnie who finally gave up on life. As she misses each Johnnie, does she become better able to bear her loss? This can be thought of as the "work" of mourning (Freud, 1917). But can this work be done without finding words for each aspect of loss? Or does it help to verbally formulate who all our Johnnies were to us? If so, is it necessary to communicate each detail to another person?

These questions are of obvious importance to the clinician. After all, we are the "talking" profession. But, ordinarily, words are limited tools. If we want words that actually evoke experiences, we may be best off looking to poetry. In an unusual memoir, told via the poems that deeply affected her at various points in her life, Jill Bialosky (2017) expresses this well: "Perhaps we turn to poetry because it can fathom and hold the inexplicable, the gasp between words, the emotional hues impossible to capture in everyday speech or conversation" (p. 180). In another interesting passage, she quotes the poet Jean Valentine, who said, "The likeness lies in poetry and meditative prayer and dreaming all being (potentially anyhow) healing, and all being out of our hands. For me poetry is mostly silence. The deeper the better" (p. 36). Should the clinician aim to "fathom and hold the inexplicable, the gasp between words"? Are our best interpretations "out of our hands"? I return to the power and shortcomings of words throughout this book and the implications for training in its last chapter.

Should we aim to decrease sorrow's intensity?

> Our instinct should not be to desire consolation over a loss, but rather to develop a deep and painful curiosity to explore this loss completely, to experience the peculiarity, the singularity, and the effects of *this* loss in our life. Indeed, we should muster the kind of noble greed that would enrich our inner world with *this* loss and its significance and weight . . . The more profoundly we are affected by such a loss and the more painfully it concerns us, the more it becomes our *task* to claim as a new, different, and definitive possession that which has been so hopelessly emphasized by this loss.
>
> (Rilke, in Baer, 2005, p. 109, italics in original)

I find Rilke's comments both beautiful and persuasive. I discuss the issue of leaning into pain, rather than escaping it, in a subsequent chapter on the topic of suffering. Briefly, I understand Rilke's philosophy as a valid perspective on dealing with loss. I appreciate his advocacy of "noble greed" toward potentially internalized loved ones, as well as his argument for a "painful curiosity" about the particular, personal meaning of the loss. I hear his plea for delving into our experience, rather than trying to escape it, as a deeply meaningful statement. It reminds me of emotion theory's (Buechler, 2008; Izard, 1977) tenet that our feelings are potentially valuable communications to ourselves (and others), and efforts to escape them often render us alienated from ourselves.

Returning to the emotion theory (Izard, 1972, 1977) that suggests that feelings always exist in a system, so an experience of sorrow is modulated by all the other emotions occurring at the same time, we might believe that we can modulate sadness by helping the mourner connect with what else is true. But, once again, this raises the issue of whether our aim should be "modulation" of sadness, by whatever means. Elsewhere (Buechler, 2010), I have described three attitudes toward this issue that are present in the analytic culture and the wider culture. I will revisit it in chapters on resiliency and suffering in this book.

In a more general sense, to what degree should we try to help someone in pain, of any kind, by directing their attention elsewhere? Traditionally, clinicians have differed markedly on whether it is best to direct the patient's attention at all, let alone in which direction. Communicating some equivalent of "we have to take the bad with the good," or "look on the bright side," or "make lemonade out of lemons," is a popular self-help principle. I see it as in tune with adaptation models of health, and assumptions that muted affective intensities are preferable, and "getting it out" in words is therapeutic. The mourner is expected to self-regulate sorrow by focusing on positive feelings or exerting willpower. Sometimes, shame or guilt is invoked, and the mourner is led to feel noble if he or she verbally "shares" and, while palpably suffering, remains in emotional control.

Many outcries against this attitude could be cited, but I will limit myself to one. In the story "The Management of Grief" by Bharati Mukherjee (1992), the author addresses the issue of "normal" emotionality in the face of loss. Shaila is living in Canada with her husband, Vikram, and their two sons. Vikram and the boys are returning from a trip to India when the plane is bombed and splits in half just a short distance from Heathrow Airport. Along with the other relatives, Shaila is taken to Ireland to identify photographs of the victims. Judith, a social worker, tries to enlist Shaila's help in dealing with the other grief-stricken mourners. Judith calls on Shaila because she is a "pillar," having taken the news calmly. Shaila refuses to see her outward calm as superior to the more intense grieving of the others. Each person must grieve in their own way. By the standards of some of the other survivors, she is behaving oddly and badly.

How does someone "cope well" with losing her husband and sons? What is a "normal" reaction? How much do cultural and religious teachings affect the definition of "healthy" sorrow? Is it normal to hear your loved one speak to you after he is dead? Is it normal for some people, given their religious backgrounds, but not for others? More generally, can one person ever really understand the grief of another or the best "management of grief"? This story suggests that harm can be done to the bereaved by intimating that expressions of sorrow can and should be controlled. The implication is that a stronger person would master grief or, at least, subdue its expression.

Previously (Buechler, 2010), I noted my own objections to this slant in my reaction to a book by Richard Taylor (2002) titled *Virtue Ethics*. Taylor describes the "healthy" response to adversity as privileging pride in one's fortitude over emotional expressions of grief. He writes of the "great test" of responding to the "death of a son or daughter who was intelligent and strong, and filled with promise of great achievement" (p. 103). Taylor contrasts a strong, noble response with the reaction of those who "collapse into whimpering and self-pity" (p. 103). In my comments on this statement, I said that I would fail most of Taylor's tests.

> Even if a son or daughter of mine were not exceptionally intelligent, strong, or filled with promise, on his or her death I would certainly whimper, and do plenty more. Taylor's language contrasts nobility, at one end of a spectrum, with whimpering self-pity at the other. What he elevates as healthy pride and fortitude I see as a kind of schizoid narcissism.
>
> (Buechler, 2010, pp. 341–342)

I also suggested that this approach may have the opposite effect from the one intended. For example, if we influence a patient to mute sorrow they may miss its positive potential, such as the possibility, in a state of sorrow, to connect with others who offer empathy.

In the language of Rollo May (1991), we might see Taylor's approach as an expression of a culturally scripted idealization of stoicism. A somewhat more palatable approach is the idea of gradual relinquishing of the lost object. This, again, accords with Freud's (1917) model of the work of mourning. While not as extreme as Taylor's, it still elevates "letting go" as an emotional achievement.

It seems probable that one's point of view about healthy mourning accords with one's more general attitudes about bearing life's pain. My 2010 paper (cited earlier) contrasts three views: the attitude that strong, painful affect is a symptom and we should aim to diminish it; the attitude that the defensive avoidance of pain is more often problematic than the pain itself; and the attitude that suffering frequently connects us with each other and acquaints us with the human condition. I argue that clinicians often hold one of these views without necessarily becoming aware of it. Each of the three attitudes affects how we work with defenses and, more generally, impacts our therapeutic stance.

Given that there is no universally optimal "management of grief," how can we recognize "normal" as opposed to pathological sorrow? *The Loss of Sadness* (Horwitz & Wakefield, 2007) deals with that question. Briefly, these authors suggest that if we concentrate on symptoms, such as the duration of grief or its intensity, we tend to pathologize normal sorrow. Sadness is a normal response to loss, whether it is loss of a person, a dream, a profession, a belief, or any of the other significant attachments human beings make. Normal sadness can last a lifetime and can be extremely intense. We must look for another way to distinguish normal sadness from pathology.

Elsewhere (Buechler, 2015), I have suggested that those suffering from normal grief generally do not feel ashamed of themselves in addition to their sorrow. In contrast, in a pathological state, the person has lost self-love along with the loss of the beloved. Both the outer and the inner worlds are impoverished. This belief has led me to focus on the emotions accompanying sorrow, rather than the sorrow itself. Both theoretically and clinically, I consider ways that shame, regret, guilt, or other feelings may be compromising the mourner's strength to bear the inevitable pain of loss. The sorrow is unavoidable, but we may be able to have an impact on the shame, regret, or guilt that is complicating it. As noted earlier, Freud (1917) focused on ambivalence as the key problem that renders mourning into melancholia. While this certainly occurs, I think other emotions just as frequently play a role.

A clinical approach

My personal as well as professional experience tells me that holding a standard for "healthy" sorrow is counterproductive. There is no "right" intensity or duration for grief. Communicating that a patient's pain is problematic, in itself, often adds shame and, perhaps, loneliness to the patient's feelings. With this added burden, the patient may be even less able to muster the strength bereavement requires. I think there is an inevitable loss of aspects of self, in addition to the loss of the other. For example, when a good friend dies, I may lose that person's ready understanding of my sense of humor. Perhaps I don't joke, in just the same way, with anyone else. I have lost that "jokester" aspect of myself, along with the loss of my friend.

But, while this is an impoverishment of the self, along with the impoverishment of my outer world, I don't necessarily feel shame or guilt about it. I may well feel intense, abiding sorrow and loneliness, but not self-blame. This is a vital difference, from my point of view. The sadness of grief is no different in intensity or duration from the sadness in depression. But the emotions that accompany the sadness are often different. Thus, clinically, it is those accompanying emotions that are my focus.

Therapeutically, I don't communicate that it is time to "move on" from sorrow, but I do take an interest in the patient's self-regard. I also wonder about other emotions that are, or are not, present. Is there (rather than shame or guilt) a nurturing attitude toward oneself, as one goes through a difficult time? Is there a sense of deepening awareness of the human condition, of the sorrow that is our inescapable fate? Is there a sense of oneness with fellow sufferers? Is there a feeling of connection with what is still alive in oneself and others?

To return to the poem by Marie Howe (2016), as already noted, the sister ends her "letter" to her dead brother, Johnnie, with the following lines:

> there are moments, walking, when I catch
> a glimpse of myself in the window glass,

say, the window of the corner video store, and I'm
> gripped by a cherishing so deep
for my own blowing hair, chapped face, and
> unbuttoned coat that I'm speechless:
I am living, I remember you.

(pp. 63–64)

Alongside her grief for the many Johnnies she has lost is a profound surge of joy in her own aliveness. One doesn't cancel the other out. Howe does not seem ashamed of her complicated emotions. She is not telling herself to sorrow less, or more, or to be ashamed of her vibrant joy. The sorrow and joy exist side by side, good neighbors that don't threaten each other.

For me as an analyst, and as a human being who has suffered her own losses, it is important to affirm that pain is part of being human. Its intensity and duration do not mark it as pathological. It links me with all who have come before me and all who will come to life in the future.

In terms of this book's main themes, I do not hold, as a goal, to "adapt" to loss or to decrease its intensity, but I do believe that finding words for it sometimes helps. The discovery, in a poem, or in a friend's compassion, or an analyst's or patient's empathy, of a word that encapsulates my experience palpably tells me I am not alone. Howe's last line, "I am living, I remember you," validates the juxtaposition of sorrow and joy that I have often felt. When I read it, I feel understood. Perhaps, more importantly, I feel less lonely, because her words tell me that I *can* be understood. Howe found the "right" words to describe my own experience and, in that formulation, she gave me a precious gift. Once I read her words, I had a verbal structure for my feelings, as well as a kind of seal of approval. This lightens my burden in several ways. I am less likely to complicate my sorrow with shame, guilt, regret, or loneliness. And I am more likely to access joy and a desire to handle myself with care, to see myself through a difficult passage.

Whether I am the sufferer or it is someone else, compassion is essential and not to be confused with pity. The sufferer is challenged to rise to the occasion. Compassion toward myself (or another) registers respect for this effortful exertion. Bearing loss can take all we have, every ounce of strength, every source of inspiration and determination. We need to be functioning on all cylinders, just as we do when swept up in writing or fully engaged in a physical activity, among other immersive experiences.

When people try to hide suffering, I think it shows a lack of comprehension of its power to bring out the best in us. Of course, it doesn't always bring this out. But courage and fierce determination often punctuate stories of terrorist attacks, floods, and other tragedies. And even when the response is not dramatically heroic, there is still a human being struggling to bear being a human being, pushing him or herself to find the strength.

A poem by Mary Oliver (1983), "Blackwater Woods," honors fully inhabiting this part of our task. To me, it affirms that in our loving relationships, including self-love, we mustn't hold back any part of ourselves just because loss is inevitable. I would say that this humility does "adapt" in that it bows to nature, but it does so with no loss of self-respect. Here is part of Mary Oliver's poem.

> Every year
> everything
> I have ever learned
> in my lifetime
> leads back to this: the fires
> and the black river of loss
> whose other side
> is salvation,
> whose meaning
> none of us will ever know.
> To live in this world
> your must be able
> to do three things:
> to love what is mortal;
> to hold it
> against your bones knowing
> your own life depends on it;
> and, when the time comes to let it
> go, to let it go.
>
> (pp. 82–83)

References

Agee, J. (1957). *A death in the family*. New York: Penguin Books.

Alexie, S. (2016). Grief calls us to the things of this world. In H. M. Seiden (Ed.), *The motive for metaphor* (pp. 1–2). London: Karnac.

Auden, W. H. (2010). Musée des beaux arts. In K. Young (Ed.), *The art of losing: Poems of grief and healing* (p. 3). New York: Bloomsbury.

Auden, W. H. (2017). Funeral blues. In J. Bialosky (Ed.), *Poetry will save your life* (pp. 180–181). New York: Atria Books.

Baer, U. (2005). *The poet's guide to the wisdom of Rilke*. New York: Modern Library.

Bayley, J. (1999). *Elegy for Iris*. New York: W. W. Norton & Company.

Bialosky, J. (Ed.) (2017). *Poetry will save your life*. New York: Atria Books.

Bromberg, P. (1998). *Standing in the spaces: Essays on clinical practice, trauma, and dissociation*. Hillsdale, NJ: Analytic Press.

Buechler, S. (2004). *Clinical values: Emotions that guide psychoanalytic treatment*. Hillsdale, NJ: Analytic Press.

Buechler, S. (2008). *Making a difference in patients' lives*. New York: Routledge.

Buechler, S. (2010). No pain, no gain? Suffering and the analysis of defense. *Contemporary Psychoanalysis, 46*, 334–354.

Buechler, S. (2015). *Understanding and treating patients in clinical psychoanalysis: Lessons from literature*. New York: Routledge.

Didion, J. (2005). *The year of magical thinking*. New York: Alfred A. Knopf.

Freud, S. (1917). Mourning and melancholia. In J. Strachey (Ed. & Trans.), *The standard edition of the complete psychological works of Sigmund Freud* (Vol. *14*, pp. 237–258). London: Hogarth Press.

Gunther, J. (1949). *Death be not proud*. New York: Harper & Row.

Horwitz, A. V., & Wakefield, J. C. (2007). *The loss of sadness*. New York: Oxford University Press.

Howe, M. (2016). What the living do. In H. M. Seiden (Ed.), *The motive for metaphor* (pp. 63–64). London: Karnac.

Izard, C. (1972). *Patterns of emotion*. New York: Academic Press.

Izard, C. (1977). *Human emotions*. New York: Plenum Press.

Marquez, G. G. (1985). *Love in the time of cholera*. New York: Penguin Books.

May, R. (1991). *The cry for myth*. New York: Dell Publishing.

Mukherjee, B. (1992). The management of grief. In J. C. Oates (Ed.), *The Oxford book of American short stories* (pp. 697–713). New York: Oxford University Press.

Oliver, M. (1983). Blackwater woods. In *American primitive* (pp. 82–23). Boston, MA: Back Bay Books.

Shakespeare, W. (1972). *King Lear*. In *The Arden edition of the works of William Shakespeare* (pp. 1–206). London: Methuen Drama.

Taylor, R. (2002). *Virtue ethics*. New York: Prometheus Books.

Chapter 3

Healthy aging

How can we help people navigate aging and approaching death? This chapter first lays out some of its inherent challenges. I think it is especially interesting to look at issues that seem to regularly evoke contradictory advice from commentators. For example, should we fight aging, holding onto our present state with all our might? Or is it better, in some sense "healthier," to gracefully adapt? Attitudes about adaptation and emotional intensity factor into how each of us wants to approach our own aging and death. Do we see death as more bearable if we decrease or try to maintain our investments in life to the very end? Do we believe we will be better off if we focus our attention on the past, present, or future? As we age, is it time to free ourselves from conventions? What causes shame and self-disgust about aging? How is aging colored by the individual's lifelong defensive patterns? How can those of advanced age best bear their envy of the young? Of course, these questions are expressed as choices for clarity. Each is a much more complicated array of conscious and non-conscious issues. The beliefs at the heart of this chapter include:

1   How we each have viewed health, throughout our lives, affects our approach to aging. In particular, our attitudes about adaptation play a role in how we each would respond to the issues raised in the previous paragraph.
2   Basic attitudes about emotional intensity also figure into our ways of dealing with aging. For example, if we generally tend to avoid intensity, we might see aging well as developing the capacity to delimit experiences of sorrow at its losses, shame at physical alterations, envy of the young, and other potentially keen feelings.
3   We differ in how much we each trust words to modulate experiences in general and the concomitants of aging in particular. Many have turned toward words to express how they feel about advancing age, and others have hungered after their words to better bear their own process. I cite a number of authors who count on words to help, but I also ask where words might be inadequate or even unhelpful.
4   Treatment includes a dialogue, most often unspoken, about coping in general and coping with aging in particular. I suggest ways the two participants in treatment affect each other by transmitting their coping styles, most often outside their own awareness.

Should we fight aging or adapt to it?

> Do not go gentle into that good night
> Old age should burn and rave at close of day;
> Rage, rage against the dying of the light.

(Thomas, 2010, p.19)

Should we "go gentle"? Or should we "rage against the dying of the light"? Just what can each of these attitudes translate into behaviorally? More generally, what do we mean by healthy aging? Is there a way to live this part of life well? How can we help people live aging as well as possible? For each of us, our overall attitude about tailoring ourselves to fit easily into our circumstances impacts our approach to aging. Most especially when we are trying to help a patient face aging but, I suggest, at all other points as well, treatment participants display their feelings about adaptation (usually outside their awareness). This is an issue I explore in each chapter of this book.

As I read it, Dylan Thomas's poem contains a whole philosophy of life. It exhorts us to go down fighting. Others would say that it might be better to gracefully, gradually accept the inevitable. Thomas opts for the former and, at least in my understanding, suggests what might make death particularly unbearable.

> Though wise men at their end know dark is right,
> Because their words had forked no lightening they
> Do not go gentle into that good night.
> Good men, the last wave by, crying how bright
> Their frail deeds might have danced in a green bay,
> Rage, rage against the dying of the light.

(p. 19)

Even the wise can't accept the unavoidable and go quietly when they have to shoulder deep regrets. If life didn't afford us a fair chance to shine bright, or wisdom came too late, and we feel we have not taken full advantage of our talents, death is too painful to accept.

This reminds me of Henry James' (1992) great story "The Middle Years." James explores the disastrous effect of an aging writer's awareness that his life is nearly over. Dencombe is convalescing at a health resort after a bout of a debilitating illness. He has just received a copy of his new book from his publisher and realizes, with distress, that he doesn't remember the book's contents. He struggles with what this means about the functioning of his mind.

Dencombe suffers from a sense of shrinking opportunity. He feels not so much that his last chance is going as that it is gone. He has done everything he would ever do and yet hasn't done what he most wanted. He yearns for "another go, ah for a better chance" (p. 174). Dencombe feels sure he can see his future, and it is empty of all that has brought him joy. But then, by chance, he meets a young man who knows and admires his work.

The young man, a doctor, imagines that Dencombe derives satisfaction from his accomplishments, but the writer speaks only of regrets. Dencombe pleads with life for an "extension" that would allow him to more fully realize his talents. But that is not to be. When he realizes that no extension will be granted, his illness escalates and he soon dies. Is James holding Dencombe up as an example of the price of fighting decline? If Dencombe were in treatment, would we advise him to go more gently into the "good night" awaiting him?

But even for those naturally inclined toward adaptation, the fear of losing the *essence* of who we have been can make it hard to adapt. And yet, to some degree, we must adapt. Ann Burack-Weiss (2015) asks "what can we keep of all that has passed between then and now? What is the balance of fluidity and permanence in the identity of an old woman?" (p. 19). About a friend who is facing the necessity to "downsize" her cherished possessions, she asks:

> How is my friend, how am I, how are other old women now in the first (or second, or third) flush of downsizing to meet the increasing losses of people, places, and things that are now our lot? How are we to face our own declining attractiveness, health, and ability to function day to day? How are we to face our own death that no longer hovers in the distant future but is now too close for comfort?
>
> (p. 20)

Profound regret, lost opportunities, can play important roles in how we feel at life's end. The rest of Dylan Thomas's (2010) poem expresses some of the regrets of the wild and the grave. At last, the poet comes to his own father.

> And you, my father, there on the sad height,
> Curse, bless me now, with your fierce tears, I pray.
> Do not go gentle into that good night.
> Rage, rage against the dying of the light.
>
> (p. 19)

I am sure there are many ways to understand these lines. For me, they express the author's wish to avoid the pain of seeing in his father a defeated, hangdog, emotionally muted response to life's end. He begs his father for a memorable legacy. Whether the father's tears curse him or bless him matters less than that they issue from a man who is fierce, vivid, passionate until the last breath. He doesn't want his father's attachment to life to be weak and tenuous. He wants to remember him in all his intensity. It matters less whether it is a loving or hating father, so long as it is a father full of life.

Among the poets, there are many who champion adaptation rather than protest. Yeats' (1996) poem "When You Are Old" recommends the company of memories to help us *adapt*. Most especially, we can turn to memories of being young and being cherished.

When you are old and gray and full of sleep,
And nodding by the fire, take down this book,
And slowly read, and dream of the soft look
Your eyes had once, and of their shadows deep;
How many loved your moments of glad grace,
And loved your beauty with love false or true;
But one man loved the pilgrim soul in you,
And loved the sorrows of your changing face.
And bending down beside the glowing bars,
Murmur, a little sadly, how love fled
And paced upon the mountains overhead
And hid his face amid a crowd of stars.

(p. 7)

Of course, it is easy for many to love youthful beauty. But it is much more memorable when we have been loved for deeper qualities. We are lucky if we can remember someone who loved the seeker in us, however inconvenient that seeker might have been. And few love us enough to really want to see the tragic toll of time as it is reflected in our faces. But those few may be able to leave ever so gently, surreptitiously, for they will hold as their highest value making sure they don't disturb us. Those few can accompany us as we age, if we call upon them. We are still left with a little regret for lost opportunities, but it is a soft, mellow regret. Perhaps it is more like a wistful nostalgia than a sharp or searing pain.

In his poem "Terminus," Ralph Waldo Emerson (1996) expresses a more extreme philosophy. We should go beyond *merely accepting* aging and death. We should *embrace* them gladly. As opposed to Dylan Thomas, Emerson guides us to acquiesce as quietly as possible. In his own words:

It is time to be old,
To take in sail . . .
Fancy departs: no more invent,
Contract thy firmament
To compass of a tent.
There's not enough for this and that,
Make thy option which of two;
Economize the failing river,
Nor the less revere the Giver,
Leave the many and hold the few.
Timely wise accept the terms . . .
As the bird trims her to the gale,
I trim myself to the storm of time,
I man the rudder, reef the sail,
Obey the voice at eve obeyed at prime:
Lowly faithful, banish fear,

Right onward drive unharmed;
The port well worth the cruise, is near,
And every wave is charmed.

(pp. 7–8)

So it is up to us to "trim" ourselves "to the storm of time." It is our duty to march to death unafraid and unresisting. Anything less is sacrilegious. To fear or regret death is to fail to have faith in heaven and, ultimately, in God.

But, perhaps, the option of accepting death graciously depends on whether or not we have been able to remain ourselves, at least in our own eyes. If we feel as though aging has robbed us of precious aspects of our identity, it may not be possible to "trim ourselves . . . to the storm of time." This reminds me of one of the two fundamental sources of joy for human beings (as posited by emotion theory; Izard, 1977): the pleasure of self-recognition. I think there is some truth to the concept that human beings experience joy from recognizing our common humanity *and* from recognizing our particularity. We easily feel a joyful rush when our human experience resonates with another's. Moments of feeling "more simply human than otherwise" (Sullivan, 1953) can give us comfort. But we are also likely to smile when confronted with our particularity. When I see evidence of my characteristic responses, I am likely to enjoy the self-recognition. Hopefully, I feel some warmth when I catch Sandra being Sandra.

In her insightful book *The Lioness in Winter*, Ann Burack-Weiss (2015) articulates a way of looking at aging based on her own experience and the words of an array of women writers. She concludes that the ability to remain oneself is very significant. The aging person who can maintain a consistent sense of self has a better chance to find meaning in life, even if that life is highly compromised. There is a vital story about ourselves that we each tell ourselves all our lives. It offers sustenance.

A few years ago, I wrote a paper about aging and titled it "Will I Still Be Me?" (Buechler, 2015b). The paper delineates some of the ways aging challenges identity. I ask whether I will still see myself when I look in the mirror. Will I recognize and respect her, or is it inevitable that I will be ashamed of aging and alienated from myself? As in adolescence, when we age, an identity that has been firmly in place is challenged from without and within. In both eras, we may mourn the loss of the familiar self and feel palpably insecure about the person we are becoming. We may look in the mirror and find ourselves changed, perhaps even unrecognizable. In both eras, rebellion is one form that mourning can take. Adolescents often paint, pierce, and otherwise decorate their bodies as posters to advertise that they don't identify with their elders. Similarly, as we age, we may use our bodies to express our reluctance to identify with the changes that are occurring. In both adolescence and aging, we may be clearer about who we don't want to be than who we are now. In a later section of this chapter, I will address the shame-inducing messages we may receive from both the outside world and the internal world. They are likely to challenge our ability to feel we are still our familiar, good enough selves.

And the challenges may not be limited to those affecting our bodies. For me, personally, an aspect of my identity was the strength of my memory. When I was young, it was a very reliable part of my "equipment for living," to use Sullivan's (1953) term. As I lose that capacity, can I still feel like myself?

Challenges to recognizing ourselves can come from other sources as well. As we get older, it is impossible to avoid suffering losses. Loved ones die, and the world becomes a place primarily designed by younger people. Opportunities shrink, and roads not traveled become permanent regrets. We are challenged to bear loss without succumbing to depression and to recognize our familiar selves in the process. That is, as I come to terms with my own losses, can I still be me? Can I laugh as I have laughed, get angry as I have in the past, and be as curious as ever? If, with age, my emotional patterns change, can I still recognize, accept, and adequately admire and love myself?

A marvelous short story, "Little Selves" (Lerner, 1999), beautifully illustrates our need to hold on to previous versions of ourselves. Lerner portrays the potential joys and sorrows of aging. She emphasizes the meaning to be found in remembering our younger selves as we let go of life. I read her as leaning toward "adaptation" to aging and dying, rather than advocating going down fighting.

In the story, Margaret O'Brien is 75, a great-aunt, devout, and clearly dying. She feels weary enough to be ready to die, and yet she seems to have one last purpose. Even in the midst of company, her eyes turn inward, and she struggles mightily to remember her earliest days. In her words, "I must be getting back to the beginning" (p. 9). She strives to recover earlier and earlier memories, straining backward, reaching for her earliest conscious awareness of herself. She is shocked at the changes she sees. "How full of verve and life were all those figures! That glancing creature grow old? How could such things be!" (p. 13).

At last, Margaret recaptures the touchstone memory of herself, at nine or ten, rebelliously restyling her coat, despite knowing how her mother will feel about it. Remembering this little self brings old Margaret O'Brien great joy. "With its fullness of detail, it achieved a delicious suggestion of permanence, in contrast to the illusiveness of other isolated moments. Margaret O'Brien *saw* all those other figures, but she really *was* the child with the red coat" (p. 15).

Most of all, the old woman wants to tell her niece, Anna, about her little selves, so that they may be remembered and live on. She is afraid Anna will laugh at her, but Anna fully comprehends. Margaret is overjoyed at Anna's compassionate understanding and confesses that she sometimes hears her little selves in her head, pleading not to be forgotten. She worries that the little selves will die if no one continues to remember them. But Anna promises to sit beside Margaret every night, so Margaret can acquaint her with all the "lasses." Anna's mother had already told her stories from that earlier time, so she reassures Margaret that her mind is well-prepared to receive the little girls. She vows to call them up often, after Margaret is gone. So, the old woman "had her heart's desire. She recreated her earlier selves and passed them on, happy in the thought that she was saving them from oblivion" (p. 16). It is hard for me to imagine a more poignant expression of our need for the sense that we will live on, in the legacy wrought by finding words that capture the essence of our former selves.

Perhaps, emotionally, we feel our losses differently when we can weave them into an overall pattern. At least sometimes, their pain may be modulated against a backdrop of other kinds of events. But, more importantly, patterns evoke a sense of having meaning. For example, if I see myself as one who always had to come up from behind, I give a particular significance to my actions today and, more generally, to my life.

Of course, there are some who tell themselves devastating stories about themselves. To me, an identity is like the through line of a book. It is a pattern that creates coherence. That, at least, is the cognitive aspect of it. But there is also an emotional aspect. Having an identity gives us someone to love. Just as we may feel love when we see our child repeat a familiar gesture, we may feel self-love when we recognize we are, once again, being just like ourselves. Frank Sinatra's popular song declares, with some pride and, I would suggest, self-love, that "I did it my way."

But, still, even a negative sense of self may be better than no sense at all, just as a painful attachment style may be healthier than complete disorganization, and having costly neurotic defenses is no doubt better than being lost in a psychotic haze. Each of us ages in a way that is characteristic, so generalizations about universal experiences fall short of lived reality. "Aging" is no more uniform than "mothering." But I do think there are challenges that frequently occur in each, so that writing my experience may help you name yours, to some degree. This is true about so many patterns in life. The person who believes she is being stalked by green aliens is probably projecting aggression, as is the wife who reads anger in her husband's every facial gesture. Both may well be using the defense called "projection," and it can be useful to recognize this pattern. In fact, elsewhere (Buechler, 2008, 2012, 2015a), I have written about pattern recognition as a key factor in what we offer in treatment. But the "stalked" woman and the troubled wife are likely to be caught up in their projections differently. And each anxiously projecting wife is anxiously projecting in her own way, to echo the famous quote from Tolstoy.

These seemingly contradictory truths both exist. That is, there are universally recognizable patterns in how human beings live the recurrent challenges of life, as well as significant individual variations. Sullivan (1953, 1954, 1956) was most interested in the regularities, believing that the clinician can become familiar with them and help people cope better. Consistency in the patterns allows us to learn from each other, to some extent. For example, my aging has some things in common with someone who grew older in the nineteenth century, or in Sweden, and so on. This is the basis for there being profound insights that span cultures and time periods. But it is equally true that we each have to forge a qualitatively different, idiosyncratic, personal style of aging. One of the most interesting threads in these writings is the question of how much it promotes our health to keep track of time's inevitable alterations of us. If we keep our former "little selves" vivid, can we more easily adapt to change as we age? Should that be our goal, or should remembering serve the function of holding fast to what is familiar? And, once again, I repeat that these are not, really, binary choices, but rather points on a continuum. But I think it is a meaningful dimension, relevant to every life.

As we age, should we decathect (invest less) in life in order to bear its loss?

This issue can be thought of as a subset of the initial question, about adapting versus fighting aging. Decathecting life, in order to bear leaving it, might be seen as a way to adapt. It also asks us about our attitude toward emotional intensity. Decathecting life, hungering for it less, in order to bear losing it, might be seen as a variant of the general goal of diminishing emotional intensity as a coping style. Another approach says we are better off if we stay intensely invested and fully participating in life, even as our losses mount. The first approach is expressed in Joseph Campbell's (2004) *Pathways to Bliss*. According to him, an important psychological function of myth is to carry the individual through the stages of life. At life's end, the myth functions to help the aged *become disengaged*. In his words, as we age, we begin to lose our grip, in many senses, and long for sleep. Faced with a vigorous younger generation, the wise elderly think, "Well, let them have it." In a similar vein, Campbell summarizes one of the precepts of the religion of Jainism by saying that an aim is to lose all desire for life. The idea is to make the loss of all desire to live coincide with your death.

But I wonder how we can remain *generative* if we have decathected life in order to be better able to let go of it? Personally, while I think decathecting might decrease some of the pain of leaving life, I can't see it as a full answer. I come back to the short story by Tolstoy (1886/1982) that helped me find my personal response to this challenge. In "The Death of Ivan Ilych," the title character leads a dull, servile clerk's life, obeying every societal imperative, until he suffers a seemingly minor mishap and begins to die. His dying is implacable. His wife and daughters gather around him, waiting for the great event. As he slowly accepts that his dying is real, as he moves from bewilderment, through fear and shock, and past hope, he discovers what can help him bear it. He understands that, by making his death into a gift to his beloved family, he transforms it. "There was no fear because there was no death. In place of death there was light" (p. 279).

Thus, it is actually his *cathexes*, or investments in loved ones, that enable Ivan to give up life. His last gift to them is his own death, which will free them to enjoy their lives. Decathecting would be precisely the wrong answer, from this point of view. At age 71, as I write this, I am personally in agreement. To me, "decathecting" in order to bear death is another version of the schizoid attempt to cope with life by feeling less intently. Of course, this is not an approach consciously chosen, but I think it is a common attitude, an outlook that can exact a steep price.

Coming at the question from another angle, as we age, how could we retain a sense of purpose (Buechler, 2004) if we decathect life? In a sense, Ivan had to "decathect" *an aspect* of life (his own existence) and "cathect" another (the lives of those he loved). His purpose shifted, but the strength of his attachment to life did not diminish. If anything, I believe it grew stronger, and that is what enabled him to let go. It might also be true that, finally, Ilych was an individual, not a functionary, living this last passage of life in his own way.

The question of how much to remain fully attached can extend to the body itself. When our bodies ache, are we better off dissociating? Is health being able to dissociate enough from the body? Are there times when we are better off if we can identify with our spirits and not our bodies?

Sexuality can raise similar issues. Once again, I turn to the work of Burack-Weiss (2015), who quotes Nancy Mairs, who was diagnosed with multiple sclerosis at the age of 29. Mairs eloquently describes how men have stopped seeing her as a potential sexual partner. In her words, "my wheelchair seals my chastity" (p. 52). Mairs has gotten a painfully early experience of sexual irrelevance, but we all can anticipate becoming invisible, in that sense. Commenting on these remarks, Burack-Weiss says she does not miss being the object of sexual interest. What she does very much miss is simply walking without anticipating aches and pains.

I would imagine that what we each miss most has to do with what we have treasured and what is crucial to our identity. Thus, I have always found it particularly sad that Beethoven lost his hearing. The capacities we depend on don't bring fame to most of us. But they are still integral to our sense of self and our relationship to the world. For some of us, being seen as a viable sexual partner is an important aspect of who we are. I think this is a component of what they mean when older women complain of having become invisible.

Should we try to remember the past or focus on the present and future?

I would suggest that unbearably intense regret, shame, and/or guilt often block our ability to remember the past. And, as an old saying (and psychoanalytic theory) suggests, those who are ignorant of the past are doomed to repeat it. But, I believe, those who are afraid of remembering, because they believe it could lead to devastating, depressive sorrow, have to waste energy avoiding their memories and are unable to change the impact of the past by finding new meanings in it and learning from it. For example, in my book (Buechler, 2008), I wrote about an inpatient at my first hospital job who committed suicide shortly after I met with him. Of course, nothing changes the pain, self-questioning, and regret that memory will always hold. But, now, added to those feelings is the sense that, having combed the memories often, I have become better able to use that experience to grow and to teach others.

In her somewhat ironic poem "One Art," Elizabeth Bishop (2010) invites us to practice loss so we become better able to bear all that it implies. I would suggest that the ability to practice loss requires us to be relatively comfortable with intense feelings.

Bishop asserts that, since all losses have something in common, we get ample chances to practice losing. But do we really become more adept? Is losing a skill that can be learned, in any sense? Bishop outlines what I would liken to a therapeutic program of systematic desensitization. The behavioral therapist presents the patient with a series of stimuli, from less to more threatening. Similarly, Bishop asks us to start by tolerating lost door keys, wasted time, and, eventually, the loss of cherished places and loved ones. While I doubt the poet meant us to think that minor losses really prepare us for catastrophes, I believe this sly poem has a subtle point. Over time, losses may acquaint us more nearly with some of life's most bitter lessons. We do have opportunities to learn how little we really control, how much we can do without, and what does and does not matter. But even with the benefit of experience, some losses present as disasters. Is there anything we can do to become ready to face the ultimate losses?

I agree with Bishop that bearing loss can take a lifetime of inner preparation. By definition, at the time of our deaths, we lose everyone we have ever known, everything we have ever been, and life itself. Personally, I think the "art" of losing, if it is any type of inner capacity, requires a relatively loving superego. When we look back and see opportunities squandered, promises unfulfilled, love incompletely recognized, can we bear it? Can we make uncompromising self-reflection bearable for someone else?

As we age, physical limitations may decrease our opportunities for exploring the outer world, but, as T. S. Eliot (1943) suggests, it can be a time for voyages into the inner world. With sublime acuity, Eliot challenges us to explore our internal sub-continents. Aging can occasion exciting adventures as we discover our own hidden depths. Reading Eliot, I think of the tendency, as we age, to lose ourselves in memories. Are we substituting insight for sightseeing? When infirmities make tours less appealing, do we turn toward time travel? Of course, as an analyst, I can see potential benefits in this shift. But to the extent that we don't feel able to look back or can't recognize the potential for internal expansion, aging may simply feel like a series of physical and other losses. But if we are becoming vast, containing more of Walt Whitman's "multitudes," we can feel that our losses are only part of the picture. So as the aged look toward the future, which losses are avoidable and which are unavoidable? Can the gains balance the losses, if the losses are kept to a minimum, and the gains are lived to their fullest?

In an essay on his own experiences of aging, published when he was nearly 100 years old, Martin Bergmann (2014) wrote, in a rather matter-of-fact statement, that he had lost the future tense. Does that have to happen? How do we help ourselves and others bear it? I turn to ideas about human feelings that have helped me in countless situations (Buechler, 2004, 2008, 2012). I wonder how the feeling of loss can be balanced by other feelings, since I believe that our emotions always exist in balance, with every feeling modulated by the presence or absence of all other possible feelings. So, at least in the abstract, what internal and external relationships can balance the inevitable losses? For myself, I believe that if I admire my courage in facing my losses, I may love myself just enough to bear them.

In a paper I wrote (Buechler, 2015b) on the question of whether, as I age, I can still remain myself in my own eyes, I suggested some ways balance could be achieved.

> If the joy of passing something on heartens me, I may accept the loss of a future tense for myself. If curiosity still excites me, I may open new doors when fading memory closes others. I differ with Bergmann's words, but, perhaps, not his spirit, when he says that in old age the future dimension disappears and there is nothing to hope for. I think and hope about the future all the time. In that future my own body, mind, and heart will be altered and, eventually, absent. But in my attachment to that future, in my hopes for it, in my work toward it, I am still me.
>
> (p. 4)

As is generally true, the clinician can hinder the patient's reflections on life's trajectory out of a personal need to deny the depth of the losses that aging often brings. But, I hope, more often, we can be helpful by focusing on both the gains and losses. One of those gains, for us all, can be the development of generativity, as Erikson (1968) suggests. I think of this state as similar to the ideal motivational state of the clinician. Elsewhere (Buechler, 2011), I have defined the clinician's most productive motive as a relatively non-narcissistic investment in the life and growth of patients. Briefly, the clinician should care about the quality of the patient's life for itself and not as a proof of the clinician's talent. The relatively non-narcissistically invested clinician can derive both joy and curiosity from this investment. Similarly, the generative person (whether clinician or non-clinician, older or younger) is relatively non-narcissistically invested in the quality of the lives others lead.

It is well known that generativity can play an especially vital, and vitalizing, role in our older years. Vaillant (1993) defines it as follows: "Generativity means assuming sustained responsibility for the growth and wellbeing of others" (p. 150). Of course, that sense of responsibility can be expressed in numerous ways. Whether we care for a community or a grandchild makes no difference, in this understanding of the term. Generativity is one way we can reach equilibrium, in more than one sense. Its joys exist alongside some of our losses. Generativity can be seen, in emotion theory terms (Buechler, 2004, 2008; Izard, 1977), as providing positive feelings that balance negative emotions. Or, from another angle, generativity can give us a sense of purpose and lend greater meaning to our lives. Life's "glass" becomes a little more than half full, so to speak. I think of generativity as one way to resolve self-esteem problems that can complicate aging. It can balance feelings of loss and make it possible to look into the future with a sense of accomplishment. But for those whose emotional balance is upended by intense envy of the young, generativity may be an unrealistic goal or, at least, a very challenging one. And for those terrified of depression, generativity's joys may not even register. I think of the ability to benefit from generativity as taking a lifetime to hone.

Should we relate differently to customs as we age?
Can lifelong adapters learn to flout rules?

When I am an old woman I shall wear purple
With a red hat which doesn't go, and doesn't suit me.
And I shall spend my pension on brandy and summer gloves
And satin sandals, and say we've no money for butter.
I shall sit down on the pavement when I am tired
And gobble up samples in shops and press alarm bells
And run my stick along the public railings
And make up for the sobriety of my youth.
I shall go out in my slippers in the rain
And pick the flowers in other people's gardens
And learn to spit.
You can wear terrible shirts and grow more fat
And eat three pounds of sausages at a go
Or only eat bread and pickle for a week
And hoard pens and pencils and beer mats and things in boxes.
But now we must have clothes that keep us dry
And pay our rent and not swear in the street
And set a good example for the children.
We must have friends to dinner and read the papers.
But maybe I ought to practice a little now?
So people who know me are not too shocked and surprised
When suddenly I am old, and start to wear purple.
(Joseph, 2013, pp. 124–125)

We associate freedom with youth. That is a limited and limiting view. In some ways, the young are the least free. So often, they feel bound by pressure to prove themselves, to themselves and to the world. They are conflicted, buffeted by society's rules and the need to rebel against them. They feel themselves to be pinned at the low end of hierarchies, always chasing something just out of reach.

In contrast, what are some of the freedoms aging can bring? As Jenny Joseph suggests in "Warning" (above), some rules no longer apply, which, I would say, is both the good news and the bad news. Why be sensible when there is no one left to impress? Why sacrifice to how we look? Why be reticent? Why try to fall within the "normal" range when no one is watching?

But this freedom is, itself, a delicate matter. If it is expressed with an over-the-top air of flouting, I think it can't be joyous. It would then feel absurdly adolescent. We are too old to be rebellious teenagers, and it is unseemly to look like we aren't aware of trying to look young. The older man or woman dressed in skimpy, revealing clothing is pitiful. They are advertising their inability to bear their place in the food chain. But, Joseph might say, why care about that? Why bother to advertise at all, when the days of impression management are over?

Freedom, in this sense, is being unencumbered by the future, even though we may care about it in other ways (see previous section). When we are young, we can be persuaded to save for the future, to sacrifice now for tomorrow. But when, for me personally, there may be no tomorrow, this deal is less appealing. Perhaps, to some of us, it never had much appeal. But now we may feel more justified in refusing it. What pleasure can we derive from the freedoms that come with advancing age? How do lifelong habits affect our ability to find genuine joy (and not just nose-thumbing spite) in wearing purple?

The young, who have not yet proven themselves, may feel they have to live up to standards, which were set by their elders and were appropriate and achievable in the past. It takes time for a society, or a profession, to recognize that their standards are out of date. Meanwhile, the young are still measured by them. To refuse is to step outside the system and bear the price. But, as we age, stepping outside may be seen as an achievement, rather than as a failure to conform. Society may no longer need us to confirm by conforming. We are no longer taken seriously enough to pose a real challenge. We might even be encouraged to wear purple, to signal our acceptance that we no longer matter.

Is there something inherently shameful about aging?

> Shame occurs typically, if not always, in the context of an emotional relationship. The sharp increase in self-attention (and sometimes the increased sensitivity of the face produced by blushing) causes the person to feel as though he were naked and exposed to the world. Shame motivates the desire to hide, to disappear. Shame can also produce a feeling of ineptness, incapacity, and a feeling of not belonging.
>
> (Izard, 1977, p. 92)

Is there anything inherent in growing old that inevitably evokes shame? Or do certain cultures, including our own, implant the idea that we should be ashamed of aging and its concomitants? In the definition cited above, Izard, an emotion theorist, describes experiences shame *produces*, including feelings of ineptness, incapacity, and not belonging. But it seems clear that, at least when it comes to aging, feelings of ineptness, incapacity, and not belonging can *cause* shame, as well as result from it. I think it is especially crucial for us, as clinicians, to consider how best to deal with patients' feelings about the changes wrought by aging. Shame is known (Izard, 1972) to be the only negative emotion that consistently increases when we focus on it. What are the clinical implications of this? What role can verbalizing shame-related feelings play in helping the aging patient cope?

In my book *Still Practicing: The Heartaches and Joys of a Clinical Career* (Buechler, 2012), I used T. S. Eliot's (1930) poem "The Love Song of J. Alfred Prufrock" to describe the agonizing, humiliating yearning that can accompany aging. I still find no better words, so I quote my own comments about that poem's depiction of aging desire.

For me, it is T. S. Eliot who best expressed the position of the old who still want, much to their shame. In "The Love Song of J. Alfred Prufrock" (1930), we have a perfect representative of aging desire as mortification. Having already measured out his life in coffee spoons, how can he dare to presume anything? Perhaps, after all, it is better not to venture out. What if he has let himself desire, only to be told, by someone settling a pillow by her head, that he has misread the situation, and what he is thinking is not at all what she meant. What utter and complete humiliation! No, he can't take this chance, for he is already sometimes "almost ridiculous" (p. 15). This is the time when he shall wear the bottoms of his trousers rolled, giving in to aging. Any effort to still enjoy the pleasures of the young brands him as a fool. To dare to eat a peach in the open shows that he is unaware that peaches are for the young, and he is no longer young. While he has heard the mermaids sing to each other, he knows they will not sing to him. I imagine him accepting this with sad resignation. Resignation, and not peaches, or love songs, is appropriate for a man Prufrock's age.

(p. 153)

Perhaps it is inevitable that sorrow accompanies knowing we have outlived our right to eat peaches and hear mermaids sing to us. But is it also inevitable that we feel shame? I think it is deeply ingrained in us to be ashamed when we are found wanting what we can't have. I use the phrase "found wanting" for its double meaning—found to be wanting what is unavailable to us, and found to be inadequate. I don't know how much our shame reactions to being "found wanting" are culturally driven. But I can certainly say that they are present in many contexts. A child who intensely wants another's toy but can't have it may deny the wish, saying they don't want it at all, thus using "sour grapes" to save face. An older single woman (or man) who despairs of finding a partner may hide the desire, as though the wish is shameful if it is not fulfilled. So it is not just when we are old that we feel ashamed of unfulfilled yearnings. But I suggest that in our last years we are especially vulnerable to this feeling. Here is another place where lifelong attitudes make a difference in how we age. Elders who have always avoided the humiliation of ungratified yearning are more likely to suffer shame since, as we age, our opportunities for gratification often constrict more quickly than our desires.

It seems to me that when we feel inept, incapacitated, or excluded, it is always in comparison with someone else, even if the "other" is merely implied and not a specific person. As we age, we may compare ourselves to our own younger selves, as well as others. In his *Essays after Eighty*, Donald Hall (2014) offers some striking imagery of how age reduces us, compared with our younger selves. "When I was fifty and sixty, the day of love and work repeated itself year after year. Old age sits in a chair, writing a little and diminishing" (p. 122). I notice that he doesn't say *he* sits in a chair, but "old age" sits there, as though his age is who he is. It is his total identity.

Hall is explicit about the "otherness" of the old.

However alert we are, however much we think we know what will happen, antiquity remains an unknown, unanticipated galaxy. It is alien, and old people are a separate form of life . . . they are permanently other. When we turn eighty, we understand that we are extraterrestrial. If we forget for a moment that we are old, we are reminded when we try to stand up, or when we encounter someone young, who appears to observe green skin, extra heads, and protuberances.

(pp. 7–8)

But, for me, his most evocative image comes from memories of his wife, the poet Jane Kenyon, who died of leukemia at 47. Shortly before her own illness and death, Jane likened Hall's elderly mother to a horse "running in wide circles, the circles growing smaller until they ceased" (p. 4). Hall continues: "Twenty years later, my circles narrow . . . I feel the circles grow smaller, and old age is a ceremony of losses . . ." (p. 4).

There are implicit comparisons in each of these images of diminishment, narrowing, and shrinking. Though a ceremony, it is hardly a celebration! It is in our natures to respond to *expansion* of who we are with joy. Elsewhere (Buechler, 2008), I have written that one of the fundamental sources of human joy is the feeling of having transcended obstacles to become more than you were before. I wrote of transcendent joy as "a kind of affirmation of life's possibilities" (p. 135), a manifestation of the potential for the future to be different and more expansive than the past. So, just as we respond to widening of our possibilities with joy, it is logical that we would respond to their diminishment with sorrow. But, I am suggesting, aside from sorrow, we also respond with shame to being "found wanting." By still wanting the wider circles of youth, we collaborate in defining our aging selves inadequate. Can we do otherwise? Is our lingering desire for wider circles, for peaches, for mermaids, the problem? Or can we see the problem as stemming from the association of shame with unfulfilled desire at any age? And, if we look at *that association* as the problem, can that change? Or is it as immutable as the joy that seems naturally to come on the heels of self-expansion? The child who takes her first steps beams and is beamed at. So, at the other end of the spectrum, when we can no longer take unaided steps, what is it inevitable to feel?

Ann Burack-Weiss (2015) says, "We old women are also stigmatized selves" (p. xv). She mentions how many products exist to mask the passing of the years. She suggests that we are often "fearful that we will be considered past consideration as fully functioning adults . . ." (p. xv). Although she goes on to say that some of us are relieved at not having to care how we look, for many, this is clearly painful. Society certainly validates the shamefulness of looking old, whether or not we consider it to be the main culprit. It is as though we have proven ourselves to be insufficient, in some way, by having gotten older. One response is to try to cover up telltale signs. I wonder about the psychological effects of the cover up, itself. My guess would be that it brings up (consciously or unconsciously) other "cover ups" we have engaged in and may still try to perpetrate. In addition to trying to look younger than I am, do I also try to sound smarter? Did I "fix" my nose so I wouldn't look as "Jewish"? Masking aging may be a somewhat different experience for those who have felt required to cover something up, for one reason or another, all their lives. For example, for those who felt they had to closet their sexuality, what is it like to veil their aging?

Since so many women (and, increasingly, men) use cosmetic and surgical procedures to cover up signs of aging, there must be benefits. I don't think they are just about how the world responds. While it is true that they may help us "pass" for younger (for a while), I think they may also foster the illusion that we have some *control* over the process. Probably that is anxiety-reducing, until life shows us just how little we control. If that awakening comes suddenly, it might be more of a shock if we have been able to delude ourselves that "70 is the new 50."

Trying to look younger may also rob us of the chance to wear the "old lady shoes" that actually accommodate best to our feet. I imagine this to have physical and psychological meanings. Every achy moment that I wear shoes that strain my feet, I am reminded of my age. I get definite signals from the painful blisters my thinning skin is prone to. Ironically, perhaps, I *feel older*. M. F. K. Fisher wrote, in her 80s, that she could not face looking at the "strange, uncouth, ugly kind of toadlike woman" (Burack-Weiss, 2015, p. 46) she had become. This is hardly a positive self-image! Surely, along with such self-perceptions one would feel some of the "insufficiency" that is a component of intense shame (as I have already suggested). But is it inevitable that we come to feel this way about so many aspects of aging? Are hearing losses, visual impairments, and mobility problems destined to make us feel inadequate? Does it help to put these feelings into words? As noted above, the child, newly able to walk, is proud of this achievement and feels superior to the still crawling infant. But does that have to mean that the older adult who can still walk with a cane will feel smug and superior to another who relies on a wheelchair to get around? Of course, this "superiority" is temporary. This reminds me of a patient of mine, wheelchair-bound, who called me "TAB": temporarily able-bodied. She longed for the day when I would get a taste of what life was like for her. And she was open about her hope that day was close at hand. In some (or, perhaps, all) of us, painful shame begets spite and other potentially interpersonally destructive feelings, adding to the sense of isolation.

Should we believe in "mind over matter"?

What is the price tag of believing we can "tough out" pain, as compared with the price tag of not believing it? I think it can cut both ways, in many senses. As is true for cancer, for example, to feel we can avoid it by "positive" thinking implies, when we are diagnosed, that we caused our illness. This can (literally) add insult to injury. But it can also be true that a belief in our agency contributes to coping well.

Burack-Weiss (2015) writes of her own journey, from believing in the power of attitude to understanding its limits.

The idea that everyone can "do whatever they want to do" and "be whoever they want to be" is underscored by all the healthy living advice that pours over us from our teens onward. By the time we reach old age, the message is ingrained: proper diet, appropriate exercise, socialization, and a positive attitude are all it takes to live long and well.

(p. 45)

What a shock reality can deliver, for those who bought this message!

But other feelings are also common, including a sense of comradeship with those in a similar position. Sometimes, our attitude about aging can resemble the analyst's analytic attitude, in the sense that we look at what is happening at the same time as we are living it. The attitude with which we observe ourselves may be more within our control than *what* we observe. At least theoretically, it is possible to be curious and to observe ourselves at any age. I am reminded of the powerful work of Victor Frankl (1946), a concentration camp survivor, who wrote that the one freedom that can't be taken from a human being is the capacity to color our experiences with personal meanings. Here is a great example of this, from *Coming into the End Zone* by Doris Grumbach:

> Old age is both the final limitation and the ultimate prison. From it there is no chance for escape or improvement. It is beyond pardon or commutation, it is the period to the sentence of change. Nonetheless, I have decided to have a celebration, as if these dire bounds did not exist, as if hope of some small future was still a thing with feathers.
>
> (Burack-Weiss, 2015, p. 147)

Sometimes, curiosity can add a grace note, and determination to "celebrate" can transform the feel of aging, to some degree. In *Essays after Eighty*, Donald Hall (2014) puts it succinctly: "When I lament and darken over my diminishments, I accomplish nothing. It is better to sit at the window all day, pleased to watch birds, barns, and flowers. It is a pleasure to write about what I do" (pp. 4–5).

How much can humor leaven the seemingly unavoidable sense of diminishment? How much can humility make bearable an ever-increasing need to rely on others? I believe there are some antidotes to shame about aging, and a lifelong habit of humility is one of them. Ideally, we can feel both deserving of help and able to maintain healthy self-esteem while receiving it. But, inevitably, our longstanding relationship with the issue of dependency accompanies us as we age. Have I always reveled in being taken care of? Did I always seize on chances to get tended to? Or have I avoided them like the plague? Have I thought of nurses as angels of mercy or guardians of the gateway to hell?

Wanting to avoid "being a burden" is, sometimes, a rationalization for a lack of healthy entitlement. What are healthy expectations of help and healthy ways of accepting it? What do caregivers get out of caring for the aging?

These and other issues help shape the experience of aging for many. Alice Munro's (1991) great short story "Mrs. Cross and Mrs. Kidd" illustrates various attitudes toward giving and receiving help as we age. The story centers on two elderly ladies who knew each other as kindergarten buddies and meet 80 years later as fellow residents of a nursing home. Each is better at giving help than at receiving it until, at the end of the story, each is forced to accept her limitations. In the chapter on generative aging in my own book (Buechler, 2015a), I suggested a reason Mrs. Cross is better able to deal with needing help. Mrs. Kidd, whose adult identity is based on her self-reliance, has to struggle to bear her prideful terror of being helpless. Fortunately, she finds an empathic listener in her old friend, Mrs. Cross. Because of her different makeup, the situation is less dreadful for Mrs. Cross. She is better able to be open about her cognitive and physical failings. Her pride is not as dependent on retaining any one attribute, so it is easier for her to give and receive help.

How do lifelong patterns of coping with emotions affect aging?

My sense is that certain characteristic ways of coping interfere most with the capacity to bear aging. I think this occurs most often when the sense of self-esteem is extremely fragile (so shame is a deadly enemy) or when security is based on a schizoid, affectless, emotionally contained self-sufficiency. Thus, narcissistic and schizoid coping styles may especially complicate aging by making it very challenging to accept necessary help. For some, the price of accepting help is forfeiture of the sense of self. But I would say that every coping style complicates aging in some way, and the individual's lifelong patterns of relating interpersonally and functioning intrapsychically will affect what aging means. More specifically, these patterns, along with many other factors, will help shape how much a person can still feel like themselves, regardless of the changes aging brings. In addition, coping patterns will affect the degree to which one can develop passionate generativity (as discussed above). As I have said elsewhere (Buechler, 2015a):

> Whatever form they take, these passionate investments can shift my focus. With generativity, the ground I have lost is balanced by the ground I am gaining. Through it I become a means to an end, as well as an end in myself. I become an instance of life.

> (p. 137)

Treatment: An interplay of coping styles

Since aging is not a condition, it is inappropriate to write about treating it. Nevertheless, people do go into therapy hoping for help with their feelings about growing older. What contribution can the clinician make?

In my book (Buechler, 2015a), I wrote a chapter on aging as it is portrayed in short fiction. Cather (1994), Day (1952), James (1992), Lerner (1999), Melville

(1994), Munro (1991), and Paley (1966), among many others, have given us vivid portraits of characters facing the end of their lives. I looked at some of the central challenges these characters confronted, including maintaining and modifying identity, meeting challenges to self-esteem, forging a sense of purpose, developing generativity, and strengthening emotional balance.

In the present chapter, I have focused on other questions that can confront us as we grow older: whether to fight aging or adapt; whether we should aim to decathect life to make it easier to lose it; whether it is healthy to revive memories of the past; how we might best relate to conventional rules; what makes us ashamed about aging; what are the consequences of believing that our attitudes shape our experience of aging; and how do our defensive relational styles affect our experience of growing older. In this chapter's concluding section, I address how the clinician can help the patient face these issues. Briefly, I suggest that the clinician implies a stance toward these issues throughout treatment. Regardless of the ages of the participants, despite countless differences in content and process, I believe that every session "comments" on what it means to be a human being and live a human life. For example, even though, most of the time, the overt agenda varies tremendously, I believe that every treatment takes positions (implicitly) about the advantages and disadvantages of adaptation as a way of life. Similarly, although it is frequently left unspoken, every session "says" something about desire, the value of remembering, relating to rules, the role of shame in our lives, how attitudes affect experience, and the impact of patterns of relating and defending oneself. Treatment can be considered an encounter between two approaches to the human condition. More specifically, the treatment interaction subtly enacts how much we each feel health hinges on adapting well, how much it involves comfort with intense feelings, and how much it depends on finding words that adequately express experiences. Most often this "dialogue" about healthy living and healthy aging is enacted by each person's focus. What each of us pays attention to, responds to, forgets, remembers, and misunderstands says a great deal about who we are and what we think is important. So, often without realizing it, in sessions we are always "addressing" the aging-related questions I raise in this chapter.

Just as children learn more from what adults do than what they say, similarly, some of the most indelible lessons in adult life come from being in the presence of someone with integrity. Integrity can be defined as a kind of wholeness, unity. I think of it as a seamlessness between one's words and actions. In analytic supervision, it is manifested when the supervisor treats the candidate in a manner that is consonant with the supervisor's recommendations for the treatment of the patient. In other words, in every walk of life, as clinicians, supervisors, parents, patients, supervisees, and so on, we have opportunities to impact others through our integrity. When our actions match our words, we have our greatest chance to effect change.

What I am suggesting is that, regardless of the age of the clinician and patient, our work often takes implicit positions about the issues raised in this chapter.

If the position expressed by our *words* matches the position expressed by our *actions*, our impact is enhanced. For example, in our words and our actions, we often implicitly "vote" for remembering the past, as an aspect of healthy living at every age. As another example, most often clinicians (implicitly) side with the belief that attitudes toward events in our lives make a difference in how these events are experienced. Furthermore, some analytic orientations privilege adaptation, while others seem more likely to inculcate a fighting spirit. I think most embody a stance against feeling shame about being oneself. And, it seems to me, embedded in most theories is a leaning toward "cathecting" life at every age. Of course, each individual clinician lives these values in a personally resonant way. I may (perhaps unconsciously) promote adaptation more than you do, or privilege emerging from being ashamed. While we each have our own "spin," I think there are certain inclinations built into the therapeutic culture. Elsewhere (Buechler, 2004), I have named a set of "clinical values" (curiosity, hope, kindness, courage, a sense of purpose, emotional balance, an ability to bear loss, and integrity). In a sense, in this book I am expanding the list.

Regardless of the analytic orientation of the author, we can read any discussion of clinical material as a commentary on these fundamental clinical values. In this chapter, I suggest that sessions also comment on the "value," as we age, of adaptation versus protest, intense versus muted desire, remembering versus moving on, obeying versus defying rules, exploring versus avoiding shame, self-determination, and the strengths and liabilities of formulating lived experience into words. While these questions form a backdrop in every treatment, I am suggesting their heightened relevance when the treatment deals with aging.

Toward life's end, it becomes crucial for the treatment partners to create a way the patient can live the central challenges of growing older. In other words, while the issues of adaptation versus protest, desire, remembering, and so on can be pivotal at any age, as we get older they attain greater centrality in our lives. Does this patient, in this life circumstance, need to "adapt" to physical, emotional, and spiritual changes? As always, there are no pre-determined "right" answers. No way of coping works for everyone. The only thing a clinician can know in advance is that, in some sense, the question of how much to adapt will come up (explicitly, implicitly, or both). I am suggesting that the best preparation for the clinician is to raise our own awareness of our personal/professional attitudes about these fundamental human issues. How much do I tend to adapt to new circumstances, however troubling they may be? Perhaps without full awareness, I lean toward adaptation in what I privilege in a session? Do I (perhaps unconsciously) respond to the patient's unwillingness to adapt as a "problem" that treatment should address? Or do I, implicitly, react as though it is a strength to be nurtured? When the patient tells me about "successfully" adapting to new circumstances, do I remember this in the next session? Do I relate it to the patient's next dream, and do I refer to it a year later? What does each of these choices tell the patient about my way of being a human being and living life? How does my orientation toward adaptation, emotional intensity, and verbal formulation affect my moment-to-moment focus in a session?

Of equal importance is the attitude toward adaptation, desire, memory, formulation, and so on that I express in my understanding of my role. For example, when my patient repeats admittedly self-destructive, physically self-injurious behavior, how do I respond? What does my response (perhaps unwittingly) tell her about my priorities? Do I seem to privilege accepting her as she is, rather than trying to influence her to change? Or do I seem more intent on getting her to stop harming herself? I hope I am being clear that this "dialogue" is usually unspoken and, often, unrecognized by both participants. But that may only strengthen its impact, since the patient has no conscious opportunity to examine and, possibly, refute it.

I am suggesting that, with aging, added meaning accrues to questions about adaptation, defensive decreases in "cathexes," the value of remembering, pervasive shame, relating to conventional rules, personal agency, verbally labeling experiences, and the intrapsychic and interpersonal costs of defensive strategies. As these issues become salient in new ways, they are lived out in the treatment relationship with greater frequency and, sometimes, at a higher level of awareness. But, I want to stress, *they have always been there.*

A patient worries about whether her colleagues think she should retire. She wonders aloud about whether she should raise the issue herself, whether she is resisting retiring for "unhealthy" reasons, whether continuing to work reveals her shame about aging, whether her colleagues will "punish" her for selfishly hanging on to her position, whether accepting retirement is a matter of changing her attitude, and how her lifelong aversion to change is affecting her vision of her situation. The fundamental issues about her characteristic responses to the human condition have been present throughout her life. But, as she gets older, they accrue new significance.

In the interaction that follows, my own attitudes inevitably affect my behavior. What do I ask or choose not to ask? For example, do I connect her suspicions about her colleagues' feelings with other instances where she has worried about what others think of her? If I make this connection, what am I (implicitly and explicitly) communicating? How am I (perhaps inadvertently) defining her "problem"? Most importantly, what values do I express in choices that stay under my own radar? That is, in the way I react, what do I say to my patient about my own answers to life's fundamental questions? In how I respond to her, what do I tell her about my coping style? For example, do I seem preoccupied or unconcerned about whether she thinks it is time for me to retire as her analyst? If she actually brings up termination, how do I respond? Do I seem to "decathect" her and the treatment, perhaps as a way to defend against feelings of hurt, or loss, or other painful affects? How do I live my attitudes about rules in the way I relate to the "rules" of my profession in my behavior with her? How much do I seem to believe that the power to shape my experience of the session resides within me? How much do I "adapt" to her as a milieu? More generally, what do I show her about my way of living life, in how I live with her?

References

Bergmann, M. (2014). Psychoanalysis in old age: The patient and the analyst. In S. Kuchuck (Ed.), *Clinical implications of the psychoanalyst's life experience* (pp. 237–245). New York: Routledge.

Bishop, E. (2010). One art. In K. Young (Ed.), *The art of losing: Poems of grief and healing* (p. 215). New York: Bloomsbury.

Buechler, S. (2004). *Clinical values: Emotions that guide psychoanalytic treatment.* Hillsdale, NJ: Analytic Press.

Buechler, S. (2008). *Making a difference in patients' lives.* New York: Routledge.

Buechler, S. (2011). Losing myself. Paper presented at the New Directions Writing Workshop, Baltimore, MD.

Buechler, S. (2012). *Still practicing: The heartaches and joys of a clinical career.* New York: Routledge.

Buechler, S. (2015a). *Understanding and treating patients in clinical psychoanalysis: Lessons from literature.* New York: Routledge.

Buechler, S. (2015b). Will I still be me? Paper presented at Adelphi University, Garden City, NY.

Burack-Weiss, A. (2015). *The lioness in winter: Writing an old woman's life.* New York: Columbia University Press.

Campbell, J. (2004). *Pathways to bliss.* Novato, CA: New World Library.

Cather, W. (1994). Neighbor Rosicky. In A. W. Lidz (Ed.), *Major American short stories* (pp. 301–326). New York: Oxford University Press.

Day, C. (1952). Father wakes up the village. In M. Crane (Ed.), *Fifty great short stories* (pp. 315–321). New York: Bantam Dell.

Eliot, T. S. (1930). The love song of J. Alfred Prufrock. In *Selected poems* (pp. 11–16). New York: Harcourt, Inc.

Eliot, T. S. (1943). East coker. In *Four quartets* (23–32). New York: Harcourt, Inc.

Emerson, R. W. (1996). Terminus. In S. A. Stuart (Ed.), *A treasury of poems* (pp. 7–8). New York: BBS Publishing Corporation.

Erikson, E. (1968.) *Identity: Youth and crisis.* New York: W. W. Norton & Company.

Frankl, V. (1946). *Man's search for meaning.* New York: Simon and Schuster.

Hall, D. (2014). *Essays after eighty.* New York: Houghton Mifflin Harcourt.

Izard, C. (1972). *Patterns of emotion.* New York: Academic Press.

Izard, C. (1977). *Human emotions.* New York: Plenum Press.

James, H. (1992). The middle years. In J. C. Oates (Ed.), *The Oxford book of American short stories* (pp. 171–190). New York: Oxford University Press.

Joseph, J. (2013). Warning. In A. Sampson (Ed.), *Poems to learn by heart* (pp. 124–125). London: Michael O'Mara Books.

Lerner, M. (1999). Little selves. In J. Updike & K. Kenison (Eds.), *The best American short stories of the century* (pp. 7–18). New York: Houghton Mifflin Company.

Melville, H. (1994). Bartleby the scrivener. In A. W. Lidz (Ed.), *Major American short stories* (pp. 135–167). New York: Oxford University Press.

Munro, A. (1991). Mrs. Cross and Mrs. Kidd. In *The moons of Jupiter* (pp. 160–181). New York: Vintage.

Paley, G. (1966). Distance. In J. Moffett & K. R. McElheny (Eds.), *Points of view: An anthology of short stories* (pp. 227–236). New York: New American Library.

Sullivan, H. S. (1953). *The interpersonal theory of psychiatry*. New York: W. W. Norton.

Sullivan, H. S. (1954). *The psychiatric interview*. New York: W. W. Norton.

Sullivan, H. S. (1956). *Clinical studies in psychiatry*. New York: W. W. Norton.

Thomas, D. (2010). Do not go gentle into that good night. In K. Young (Ed.), *The art of losing: Poems of grief and healing* (pp. 19–20). New York: Bloomsbury.

Tolstoy, L. (1886/1982). The death of Ivan Ilych. In A. Maude & L. Maude (Trans.), *The raid and other stories* (pp. 228–280). New York: Oxford University Press.

Vaillant, G. (1993). *The wisdom of the ego*. Cambridge, MA: Harvard University Press.

Yeats, W. B. (1996). When you are old. In S. A. Stuart (Ed.), *A treasury of poems* (p. 7). New York: BBS Publishing Corporation.

Chapter 4

Cognitive, emotional, and interpersonal sources of resilience

On January 8, 2017, in the *New York Times Magazine*, Jan Mooallem published an article titled "The House at the End of the World." It is the story of a college student named B. J. Miller who went out for drinks with friends and had a terrible accident that landed him on a burn unit, near death. He lost both legs and one arm just below the elbow. When Miller was rolled out of surgery, he said to his wheelchair-bound mother that now they had more in common. According to the article, Miller didn't suddenly experience a state of spiritual clarity. Rather, he felt himself to be in tremendous turmoil. But, looking back at that time, Miller feels he found a good perspective on his situation, and he was determined to *fake* that attitude until he could really feel it. From Miller's point of view, he is no different from others, in that each human life, including his, is difficult in its own unique way.

I might call this a "fake it 'til you make it" approach to cultivating resilience. Of course, this is not psychoanalysis, but I think it is very interesting to contrast it with the values many analysts implicitly hold. My goal is to explore and, in some cases, challenge the values about healthy resilience that I believe are embedded in our theories and in the clinical work we do.

Miller saw himself as somewhere on a continuum between a person on their death bed and someone who had misplaced their car keys. He believed that, mistakenly, we treat suffering as a disruption of the life we are supposed to have, instead of as an inevitable part of life. Miller says he tried to get *into* his injuries, rather than *over* them, as he feels the medical profession implicitly recommends. What attitude toward suffering does our psychoanalytic profession hold?

Eventually, Miller went to medical school and specialized in palliative care, focusing more and more on the end of life. He became executive director of Zen Hospice Guest House, a small residential care facility in San Francisco. With six beds, the program helps each patient find their own way to die. In an interview, Miller described helping some terminal patients "recalibrate" hope. When living another year is unrealistic, making it to a grandchild's birthday can become a meaningful goal. Aside from a regular medical and nursing staff, Zen Hospice operates with a team of volunteers: an assortment of retired business people, bakers, underemployed youth, empty-nesters, and so on. Miller trains them not to run away from the patients' suffering, but to sit with them and let them take the lead. In the article, Mooallem wrestles with whether the staff should confront the patients more, encouraging them to express their regrets, their anguish. Mooallem comes to the conclusion that not all patients are better off if they talk about their condition and/or future prospects. With some patients, the goal may be to help them live a succession of ordinary present moments until their share of present moments runs out.

What can this moving article tell us, as psychoanalysts, about nurturing the strength life's roughest passages require? More specifically, what insight can we gather about healthy adaptation, emotionality, and the role of verbal formulation in bearing suffering? When, as in some illnesses and natural disasters, the losses are severe but not terminal, how do we help survivors find the resilience to rebuild their lives?

I think our understanding of resilience is yoked to our implicit and explicit conception of emotional health in general and, in particular, how we define the healthiest human attitude toward suffering. In the following section, I examine some analytic definitions of health and their implications for cultivating resilience in treatment and, more generally, in life. To touch on the themes that will recur in every chapter of this book, Miller's way of bearing the human condition does not take for granted the unquestionable superiority of verbalized insight. Nor does it take a stand for or against intense emotionality as part of health. But I think it does picture health as taking the form of an adjustment to reality, however complicated and painful it may be. In the history of psychoanalytic thought, seeing some form of adjustment as a goal has been an extremely controversial position. I explore just a few of the many issues this raises.

What is healthy suffering?

It would take more than a chapter to compare definitions of psychological health, emotional health, sanity, normal emotionality, and other related concepts. Since I discuss this in several chapters of this book, I will not attempt a full exploration of these issues here but merely suggest some ways analysts have understood health in general and a healthy attitude toward pain and suffering in particular.

Perhaps the best place to start is the statement by Adam Phillips (2005) that it makes no sense for clinicians to practice without a thoroughly thought-through definition of an emotionally healthy way of living. And yet, while we have devoted countless pages to defining pathology, we have given relatively little attention to understanding health in any form. Phillips spells out the problematic consequences of this neglect. In his own words, "sanity—if it is something we aim at—has to be aimed at without a target" (p. xix).

Elsewhere (Buechler, 2010), I discuss three attitudes clinicians hold toward dealing well with emotional pain. The first, the attitude that pain should be reduced as quickly as possible, has a significant impact on the analyst's focus in treatment, most especially on the timing of interpretations of defense. Briefly, from this perspective, the defenses might easily seem like allies. A quite different orientation is the fundamental attitude that pain is an inevitable part of human experience, best accepted rather than avoided. In this view, the defenses that obstruct our vision of pain are themselves problematic. A third possibility embraces suffering as not only unavoidable but a primary source of wisdom and personal identity. For those holding this view, I argue that defenses are simply not the point.

Freud's views often fall into the second category, which sees suffering as inevitable without necessarily seeing it as potentially ennobling. Unlike the first attitude, which unequivocally aims to reduce or eradicate suffering, according to this point of view the recognition and acceptance of suffering is what is crucial. This recognition can alleviate wasted efforts to deny suffering's existence. For a clinician adhering to this viewpoint, the central problem is not suffering itself but the human effort to deny its presence. I think Freud can be counted among the proponents of this idea, when he famously says to a patient:

> You will be able to convince yourself that much will be gained if we succeed in transforming your hysterical misery into common unhappiness. With a mental life that has been restored to health you will be better armed against that unhappiness.
>
> (Breuer & Freud, 1895/1957, p. 305)

This suggests an attitude toward suffering that focuses on its inevitability. The analyst should address *the way people try to avoid pain, rather than the pain itself.* Defensive avoidance of pain can greatly complicate life. I conclude that analysts aiming for the acceptance of pain would be likely to interpret defenses earlier than analysts aiming for pain's eradication or reduction since, for those analysts, costly defensive avoidances are the central problem.

Rilke tells us that while we are suffering we can't know whether or not it will contribute to our growth:

> you cannot be sure whether your heart did not also grow with it and whether this immense fatigue is not actually the heart growing and expanding. To have patience, patience, and not to judge when suffering, never to judge as long as one is bound up in suffering.
>
> (Baer, 2005, p. 98)

In the same volume, more explicitly advocating bearing difficulties, Rilke states: "Life itself is heavy and difficult. And do you actually want to live?" (p. 48).

I find it fascinating to wonder how Freud would see Miller's statement (above) after his accident that he refused "to let himself believe that his life was extra difficult now, only uniquely difficult, as all lives are." I imagine this could be one way of phrasing our "common human misery." Each of us faces uniquely difficult challenges and sorrows at one time or another. Human beings have in common the inevitability of pain, though our specific situation feels particular to ourselves.

Miller's first words to his wheelchair-bound mother (stating that now they had more in common) align with an assumption I have discussed elsewhere (Buechler, 2008) and will return to in subsequent chapters of this book. According to many varied sources, including discrete emotion theory (Buechler, 2008; Izard, 1977), pain and sorrow can function as an occasion for human bonding.

On the other hand, we can imagine how some analysts might respond to Miller's determination to "fake" an adaptive perspective "hoping that his genuine self might eventually catch up." Those who would see inhabiting that "genuine self" as health might be highly skeptical of this approach. Helping someone fake adaptation would seem contrary to the spirit of Erich Fromm's and Rollo May's analytic values, at least as I understand them (see below for a more detailed exploration of this point).

And what would clinicians from various theoretical schools make of Miller's effort to get "into" his injuries, rather than "over" them? While Miller is not a Buddhist, according to the article, Buddhism does inform the training of many on the staff. Perhaps this slant would foster resilience in the form of a relatively non-conflicted acceptance of what is, without comparing it to what should be. But this raises other extremely complicated issues. Aren't we always, implicitly, comparing what is with what should be? Whether or not we are willing to acknowledge the role values inevitably play in the analytic enterprise, as I have suggested elsewhere (Buechler, 2004), I believe we endorse such value-laden comparisons every time we are willing to diagnose or, even more broadly, every time we are willing to "treat." A diagnosis of a sprained ankle, or a narcissistic personality, or tooth decay implies a comparison with a healthier state.

Further, one of the most complicated and consequential issues, related to our conceptions of health in general and resilience in particular, is the question of the clinician's attitudes about "adjustment" as a therapeutic goal. Arguments about the value of adjustment have been explicit during some periods of analytic history and less explicit at others, but, I would suggest, they are always relevant. It seems clear that during the heyday of ego psychology, analysts lined up, declaring themselves as pro- or anti-adjustment as a high achievement. Some would see "adjustment to reality" as an essential therapeutic goal, while others would question whether such an outcome is just another form of pathology. Within the original group of Interpersonalists, there is a clear divide, as I see it. At times, Sullivan could be the ultimate pragmatist, working to help his patients become better able to fit in to society and have successful, secure relationships. Compared with his colleagues Erich Fromm and Rollo May, Sullivan was less focused on what was right and wrong than on what was acceptable interpersonally (although in one area, cultural dictates about homosexuality, Sullivan's relationship to society's rules was more complicated, as extensively discussed in Wake, 2011). Fromm and May espoused values that are universal and supersede those of any particular society, while Sullivan was often content to help patients adjust more successfully within society as it is. Fromm was explicitly critical of what he called the socially sanctioned, empty "marketing character," whose motto is "I am as you desire me." In what I hear as a similar tone, May (1953) described "other-directedness" as typical of many in modern western culture whose drive for approval can make them into "hollow" people, lacking in inner, guiding, orienting values and strong convictions.

For a humorous spoof of adaptation as a healthy way of life, I have always loved W. H. Auden's (2016) poem "Unknown Citizen." Auden's model member of society consumes exactly what modern culture dictates. He is sure to own the prescribed gadgets, appliances, and conveyance. Even his political opinions are supplied to him by society. His is a life of perfect adaptation.

In short, Rollo May and Erich Fromm, among others, openly questioned whether aiming toward "adjustment" is, in itself, problematic, since it accepts a particular society's dictates, regardless of whether or not they are (in some universal sense) "healthy." Leaving aside the enormous difficulty of trying to define a universal standard of health, does the goal of adjustment give too little credence to the possibility of healthy individual variations? Can striving for adjustment inspire, as much as other goals can? Looked at from a different angle, when we fight for our own, personal, idiosyncratic vision, do we, perhaps, have the strength to fight harder than we could if we were fighting to adjust to generally accepted norms?

As is often true for me, Emily Dickinson (1960) most succinctly summed up the problem.

> Much Madness is divinest Sense –
> To a discerning Eye –
> Much Sense – the starkest Madness –
> 'Tis the Majority –
> In this, as All, prevail –
> Assent – and you are sane –
> Demure – you're straightway dangerous
> And handled with a Chain –
>
> (p. 209)

It seems clear to me that we need a concept of health in order to understand resilience, but defining health as "adjustment" raises as many questions as it attempts to answer. These questions are at the heart of many great pieces of fiction, as well as much of our heritage of philosophical, psychological, and psychoanalytic thinking. Although they will figure into other chapters of this book (especially with regard to suffering and mourning), here I mention the play "Rabbit Hole" (Lindsay-Abaire, 2006), which explores each parent's reaction when their young son is killed in a bicycle accident. The father wants to get rid of his toys, perhaps have another child, and move on. The mother holds on tight to every memory, every sensation, everything left to her. Is one grief healthier than the other?

Cognitive, emotional, and interpersonal sources of resilience

Cognitive sources of resilience

I hasten to make clear that when I write of "cognitive" resilience, I am very aware that the cognitive, emotional, and interpersonal sources of strength are not really separable. But, to be able to discuss them, I address them separately. What contribution can our minds make when we are struggling to bounce back from severe challenges? Do we see defenses, such as rationalization, denial, even dissociation, as part of a healthy process of "adjusting" to an altered reality? When Miller (above) explains that he "faked" a positive perspective about his altered state, hoping his real self would catch up with it, do we have to alter our analytic theories in order to see this as a healthy response?

In other words, how do we understand Miller's first statement after surgery: "Mom. Mom. Now you and me have more in common"? Although I imagine Miller would not put it this way himself, I see this expression as similar to the *shift in focus* that clinicians call "reframing." Miller is focusing on what he has just gained, instead of what he has just lost. I will call that a cognitive resource, although it obviously has crucial emotional and interpersonal roots as well.

Shifts in focus form part of healthy functioning for many, both with and without the benefit of any psychoanalytic theoretical rationale. To illustrate, a poem, titled "Detail," by Eamon Grennan (2016), vividly captures the transformative power that can come from a sudden change of focus. In treatment, we might take this movement as lending experience a new perspective. In poetry, I think it can have the special sheen of magic. One way to describe its effect is that a shift in perspective creates the experience within us that life can be seen from a new angle. As we read the poem, we shift at the same time as Grennan tells us *about* the shift. His words express the experience the reader is simultaneously having. This strikes me as not unlike the most effective transference interpretations. Part of their power to change us comes from their ability to happen on several levels at once. In Grennan's poem, a robin chases a little finch, presumably about to pounce. Reading the poem, I "watched" the scene in my mind's eye, transfixed by its everyday, casual brutality. The sudden appearance of the sparrow hawk surprised me, as it did the doomed robin. Grennan swiftly comes in for the kill, simultaneously demolishing the robin and the reader's equanimity. This is Grennan's point. We fasten our focus on one of life's myriad details, just as a poem (or a sparrow hawk, or a sudden shattering revelation) wreaks havoc, and we are jolted into awareness that our perspective has been too narrow. It only takes a second for unsuspecting predator to become terminally surprised prey. Similarly, in psychoanalysis, a patient's painful story of parental neglect is unfolding until, along with Edgar Levenson (1988/1991), we ask the unexpected question: What happened to the (seemingly incidental) cat? And with attention to that detail our focus shifts, the story attains a different meaning, and, I believe, with this jolt can come a quickening of the breath, a lively awareness that our perceptions, and life itself, can change irrevocably in a second. I am suggesting that, in these examples as elsewhere, it is the *shift itself*, rather than where the shift takes us, that most contributes to the impact of the words.

As another example, elsewhere (Buechler, 2008) I have described the "analytic attitude" that Schafer (1983) advocates for analysts as potentially equally useful for the patient. In this frame of mind, we look *at* an interaction at the same time as we engage in it. Sometimes, the freedom to shift focus in this way provides a source of resilience.

In thinking about the meanings of resilience, I would also mention a concept put forth by the Indologist, Heinrich Zimmer (1948), who wrote that "[t]he true dilettante will always be ready to begin anew" (p. 6). I see this as a playful expression of resilience. Perhaps another way to express a similar idea is Joseph Campbell's (1988) sense, as described in an introduction by Bill Moyers, that "[t]he unpardonable sin, in Campbell's book, was the sin of inadvertence, of not being alert, not quite awake" (p. xviii). This way of thinking suggests that we owe it to life to be light on our feet, ever ready to be resilient in our response to the next curve ball. It privileges an *ongoing* keen attitude, rather than a capacity to respond after adversity strikes.

Emotional sources of resilience

I can't approach the question of the emotions as contributors to resilience without considering the role of curiosity as a motivating force. Seeing curiosity as an emotion, and a primary motivator, has been enormously meaningful to me. By this I mean that, from birth onward, human beings are driven to seek the new for itself and not in the service of any other drive. Because curiosity clearly moves us and has a specific facial expression, it is considered by emotion theorists (Izard, 1972, 1977) as a fundamental emotion. Personally, I find it clinically useful to think of a wide range of inherent, separable, motivating emotions that are each primary, not means to another end but ends in themselves. For example, as infants, and from that point on, we are curious beings, responsive to novelty, seeking it *for itself* and not just to obtain some other satisfaction. When this primary curiosity is missing, in myself or my patient, I wonder why, because I assume it would be there if it were not blocked.

Curiosity can sometimes push us onward, in treatment and elsewhere, even when the going gets rough. I can personally attest to this. At times, when a treatment has felt daunting, I have felt spurred on by curiosity about the patient and my own part in the interaction. For me, writing has often given structure to my curiosity. It most easily brings me to a higher level of abstraction, so not only am I involved in an interplay, but I am also looking *at* the interchange. The increased clarity this may bring has a cognitive aspect, but, at least for me, it also has emotional benefits, in that it enhances my curiosity. This strengthened curiosity can provide the impetus to keep working, despite sorrow, rage, shame, loneliness, despair, or other painful feelings I might be experiencing.

Looking at it from the opposite direction, since I believe that the emotions exist in a balance, with any alteration in one affecting the levels of all the others (Buechler, 2004, 2008), theoretically any change in the intensity of my feelings in a session would have some impact on my curiosity. I find this to be especially true with regard to anxiety. If I am anxious in a session, I am unlikely to be able to maintain potent curiosity.

I have adapted something André Green (2005) wrote to understand this better: "The primary task of the ego, then, is not predominantly that of defense, but how best to maintain aliveness while navigating 'between chaos and sclerosis'" (p. 104). I find this statement extremely resonant with my own clinical process. Often, I feel I am maintaining my own curious aliveness by navigating between the ever-present Scylla and Charybdis of chaos and sclerosis. In other words, while my own aliveness has interpersonal and intrapsychic *sources*, its *maintenance* partially depends on my ability not to succumb to either anxiously drowning in the overwhelming chaos of moment-by-moment analytic experience or stiffening and closing down in avoidance of that experience.

But, as already mentioned, it is not just anxiety that can decimate my curiosity and diminish the aliveness it can contribute. Intense shame, anger, guilt, loneliness, contempt, and other strong feelings can play this role. I have found that at some point, in most treatments, I have to call on my ability to bounce back. But, for me, questions about the nature of resilience are often too broad. I need to narrow them down by making them more emotion-specific. For example, what does it take for me to bounce back when I am primarily feeling rage in a session? What does it take when I am very anxious, or terribly sad, or achingly lonely? When I feel very ashamed of my behavior in the last session, is there anything I can do to nurture my resilience? While I am never just lonely or just anxious, I think it can be helpful to identify the predominant emotion I am feeling. For me, that is often the first step in working with my countertransference. I think bouncing back from feeling awash with grief takes something different from bouncing back from other states of mind, heart, and soul. I am assuming that for other clinicians and, more generally, for all of us as human beings, resilience comes in different flavors. Bouncing back from shame, rage, terror, and sorrow are not the same. But they do have some commonalities. They all prioritize something over something else. Essentially, they all vote for life. I think even positive emotions, such as joy, might inhibit curiosity, at times. Joy's feeling of completeness could reduce curiosity's hunger, at least in theory.

In both my clinical work and my personal experience, I have found that even short "vacations" from suffering can contribute to renewal. This is one of the great misfortunes of someone who is obsessively preoccupied. For him/her, there are no ten-minute breaks. A long-playing record of thoughts about (past, present, and future) misfortunes never ceases. I see this as different from Miller's advocacy of getting into his injuries, rather than trying to get over them (see above). In its repetitive, endless circularity, obsessive preoccupation leaves no room for Winnicottian transitional relief. Elsewhere (Buechler, 2012), I have explored how writing gives me much-needed "vacations." In my own experience, a vacation in transitional space sometimes transforms the content of my pain, thereby relieving it. Several beautiful examples of this occur in Shakespeare's (1972) *King Lear*. In one, he summons a mock "trial" of his faithless daughters. In his imagination, he temporarily "leaves" his stormy reality and lets his mind concoct a fantasy that serves to exorcise some of his rage. The fantasy of the trial is part vacation (from the "raging" storm) and reworking of the content of the worst affronts. After playing out the fantasy of a trial, Lear allows himself the sleep that renews his sanity. In Harold Bloom's compendium *Shakespeare through the Ages*, G. Wilson Knight (2008) spells out his belief that *King Lear* is a play about creative suffering. As he sees it, the good characters are purified by their adversity, while the bad are brutalized by success, and those who are able to learn from their suffering endure it stoically.

Interpersonal sources of resilience

Like Winnicott's infant who finds herself in her mother's eyes, sometimes human beings can take strength from the mirrors we offer each other. Just as Winnicott's growing child needs good enough interpersonal experience to develop the capacity to be alone and to thrive in transitional space, the clinician needs good enough supervisory experience. In much of my writing about training (Buechler, 2004, 2008, 2012), I have explored what I call the "internal chorus" that can reduce the loneliness of clinical work. Briefly, this is my way of describing the internalized voices of supervisors, teachers, and others that we can call upon in difficult moments with patients. A moment of (silently) touching base with this professional ego ideal may nurture our resilience. We need to be able to bounce back during and after trying sessions, over the course of the day, the week, the years of practice. Colleagues during and after training can become an internalized resource that enables us to experience treatment hours as a creative space. I am using the clinician as a model because it reflects my own experience, but I think the process is similar for others. We all call upon internalized interpersonal sources of strength to bear suffering with resilience.

Loving feelings about the patient can also help us bear pain. In countless mythologies, human beings and gods are rescued by love. I believe that, as analysts, we, too, can be restored to our full resourcefulness, by curious love. Adam Phillips (1994) describes the conjunction of knowing and loving in psychoanalysis. I quote from his witty and wise essay, "On Love."

> "Transference," "repression," "fetishism," "narcissism," "the riddle of femininity"—all these key psychoanalytic concepts confirm the sense that in psychoanalysis love is a problem of knowledge. That lovers are like detectives: they are trying to find something out that will make all the difference.
>
> (p. 40)

I think it can hearten us, as psychoanalysts and, more generally, as people, that knowing and loving are often seen as intertwined. For example, in the Bible, to know someone is to have sexual intercourse with them. An expression of this can be found in Genesis (4:1): "And Adam knew Eve his wife, and she conceived." Like love, knowing one another analytically is a potentially fruitful form of penetration. In psychoanalysis, knowing is the form of loving that allows both participants to conceive themselves anew. Literature, poetry, opera, art, and so many other forms of human creativity proclaim the power of love, in all its forms, to give us the strength to bear whatever life brings. For example, we can read much of the Bible as reflecting beliefs about love's eventual triumph over suffering, no matter how severe. This is one way to listen to the spiritual journey of Jesus, Job's trials, and the evolving tenderness of Shakespeare's King Lear. The triumph of love over all other forces is celebrated in much of poetry, including Shakespeare's expression of praise for the saving grace of love. Although there are countless celebrations of love prevailing over all suffering, I limit myself to just one of Shakespeare's (1997) poems, "When in Disgrace with Fortune and Men's Eyes":

> When in disgrace with fortune and men's eyes
> I all alone beweep my outcast state,
> And trouble deaf heaven with my bootless cries,
> And look upon myself and curse my fate . . .
> Haply I think on thee—and then my state,
> Like to the lark at break of day arising
> From sullen earth, sings hymns at heaven's gate;
>> For thy sweet love remembered, such wealth brings
>> That then I scorn to change my state with kings.
>> (pp. 160–163)

Numerous songs, stories, poems, sculptures, and paintings celebrate love as the balm that brings us the strength to bear sorrows with resilience. Often, we gather the forbearance to "bounce back" after catastrophes because we are loved and love others.

This brings me to the idea that, in grief, a saving grace may be the feeling of connection with other sufferers. I discuss this idea elsewhere (Chapter 2), but here I mention one story, Raymond Carver's (2002) poignant tale, "A Small, Good Thing." In this moving story, Ann and Howard are planning their son Scotty's birthday party. But then, on the way to school the day of the party, Scotty is hit by a car. Most of the story takes place in the hospital, where the desperate parents wait in vain for their son to come out of a coma. At first, the doctors hold out hope, and only the nurses seem to believe Scotty will really die. Then Scotty dies.

Meanwhile, Ann and Howard get a series of harassing calls from the baker, who demands that they pick up and pay for the birthday cake. Ann burns to confront him, so they drive to the bakery, very late at night. Ann bursts out that her son is dead. She concedes that the baker couldn't be expected to know that, but then she spits: "Bakers can't know everything—can they, Mr. Baker? But he's dead. He's dead, you bastard!" (p. 24). Her sorrow overtakes her anger and she collapses, shaking, sobbing that it isn't fair.

The shaken baker asks them to sit down, apologizes, and tries to explain that his lonely life has left him socially unfit. He doesn't have children, friends, lovers. He makes cakes so others can celebrate. He admits that he has forgotten how to act like a human being and asks for their forgiveness. All he knows how to do is bake, so he serves them rolls: "'You probably need to eat something,' the baker said. 'I hope you'll eat some of my rolls. You have to eat and keep going. Eating is a small good thing in a time like this,' he said" (p. 25). At first, they can't eat, but, gradually, they do. As they take in his offering, they recognize that grief has distorted them all, in different ways. Ann and Howard reflect that it would be just as absurd not to eat the rolls as it is to have them. So why not share a small, good thing? Carver's story vividly illustrates how one human being reaching out to a sufferer, even in a small gesture, can sometimes provide sustenance. A flash of fellow feeling often nurtures resilience during crises. At the end of Carver's story, the reader may imagine that the baker, as well as Ann and Howard, become a tiny bit better able to go on living.

Emily Dickinson (2010) wonders whether comparing one's grief to another's can ease the ache. I quote some lines of the beautiful poem (550) in which she catalogues all human grief, and compares them with her own.

> I measure every Grief I meet
> With narrow, probing, eyes –
> I wonder if It weighs like Mine –
> Or has an Easier size . . .
> I wonder if it hurts to live –
> And if They have to try –
> And whether – could they choose between –
> It would not be – to die . . .
> The Grieved – are many – I am told –
> There is the various Cause
> Death – is but one – and comes but once –
> And only nails the Eyes –
> There's Grief of Want – and Grief of Cold –
> A sort they call "Despair" –
> There's banishment for native Eyes –
> In sight of Native Air –

(pp. 250–251)

At the close of the poem, Dickinson declares that it gives her comfort to see the "passing Calvary" and to note that some of the suffering she sees on the Cross is like her own. Perhaps "misery loves company" not just because it makes suffering less lonely, and makes us feel less singled out, but, by connecting us to each other, it might help us emotionally defray some of the costs of what we have lost.

Resistances to resilience

How are remembering the past and forgiving it related to resilience? For example, is it ever better to avoid remembering, or does it facilitate rebuilding a life to retrieve traumatic memories? For a beautiful affirmation of the healing power of remembering, I turn to Anna Ornstein's (Ornstein & Goldman, 2004) poignant memoir, *My Mother's Eyes: Holocaust Memories of a Young Girl.* Writing of the dedication of the Holocaust Museum in Washington, DC, she said: "Renewal is not forgetting; renewal comes from an ever-deeper appreciation of memories that link the past with the present" (p. 163). Ornstein gathers resilience from seeing that the atrocities will be remembered. She quotes Eva Hoffman, who said: "To survivors, the permanent cording off of memory would mean an ultimately tragic alienation from their history, an excision of part of their identity, even if that is an ineradicably hurtful part" (p. 160).

But is forgiveness conducive to resilience? Obviously, this is an extremely complicated issue. I write about forgiveness in a separate chapter of this book, so I will just mention a few experiences I have had dealing with resistances to forgiving and moving on. I start with my impressions of a patient's struggle with this issue. Depression punctuates my patient's life, as it did her mother's. While she has struggled to disentangle her life from her mother's, and is (consciously) determined to do so, we both know that it is not so simple. Who would it make her if she could sleep restfully, smile easily, joke? What would it negate if she could enjoy sexual contact, when her mother didn't? What part of her own experience would be denied if she had a comfortable comrade now, when so few friends populated her lonely childhood and her mother's extreme social isolation? I see her loyalty to depression as, in part, an expression of her loyalty to her mother.

I would like to quote a phrase from Christopher Bollas's (1999) book, *The Mystery of Things.* His patient, Antonio, was deeply emotionally connected to a mother who never recovered from the loss of her family and culture. Antonio could be seen as living in a state of opposition to resilience. Waves of disturbing thoughts would completely engulf Antonio's mind. Bollas described Antonio as a "headstone for the departed" (p. 111). I find this phrase extremely evocative. I think it captures the similarity between Antonio's allegiances and my patient's way of remembering her long-dead mother. In brief, I see her depressive symptoms in at least three ways: as a firmly established identity, a form of attachment to her mother, and an assertion of her unwillingness to forgive life for all that she and her mother have endured.

Very briefly, my patient has been depressed most of her adult life and, probably, most of her childhood as well. She remembers latchkey loneliness, the long afternoons between school and her mother's return from work. She pictures herself as a child, staring out of a window, scared an intruder would come, and wondering whether her fears were realistic, wondering what it meant if they were and what it meant if they were not. Although much less isolated now, she still sees herself as that child, unsure of whether anyone will ever want to play with her. When she tries to imagine life without depression, she thinks of someone else's life.

My patient is a testament to her own childhood deprivations and her mother's suffering. *To recover would be to forgive life*. It would mean giving up hope that someone will notice the haggard child, worn down by unrelenting chores and a premature understanding of just how bleak life can get.

What would it mean for my patient to forgive life and move on? When forgiveness is mentioned in a religious context, it is usually about our being forgiven for our sins. But what about *our* forgiving life? This idea helps me understand one of the limitations of all dualisms. When we divide the world (and ourselves) into good or evil, life or death instincts (Freud), biophilic or necrophilic (Fromm), we might be distracted from the search for the side-by-side experience that could inspire us to forgive. Profound rage at life's outrageous blows and profound gratitude for its joys don't cancel each other out. Each exists horizontal to the other, better neighbors than we sometimes imagine.

I am reminded of something Bromberg (2001) said in response to Freud's case of Emmy: "Even though she welcomed his trying to 'cure' her, she didn't want him to 'cure' her of being herself" (p. 137). Sometimes, symptoms are a patient's family album, portraits of the people who have meant the most, that now determine the contours of a self-portrait. I think of resilience as often both impossible and necessary. We may know we have to carry on, but resilience seems unattainable. Like a broken record, we are stuck at the place where impossible and necessary meet.

I believe that when any of us faces something both impossible and necessary, we bring to the task our whole histories of similar moments. Many situations feel both impossible and necessary to bear. I think that we all live through times like that, but each of us brings a different set of equipment and history of previous struggles. Sometimes, what is both impossible and necessary in the present conjures up earlier situations we were too young to cope with. This is one way to think about trauma. Perhaps such situations have been summed up most succinctly by the Samuel Beckett (1955) character who declares, "I can't go on, I'll go on" (p. 414).

When does emotional intensity foster resilience?

It is easy to understand why most of us fear emotional intensity. Extreme fear, anger, shame, guilt, sorrow, and even extremely intense joy and curiosity can be very unpleasant. They can threaten our sense of being in control and trigger destabilizing anxiety. They can prompt us to act impulsively and later deeply regret it. While we celebrate passion in the opera, the ballet, theater, and other cultural venues, we worry about it (and sometimes punish it) in our children and, often, in ourselves. Along with King Lear, lowlier fictional and non-fictional characters, including us, can be undone by intense feelings, but we can also be effectively bolstered by them.

In this chapter and many to come, I argue that intensity deserves a better reputation in daily life, not just on small and large screens. I think it is frequently needed to respond to life's blows with resilience. Sometimes, when we try to tame intensity, we also cool the very passion that could enhance our ability to cope. For example, a patient who tamed her depressive feelings with medication later came to see that she had also diminished the hunger that could have led her to reach out more socially.

Many forms of treatment call upon cognitive resources to "master" negative feelings and impulsivity. Those who try to "cure" suffering addicts with reasoned arguments, or control self-destructive teenagers with limit-setting rules, know how feeble these attempts can be, unless they recruit *passionate* determination in the person we are trying to reach. The old adage that we must fight fire with fire applies here. A "symptom" born of intense emotion often doesn't yield to logic. We usually don't get far trying to persuade the depressed person that they really have a great deal to live for. And yet so many forms of treatment (and not just those that call themselves "cognitive") rely on the mind to tame sorrow and overpower impulse. We implicitly accuse the depressed sufferer of not having enough willpower to overcome their feelings. An interesting book, *Unholy Ghost*, edited by Nell Casey (2001), makes this clear. The book is a compilation of chapters written by people in significant relationships with someone who suffers from depression. Many of the chapters eloquently express how damaging this attitude can be for all concerned. The depressed person may end up feeling doubly miserable. Not only is the depression itself hard to bear, but shame and guilt about being unable to "master" it are added to the suffering. Here are a few quotes that bring this message home.

> [T]here are always private suspicions in the presence of the depressed. Is this person just spiritually weaker? Am I stronger? . . . I wondered if Maud was clinging to her sadness, stubbornly digging her heels in on a life that had become unwieldy and disappointing . . . I wondered if she just wasn't trying hard enough.

> (pp. 277–278)

These were the words of Nell Casey, sister of Maud, who suffered from severe depression. It seems clear that the suspicion that Maud just wasn't trying hard enough reflected a (not uncommon) belief that depression can be "managed" by adequate effort, so those who remain depressed are either intentionally unwell or weak. I can only believe that this attitude, itself, often adds to the pain of both parties.

In the same volume, Lee Stringer expresses a very different attitude.

And it has occurred to me that perhaps what we call depression isn't really a disorder at all, but, like physical pain, an alarm of sorts, alerting us that something is undoubtedly wrong; that perhaps it is time to stop, take a time-out, take as long as it takes, and attend to the unaddressed business of filling our souls.

(pp. 112–113)

I find in these words a much-needed corrective to the attitude that, with sufficient willpower or cognitive strategies, we can and should "master" intense feelings. To me, this can be a powerfully damaging message. Not only might it hurt the self-esteem of the sufferer who is unable to turn the pain off, but it may inadvertently diminish needed passion. Emotions are not like taps that can be individually turned off. I have long believed (Buechler, 2004, 2008) that the emotions exist in a system, so impacting one of them affects them all. When we try to diminish one feeling, even if we succeed, we may mute the whole system. Thus, for example, a patient of mine felt great sadness about the loss of her partner. The intensity of the feelings of sadness and loneliness eventually motivated her to find someone with whom to share her life.

Words that can augment or inhibit resilience

As purveyors of the "talking cure," it would be convenient to believe that finding words for painful experiences contributes to resilience. No doubt it frequently does. But I would question the assumption that it always works that way. I think it is important to challenge the idea that the clarity that words may bring enhances coping. This unquestioned assumption was part of the curriculum when I was trained although, ironically, usually it was not put into words. But, then, sometimes it was. For example, Sullivan's emphasis on "consensual validation" implies that when we can communicate experience in words that can be understood by another, we have moved in the direction of health. Like many others, Sullivan believes that having words for an experience renders it understood and, therefore, more likely to come under the healthy jurisdiction of coping devices. It is as though, when I verbalize, I have expanded the known "me," which is, in a sense, much of what analysis strives for when it attempts to make the unconscious conscious. In Sullivan's (1954) words,

Thus whenever the psychiatrist's attempt to discover what the patient is talking about leads the patient to be somewhat more clear on what he is thinking about or attempting to communicate or conceal, his grasp on life is to some extent enhanced. And no one has grave difficulties in living if he has a very good grasp on what is happening to him.

(pp. 23–24)

Perhaps this can be viewed as Sullivan's version of the idea that knowing the truth makes us free.

On the one hand, insight can be an important outcome of finding words for experiences, but not the only one, and (in my experience) not its most crucial benefit. Finding the right word doesn't just *describe* or *explain* experience, it sometimes actually *changes* it. T. S. Eliot (1943) has written of the transformative power of words in his great poem, "East Coker." The poem deals with a question significant for every clinician (as well as others). How do we communicate our thoughts, feelings, spiritual struggles, vividly enough for them to be felt by the listener? Every time we speak, we can be reminded of the imprecision of words for conveying our deepest feelings. Eliot likens our efforts to the disjointed forays of a ragtag squad of soldiers, forever striving and forever falling short. In each session, both participants strive toward articulation, often with imprecise words that are trying to express unformulated feelings. Like the poet, the clinician and patient try to get the better of words.

At our best, the words of patient and analyst transform an experience. Like psychoanalysts, poets do more than merely describe or explain. We make magic. The word creates something alive from the intercourse of two people, much like other miracles of birth. The poet, reader, analyst, and patient sometimes experience an unexpected, life-altering moment. It is the work of the poet and the analyst to find words that facilitate these potentially transformative jolts.

Sudden bolts of clarity have been called by different names. In psychoanalysis, they might be referred to as "now moments" (Stern, 1998). Hirsch (1999) tells us that Wordsworth referred to them as "spots of time," Virginia Woolf called them "moments of being," and Harold Bloom refers to the "poetic crossing." Describing the appearance of these moments in James Joyce's work, Hirsch defines them as "a sudden revelation or manifestation of spiritual meaning, an insight or revelation of truth in the commonplace, a psychological and literary mode of perception" (p. 226). Later, he goes on to say:

> The epiphanic moment always marks a crisis point in a work, a threshold experience. One notices how often, and how primitively, it is set off by the word suddenly. It is a moment of illumination that signals a dramatic turning point for the protagonist. The change is interiorized; under the pressure of insight one's mental landscape is irrevocably altered. Such moments are "visionary"; that is, they mark a crossover from one level of experience to another.
>
> (p. 242)

I have written elsewhere (Buechler, 2004) about my work with a patient I call "John." He had been released from a State hospital, and I treated him in our outpatient clinic. His history was riddled with profound neglect. His tone was matter-of-fact, devoid of affect. John's life was punctuated by rituals. He made sure he didn't get too comfortable sleeping by setting the alarm to ring every few hours. He prevented himself from enjoying washing his hair by using ice-cold water.

I was barely older than John when I began to see him, in a treatment that lasted four years. It was my first professional job, and I was still in graduate school. I really had no idea how to help him. But when he told me an experience, in his dry, emotionless tone, I guessed at what he might have been feeling. I felt the affect that was missing. A few years into the work, John began telling me something that happened with the phrase, "You would say I felt . . . " (anxious or angry, I don't remember which). I was very moved by this, knowing, in some inchoate way, that this was progress. Now, I would also say it was akin to poetry. It both marked a change and created change. It expressed John's developing awareness of me as a separate person with my own subjectivity. But the words also moved toward the creation of an "us." *We* understood that I supplied affect-laden words. This was a magical moment, for me. I think, in a way, it was the moment I became a clinician. I understood how much words can matter, and how, sometimes, they can actually change reality.

At times, words can structure experience for both the present and future. For example, with a patient who tended to minimize his childhood neglect, I (somewhat teasingly) described his wife's inattention to him as "no big deal." We both knew that I meant that this is how he would choose to see it, whether or not it really mattered. The phrase became a touchstone for us. Forever after that, it affirmed that there was an "us." That is, we could use a shorthand that reminded both of us of his history. I think the phrase also served to structure his experience, so that, after we created it, whenever he felt neglected he could ask himself whether this was another instance of trying to see it as "no big deal." The words gave him a category in which to file future moments, as well as a (somewhat rueful) sense of self-recognition, and the feeling of being understood by me. Thus, words can sometimes change experience by structuring it and putting it in a relational context. "No big deal" was *our* phrase, redolent of our ways of being with each other.

When words function in these ways, they foster resilience in that they inspire growth. But I think putting our experiences into words has its costs as well as its benefits. Words can give the speaker as well as the listener a false sense that an experience is understood. If you and I label a piece of cloth "red," does that mean we are having the same experience? Erich Fromm (2009) has eloquently argued that words can actually *alienate us* from lived experiences.

> Actually if you utter a word, by uttering the word, you alienate yourself already from the experience. The experience is really there, only just the moment before you say the word. Once the word is said, it is already over there.
>
> (p. 14)

Many patients complain about the expectation that they have to use words in order to engage in the "talking cure." Analysts often experience (and interpret) the patient's silence as a form of resistance. But I think silence can also represent the patient's sense (however inchoate) that there are no words that would be adequate to convey what they feel. In some situations, the analyst's willingness to wait for the patient to find words, however long it takes, can be the greatest possible gift. I have sometimes felt that I can best honor the patient's experience by not insisting on words at all. Words uttered may make me feel (relatively) comfortable and ensconced in my familiar analytic role. They are, in some senses, my home. What if they are not the patient's?

We assume that if the patient fits words to experience, this fosters curative insight. No doubt that is frequently true. Finding words may convince the patient that whatever he or she feels now has been felt before and adequately borne. This may well evoke the strength resilience requires. But I think this fails to credit the power of the unarticulated.

References

Auden, W. H. (2016). Unknown citizen. In H. M. Seiden (Ed.), *The motive for metaphor* (p. 11). London: Karnac.

Baer, U. (2005). *The poet's guide to the wisdom of Rilke.* New York: Modern Library.

Beckett, S. (1955). *The unnamable.* New York: Alfred A. Knopf.

Bollas, C. (1999). *The mystery of things.* New York: Routledge.

Breuer, J., & Freud, S. (1895/1957). *Studies on hysteria* (J. Strachey, Trans.). New York: Basic Books, Inc.

Bromberg, P. (2001). Hysteria, dissociation, and cure: Emmy von N. revisited. In M. Dimen & A. Harris (Eds.), *Storms in her head: Freud and the construction of hysteria* (pp. 121–143). New York: Other Press.

Buechler, S. (2004). *Clinical values: Emotions that guide psychoanalytic treatment.* Hillsdale, NJ: Analytic Press.

Buechler, S. (2008). *Making a difference in patients' lives.* New York: Routledge.

Buechler, S. (2010). No pain, no gain? Suffering and the analysis of defense. *Contemporary Psychoanalysis, 46,* 334–354.

Buechler, S. (2012). *Still practicing: The heartaches and joys of a clinical career.* New York: Routledge.

Campbell, J. (1988). *The power of myth.* New York: Anchor Books.

Carver, R. (2002). A small good thing. In A. H. Bond (Ed.), *Tales of psychology: Short stories to make you wise* (pp. 1–28). St. Paul, MN: Paragon House.

Casey, N. (Ed.) (2001). *Unholy ghost: Writers on depression.* New York: HarperCollins.

Dickinson, E. (1960). Poem 435. In T. H. Johnson (Ed.), *The complete poems of Emily Dickinson* (p. 209). Boston, MA: Little, Brown & Company.

Dickinson, E. (2010). Poem 550. In H. Vendler (Ed.), *Dickinson: Selected poems and commentaries* (pp. 250–251). Cambridge, MA: Harvard University Press.

Eliot, T. S. (1943). East coker. In *Four quartets* (pp. 23–35). New York: Harcourt, Inc.

Fromm, E. (2009). Being centrally related to the patient. In R. Funk (Ed.), *The clinical Erich Fromm* (pp. 7–39). New York: Rodopi Press.

Green, A. (2005). *Key ideas for a contemporary psychoanalysis: Misrecognition and recognition of the unconscious* (A. Weller, Trans.). New York: Routledge.

Grennan, E. (2016). Detail. In H. M. Seiden (Ed.), *The motive for metaphor* (pp. 40–43). London: Karnac.

Hirsch, E. (1999). *How to read a poem and fall in love with poetry*. New York: Harcourt.

Izard, C. (1972). *Patterns of emotion*. New York: Academic Press.

Izard, C. (1977). *Human emotions*. New York: Plenum Press.

Knight, G. W. (2008). The "Lear" universe. In H. Bloom (Ed.), *Shakespeare through the ages* (pp. 169–195). New York: Checkmark Books.

Levenson, E. (1988/1991). The pursuit of the particular. In *The purloined self: Interpersonal perspectives in psychoanalysis* (pp. 189–203). New York: Contemporary Psychoanalysis Books.

Lindsay-Abaire, D. (2006). *Rabbit hole*. New York: Broadway Production.

May, R. (1953). *Man's search for himself*. New York: W. W. Norton & Company, Inc.

Mooallem, J. (2017, 8 January). The house at the end of the world. *New York Times Magazine*, pp. 39–45.

Ornstein, A., & Goldman, S. (2004). *My mother's eyes: Holocaust memories of a young girl*. Cincinnati, OH: Emmis Books.

Phillips, A. (1994). *On flirtation*. Cambridge, MA: Harvard University Press.

Phillips, A. (2005). *Going sane: Maps of happiness*. New York: HarperCollins.

Schafer, R. (1983). *The analytic attitude*. New York: Basic Books.

Shakespeare, W. (1972). *King Lear*. In *The Arden edition of the works of William Shakespeare* (pp. 1–206). London: Methuen Drama.

Shakespeare, W. (1997). When in disgrace with fortune and men's eyes. In H. Vendler (Ed.), *The art of Shakespeare's sonnets* (pp. 160–163). Cambridge, MA: Harvard University Press.

Stern, D. (1998). The process of therapeutic change involving implicit knowledge: Some implications of developmental observations for adult psychotherapy. *Infant Mental Health Journal, 9*, 300–308.

Sullivan, H. S. (1954). *The psychiatric interview*. New York: W. W. Norton.

Wake, N. (2011). *Private practices: Harry Stack Sullivan, the science of homosexuality, and American Liberalism*. New Brunswick, NJ: Rutgers University Press.

Zimmer, H. (1948). *The king and the corpse: Tales of the soul's conquest of evil* (J. Campbell, Ed.). Washington, DC: The Bollingen Foundation.

Chapter 5

Bearing uncertainty, upholding conviction, and maintaining curiosity

It has become extremely popular in psychoanalytic circles to declare how little we know. Sometimes, I feel we are boasting about our modesty and humility. In this chapter, I ask how we can hold onto the benefits of renouncing all pretense of omniscience, without losing our place as a trusted resource for individual growth and societal betterment.

My own experience in doing treatment and training tells me that patients and beginning clinicians need to feel that it is possible for clinicians to define health, at least in broad terms. Treatment suffers (and probably ends) if either participant can't muster conviction that the work will foster healthier life. In addition, many of our forebears (e.g., Fromm, May, Winnicott) considered it part of the analyst's responsibility to use our knowledge to speak out against society's ills, which assumes we know something about healthy functioning.

It is my sense that, while not impossible, *it is difficult to maintain passionate conviction about healthy living, at the same time as we embrace full recognition of the subjectivity of all human experience and open-minded curiosity about other points of view.* In personal relationships, as well as on the world stage, at least one of these three is frequently sacrificed to maintain the others. And yet, I can't see psychoanalysis as a force for individual and societal betterment unless we can meet the challenge of holding onto strong convictions, along with awareness of the subjectivity of all perception and genuine curiosity about perspectives other than our own. If we can't maintain all three of these values, how will we help our patients live with integrity as individuals and citizens?

Holding the tension between conviction about what we *do* know, awareness of subjectivity, and curiosity reminds me of Hoffman's (1998) ritual and spontaneity dialectic. Just as analysis thrives when ritual and spontaneity are both honored, clinicians are called upon to maintain sufficient conviction, at the same time as we remain aware of the limitations of our vision and maintain enough open-minded curiosity to take in news. Bion's oft-repeated injunction to enter sessions without memory or desire is, in my opinion, only half the story. We must enter sessions both with and without memory and desire. While logically impossible, I think this is therapeutically necessary (as an ideal to approximate to). Elsewhere (Buechler, 1999), I have described a consultation with a patient who suffered from a severe eating disorder. I believe that fully meeting her required me to have an unswerving belief that I could imagine the healthier person she could become, at the same time as I accepted that my vision of her is limited by who I am, while also maintaining profound curiosity about how she sees herself. I needed the strong conviction to lend my work passion, but I also needed curiosity and awareness of my subjectivity to remain humble enough to hear who *she* wanted to become.

I am suggesting that maintaining this tension is important for several reasons. I think both partners in treatment need goals to aspire to, in order to commit fully to the work. Even if the goals change over time (as they frequently do), I think it is vital to have *some* vision of the richer life that the treatment can facilitate. Without this motivation, treatment can become a sterile exercise. But, at the same time, without sufficient curiosity and humility it can become indoctrination (Levenson, 1991).

I also believe that maintaining the tension between these ideals is a significant statement about the human condition. I have come to believe that sometimes we clinicians have our greatest impact by transparently living our values in sessions (Buechler, 2004). I think this is true in many other arenas, such as teaching, supervision, and parenting. Who we are shapes our impact. When our actions and words speak similarly—when, in other words, we maintain integrity—our messages are much more powerful.

I believe that treatment (and so much else) can't thrive without steadfast dedication to life itself, which is hard to maintain without some specificity about health. And yet, any specificity is, by its nature, shaped by the eyes of the beholder. And any vision focuses our attention on some aspects of the interpersonal situation and away from others, which affects what we can be curious about. When we struggle to maintain all three of these values, we are saying, in our action, that we believe all three are necessary to life as a human being.

I am not suggesting that the clinician should strive to be an ideal human being or that we serve as models of mental health. I know it is quite possible to hear me as suggesting this, but it is not what I mean. We are as fallible, as imperfect, as anyone else. But our work is about creating a human interaction that facilitates health. I think we each need to forge a personal style of coping with that task that optimally uses our particular "equipment for living," to use Sullivan's (1954) phrase. In this chapter, I suggest that some tension between conviction, awareness of subjectivity, and curiosity are necessary ingredients, regardless of our theoretical orientation.

In the past, analysts like Erich Fromm (1941, 1956) felt free to voice clear definitions of health, strong convictions about better ways to live, and firm beliefs that analysis had a part to play in individual and societal growth. Fromm's passionate conviction inspired many followers and influenced a generation internationally. While his critics might accuse him of grandiosity, sacrificing the benefits of analytic neutrality, being more of a prophet than an analyst, engaging in "superficial" rather than depth processes, and falling prey to logical positivism, many of his books sold in the millions, many of his students carried his messages throughout their careers, and many of his ideas touched countless lives. Can anyone today harness the power to have such an impact? In accepting the subjectivity of all human perception, have we forever lost Fromm's passionate fervor? And have we forfeited our ability to help our patients, and society as a whole, live morally committed yet profoundly open-minded lives?

Elsewhere (Buechler, 2004), I have suggested another way to describe degrees of open-mindedness. I posited a continuum between, at one extreme, curious open-mindedness and, at the other extreme, paranoia. In paranoia, we think we have air-tight explanations. Doubters are traitors. My use of terms such as *paranoia* rests on my belief (Buechler, 2015) that each of us has some potential for using para-noid, obsessive, hysteric, narcissistic, schizoid, and other ways of coping with the human condition. From this perspective, a treatment session is a meeting between two ways of coping. In the interpersonal field this creates, both coping styles are affected. Each brings out the other's proclivities. Thus, with a patient who copes obsessively (predominantly), I might be at my most obsessive, or, perhaps, my defenses against that style are recruited, but, in any case, my obsessive tendencies will be relevant. Similarly, if I have a paranoid cast, I may bring out the paranoid potential in my patients or, perhaps, some way they have resisted this potential. Of course, it is not as simple as this, as all the potential ways of coping are always available, so that in a session we each fluctuate in the degree to which we are using paranoid, schizoid, obsessive, hysteric, and other coping styles (Buechler, 2012, 2015). The *field* we create together can be characterized as predominantly para-noid, for example, but it will also have obsessive elements. Whereas most of our theories about treatment have adopted two-person models, diagnostic thinking has lagged behind. But it seems clear to me that, in a session, *the coping style of each person affects the other*, so that some sessions (or interactions) bring out the para-noid, schizoid, obsessive, hysteric, or narcissistic potential in both participants. This is really another way to say that, as Sullivan (1953) suggested long ago, we function differently in differing "me–you" patterns.

When I describe the paranoia/curiosity continuum, I see them as extremes with many shades in-between. Some points along this continuum, perhaps closer to the paranoid end, but not at that extreme, might be called convictions. Among the defi-nitions of *conviction* in my dictionary is "a fixed or strong belief" (Morris, 1978). I find the word *fixed* interesting. For example, I have a conviction that the truth is important as an end in itself, and not just as a means to an end. This belief is "fixed," in that it stays in place and would be hard to move. It could be close to the paranoid end of the continuum, depending on how I use it. The more I use it to cut off curious exploration (my version of reality is right, and that is all there is to it), the closer to the paranoid end it falls. I hope I am clear that I am *not* opposing conviction and curiosity as binaries. One can have conviction and still be curious. But there are *uses* of convictions that can block curiosity. Most important, I think that two people in an interaction affect each other's levels of "fixedness" and "curiosity." In this chapter, and throughout this book, I am asking what uses of our convictions can best facilitate the treatment process.

In this way of thinking, a strong sense of conviction, or, we might say, a high level of certainty is, in a sense, a product of an interpersonal field, in which two or more people *may* be coping with life with more "fixedness" than others might or than they themselves might with other partners or at other times. The same might be said about a strong sense of curiosity. Curious open-mindedness often inspires curious open-mindedness in others. To make it even more complex, I think we each *move*, minute by minute, on this continuum between the extreme poles of absolute certainty and curious open-mindedness. In other words, this is a fluid process. Minute by minute, my fixedness will affect where you are on that continuum in some way, although the impact may not be entirely predictable.

Let us say a patient comes into a session talking about a very firm political belief. It is a fixed conviction, connected with his or her identity, related to many other strongly held beliefs. While the strength of the conviction does not, in itself, preclude curiosity, it depends on how the conviction is being used. If it is functioning to contain projected aggression, and to rigidly explain a broad swath of reality (they all hate me because their beliefs are the opposite of mine), it edges toward the paranoid end of the spectrum. But what happens next? The clinician's position comes into play and may move the patient further toward unquestionable certainty or more toward curiosity. But the influence is mutual, not one-way, although it is not entirely predictable. Maybe, for example, the patient's strong belief calls out the clinician's defenses against fixedness. Or, possibly, the clinician counters with unusually extreme positions of her own.

Given this general framework, what are the two participants in a session likely to feel certain or uncertain about, and how is their mutual influence likely to play out? (In Chapter 10, I examine some of the roots of my own convictions about healthy functioning and my efforts to integrate them with awareness of my subjectivity.) Briefly, since the analyst is inevitably seeing the patient through a personal lens, what claims about our contributions to the process can we still make? Are there any universal truths about health that can guide the clinician, despite our irreducible subjectivity? Finally, how does the analyst's stance on these issues affect the patient's capacity to function with sufficient *conviction and curiosity* in daily life?

Before addressing these questions, I would like to turn to the wider world, as I am experiencing it in 2017. I trust that these perceptions will not become entirely irrelevant by the time this is published. An op-ed piece in the *New York Times* by Thomas L. Friedman (2017) nicely captured my feelings. Friedman described the American dilemma that we no longer share basic truths, so there is no legitimate basis for authority. He distinguishes the formal authority of our national administration from moral authority. Leaders who have moral authority understand what they can demand of others and what they must be able to inspire. They know the difference between formal authority (which can be seized or won) and moral authority, which can only accrue from good leadership. Friedman suggests that we have too few leaders with moral authority. He goes on to describe leaders with moral authority as motivated by values, such as humility, and principles, such as probity. These leaders do what is right, even when it will be unpopular. They attract people to work toward noble goals and to engage in projects that deserve dedicated effort. Friedman urges each of us to build moral authority into all our endeavors.

Earlier in psychoanalysis' history, writers like Erich Fromm (1956, 1976) took for granted that analysts should be moral authorities, in Friedman's sense of the term. But that assumption has been challenged for many reasons. Here I cite a few, but for a more extended consideration, see Mitchell (1997). I think one of the chief reasons for our reluctance to embrace moral authority is a confusion of *moral* with *moralistic*. I am addressing some of the difficulties and benefits of the analyst's assumption of moral authority in matters related to healthy functioning. While I acknowledge that there is much merit in the argument for analysts shedding the cloak of formal authority, I feel the issue of our moral authority is more complex. I would argue that the loss of moral authority is costing analysis a great deal of its relevance, meaningfulness, and capacity to inspire clinicians to want to train analytically and patients to want to enter analysis.

I am suggesting that, while our loss of formal authority was inevitable and not problematic, our loss of moral authority comes at great cost. I concede that it has saved us from charges of undue influence (to some extent). It separates us (to some degree) from hurtful aspects of our field's past, such as our pathologizing of homosexuality. We can decry the "bad old days" when we made our own subjective value judgments into objective statements about patients' ways of living their lives. This is an extremely important advance. But, I suggest, we have thrown out the baby with the bathwater.

I think several tendencies reinforce our loss of moral authority. Here I name just a few factors.

1   The interpersonal/relational "turn" in psychoanalysis prefers to focus on what is particular, rather than what is universal.
2   We are reluctant to use diagnostic terminology or think in terms of pathology. This has implications for our understanding of health, therapeutic progress, and treatment goals.
3   Many now assume (contrary to Sullivan, 1954, who defined us as experts) that the analyst is not an "expert" in anything. His or her awareness is limited, subject to unconscious forces. We are inherently flawed, yet responsible for our impact. Put succinctly by Schoen (2017),

> If our influence is inevitable, our subjectivity "irreducible," our awareness incomplete and retrospective (Renik, 1993) and everything we do will be determined and given meaning by the distinctive interactive matrix created by each dyad (Greenberg, 1995), then we rely on finding our way into, and out of, enactments as the new mainstay of therapeutic action.
>
> (p. 107)

Benjamin Wolstein (1975/2017) raised "the fundamental question of how to be both a psychoanalyst behaving as a professional expert and a person experiencing a unique psyche" (p. 51). Interestingly, then, the clinician is held responsible for the impact of his or her unconscious behavior, although it is, by definition, outside his/her awareness and control. This reminds me of a comment Donnel Stern made (2017) about Erich Fromm:

> More than we would today, Fromm and some of his students probably confronted patients with their responsibility for the nature of their own unconscious participation in the creation and maintenance of the kinds of interpersonal transactions that resulted in their own unhappiness.
>
> (p. 21)

Perhaps the differences are matters of emphasis. Fromm, in his time, was focusing on the *patient's* (conscious and unconscious) role in problematic interactions, and, today, some of us are emphasizing the *clinician's* conscious and unconscious participation in treatment interplays.

4   Whatever the analyst *can* claim to "know" is in reference to individual patients, and not society as a whole.
5   In the wider world, claims of authority of any kind are questioned. It may be said that the "information age" has leveled the playing field.

I suggest that relinquishing our moral authority has limited our ability to help patients struggle with their own questions about health, the goals of treatment, and, more generally, their goals and responsibilities as human beings. We have forfeited the opportunity to openly grapple with the human dilemma of marrying firm convictions with the humility that should accompany awareness of our limitations. I also think it has had a deleterious effect on our willingness to take positions publicly when our voices might make a difference. Further, I think it has curtailed our capacity to inspire clinicians to train analytically and prospective patients to undergo psychoanalysis. Sometimes, when we urge each other to take a stance in public about issues related to health, we do so almost apologetically, as though it is unseemly. We question whether or not, as analysts, we have anything to contribute to controversies in public forums. And yet our analytic forebears, such as Fromm (1950) and May (1953), and contemporary analysts such as Altman (1995) and Orange (2017), have felt impelled to speak out about issues that affect the health of individuals and society as a whole.

I would say that, out of concerns about our ability to be "objective," and out of fear of being seen as hopelessly out of date, we have abrogated our responsibility to contribute what we know about psychological health. While I agree that claims to moral authority are rife with dangers, I think our silence can have dangerous consequences as well. A significant problem is our lack of unanimity about what we consider universal versus culture-specific. Adam Phillips (2005) has written persuasively on the topic of our inability to define sanity. I think this stems from our reluctance to declare any qualities to be intrinsic to human health. I am aware of the dangers of imposing evaluative judgments, yet I believe we have training and experience that can allow us to make meaningful contributions to advances in human behavior in varying contexts. In my mind, this obligates us to apply our knowledge when we can. And linked to this responsibility is our capacity to see ourselves as equipped to comment on an individual's (and a culture's) strivings toward health. Our years of training and clinical experience have acquainted us with patterns of how individuals and groups can get mired in paranoid, schizoid, obsessive, narcissistic, and other perceptions and enactments. We may not always "know" or be able to formulate a path toward health, but we have a clearer sense than most about what constitutes *deviations* from that path. We are unusually acquainted with paranoid, obsessive, schizoid, hysteric, narcissistic, and other defensive coping styles. Who, other than us, can bring this perspective to bear on the significant issues of our day?

I am aware that taking this position exposes us to the danger of repeating the excesses, grandiose postures, and logical positivism of the past. I do not, at all, take these dangers lightly. But I think we risk even more if we are silent.

Among other points I am making here: I am suggesting that *our stance on our moral authority affects how we influence patients who are struggling with the continuum between certainty and curiosity*. I think if we disqualify ourselves as moral authorities, we forfeit some of our capacity to help patients with this complicated aspect of life.

For example, a patient is certain (from my point of view, too certain) that she has been unfairly treated by members of her team at work. For her, there is only one way to see the situation—her way. With colleagues, her husband, and me she repeats her complaints, varying the words but not the conclusion. But I hold as a value the capacity to "mentalize," or see a situation from another's perspective. There can be many points of view about what can go on, what should go on, and what did go on in a subsequent session with this patient. An absolute adherence to neutrality and abstinence might dictate that I say little, or refrain from "advocating" mentalizing, or anything else. Taking a neutral position, facilitating the patient's self-expression, I don't need to think about my authority—formal, moral, or otherwise. In a sense, the only value I am communicating at that moment is the potential value of formulating experience into words and, by extension, of the treatment itself. In facilitating free association, I would be representing the value of giving voice to one's inner life. As the patient tells her story to me, she would reveal her transferences and resistances, and (eventually) they would become our subject.

I think this would mean that I would take no overt position about where my patient falls on a continuum from absolute certainty to completely open-minded curiosity. These are, of course, ideal points, and not, generally, actual states of mind. But if I adhere to a standard (A. Freud, 1936) of "even hovering," my subject matter is who I become to her as she recites her position to me and how she resists the treatment process.

What happens, then, if I privilege the value of the human capacity to mentalize, and I believe this value *should* inform the treatment? I suggest that my focus on the material would have a slant, would have priorities, rather than an even distribution. In this case, my attention would concentrate on how my patient insists on seeing the situation from only one perspective—her own. I am, in a sense, processing her behavior according to *a standard I assume to be universal*. I am implicitly assuming that mentalizing is "healthier" than not mentalizing, whether we live in New York or Tokyo, whether we are working in 2017 or 1917. My behavior implies that examining her certainty is therapeutically relevant and significant. Importantly, there is, in a sense, a kind of "certainty" *in my stance*. I am speaking from a point on the certainty/curiosity continuum, as I explore my patient's position on the same dimension.

Lest this be heard as my condoning the "corrective emotional experience" of Alexander (1961), let me be clear that I am not advocating what I elsewhere (Buechler, 2008) call a puppet show. That is, I do not assess my patient as needing me to show her an example of freely roving curiosity (or unchanging certainty) and then *deliberately act the part*. That would be inauthentic and probably ineffective. On the contrary, I am suggesting that the more I can be *aware of my conviction* that healthy functioning includes mentalizing, the more I can "tune in" to our (as yet) unspoken dialogue about her certainties and my own. At this moment, we are both probably further toward the "conviction" end of the continuum, although the content of our convictions differs. We are probably influencing each other to state our cases with more certainty than either of us might express in other contexts. To take this further, I imagine that we are creating a field tilted toward certainty. We now have an "enactment" that can be unpacked and understood, probably to our mutual benefit.

Why and how does this happen? I think it is because there are certain issues, like the continuum between absolute certainty and open-minded curiosity, that are built into the human condition. When either treatment participant takes a position on that continuum, it pulls for the other to inhabit a position on the same dimension. This is a therapeutic opportunity, which can be fruitful if neither participant is wedded to seeing themselves as "pure" of the taint of values. Having explored this frequently recurring issue in the past, perhaps with this patient and/or others, I will know that inevitably I have varied, moment to moment, session to session, patient to patient, self-state to self-state, in how entrenched I am in my certainties. This helps me explore how my patient and I have contributed to our (spoken and enacted) dialogue. Hopefully, I know enough about myself to have a sense of just how "certain" and just how "openly curious" I tend to be. This awareness can help us learn about our impact on each other, as we struggle together with one of the more complex dimensions of human experience.

Balancing conviction with curiosity and awareness of subjectivity

> Consider the hopes of the obsessional patient beginning treatment. He is not interested in giving up his life's work of controlling everything that happens in his experience and that of those around him . . . Of course, the analyst does not say anything like: "Look, I understand that you are hoping I will help you repair and perfect your obsessional approach to living, but I can help you give all that up and find a much fuller and more meaningful life." If the analyst did say something like that, the patient would likely leave, and rightfully so.
>
> (Mitchell, 1993, p. 208)

This paragraph, from Stephen Mitchell's book *Hope and Dread in Psychoanalysis*, has always intrigued me. What are the convictions about health implicit in Mitchell's statement? How can they be accompanied by awareness of our subjectivity and openness to news about the patient and ourselves? For me, Mitchell exemplified these values, in the content of his work, and in his conduct. His *conviction about* our inherent subjectivity was fundamental to his thinking.

And yet, he is definitely assuming that what the patient wants (more control over his own experience and other people) is not what he *should* want. Mitchell clearly has conviction about what would constitute health for this person. Is this just Mitchell's subjective experience, and, if so, how can he adequately honor both his conviction and his awareness of its limitations?

When I read Mitchell's statement, I think about its implications for training as well as for treatment. In my experience, candidates want the clarity his conviction affords. Yet they often have a strong commitment to paying proper attention to the effect of their own subjectivity and a fervent belief in staying open to what the patient wants for himself. Holding the tension between these values is part of what makes treatment and training hard work.

I think each generation of analysts tilts in one of the possible directions, but all have to grapple with these issues. Historically, Interpersonalists, like Singer (1977) and Levenson (1978) rebelled against the classical analyst's certainties. The pendulum swung toward more profound awareness of our subjectivity and greater curiosity about the patient's lived experience. Personally, I sometimes think it has swung too far, and we need to clarify the convictions we *do* bring to the process. For example, if I try to put myself in the analyst's position in Mitchell's statement, I imagine myself holding a number of convictions about a healthier version of this obsessive patient in tension with curiosities and an awareness of my subjectivity. I believe we each bring some conceptions of health with us as we focus selectively in sessions, so the question is whether or not we choose to know them, not whether or not we choose to have them.

Further, I find myself in agreement with those analysts who, like Slochower (2017), ask:

> Might we be, at moments, too anxious to relinquish our authority and relocate it within the relational matrix? Might we overlook our patient's need for us to *know*, to comfortably hold our authority? . . . Might they sometimes long for us to be more certain, more knowing, more authoritative than our theory seems to allow?
>
> (p. 290)

In his witty and perceptive book *Going Sane: Maps of Happiness*, Adam Phillips (2005) outlines some of the problems of trying to practice without a clear definition of emotional health.

> People have never been quite sure whether madness refers to the more bizarre forms of malfunctioning, of diseases, that human beings are prone to; or whether, in fact, human beings are intrinsically mad – an exaggeration perhaps, even potentially a disability, but not essentially alien. Should the project be to attempt to cure ourselves, or to attempt to accept ourselves as we are?
>
> (p. 31)

As usual, Phillips has ironically and succinctly summed up the problem I am addressing, but from another angle. He is asking how we can define the goals of treatment if we can lay no claim to understanding emotional health.

As I spell out more fully in Chapter 10, I was trained, for the most part, by students of H. S. Sullivan. I think his way of working can reduce anxiety in both participants, in that, at least initially, it focuses on the relatively clear task of getting a history of the patient's life. History has chronology. After you look at the patient's first five years together, you know you will look at the next five. Of course, things don't always proceed in this linear fashion. But the chronology can function like an anchor or a scaffold.

I was taught to track fluctuations in the patient's anxiety, my own, and shifts in other feelings, which also gives me a pretty clear task. History-taking and observing emotional shifts are work that requires alertness, concentration, effort, and the ability to organize. But they can be done. With experience, they begin to feel more familiar.

Emotionally, having a relatively clear task helps me feel more competent and, in a certain sense, more hopeful. There is a certain "can-do" quality in this way of working. It can make you feel that it is possible, in Sullivan's language, to profit from one's experience. Embedded in this ideology is a faith that people have, in his words, a drive toward health. I think all this can lead the clinician to feel a sense of integrity or, in other words, the opposite of fraudulent. We are doing something almost tangible. The patient can gain some self-understanding, at the very least, and we can feel some measure of competence. Furthermore, when we look at what has interpersonally recurred in the patient's life, we are likely to see similar patterns in the treatment relationship and, perhaps, in our own life or the lives of others we have known. This demonstrates that we are all more human than otherwise.

It can promote a kind of carryover from what we have learned from literature, art, our personal relationships, our personal treatment, and many other sources. We can bring our whole selves to our work.

This point of view has limitations and, I would say, doesn't work equally well for every clinician and patient. Elsewhere (Buechler, 2004), I have written that it best fits the hard-working clinician with the inhibited, schizoid, obsessive patient, who secretly yearns to join the rest of the human fold but feels inadequate. But for those for whom "can-do" feels cloying, for those who find history-taking too belabored, for those who can't wait to get to the present moment with its pressing problems, for those who feel this way of working is too simplistic and smacks of logical positivism, it isn't a good fit. Personally, I feel this training is valuable to me. Even when I drastically deviate from this approach—and I frequently do for various reasons—I feel heartened that I have a basic template. But, as I will examine shortly, at what cost?

Availability of significant material as a source of optimism

From the Sullivanian perspective, significant patterns should be evident in the person's history, current life, and behavior in treatment. A thorough understanding of every recurring interpersonal pattern is a crucial aspect of therapeutic action. In this way of thinking, a significant pattern may be apparent in a first session, *without the need for regression*. I see this as a source of optimism. The material we most need is available from the beginning, if we could only focus on it. We don't need to wait an undefined period of time for it to become apparent.

Sullivan's thinking seems to me to be well-suited to the eager analyst/explorer, avid to observe, clarify, and demystify. For her or him, psychological health includes the ability to learn from new experience. This, of course, requires that the patient can come to recognize that the experience *is* new, that is, that it is different from what has occurred in the past.

The analyst's role can be described as a complicated process of self and other observation. The importance to Sullivan of being a good observer can't be overstated. Without good observation, we can't know what makes the patient anxious, we can't monitor the effect we are having on the patient, we can't modulate the inquiry to keep anxiety at tolerable levels, and we can't recognize the defenses the patient uses when he is made anxious. Through observation and inquiry, the clinician pictures the situation the patient describes, getting a feel for what the patient might be defensively leaving out of the story. Observation is, of course, central to Sullivan's conception of the analyst as a participant observer. I think of our movement in treatment as a kind of rocking motion between participation and observation. As participation gathers momentum, we begin to shift toward an observing stance, and vice versa. But I would extend this to say that participant observation is as important for the patient as it is for the analyst. Nurturing this capacity is a significant part of the work.

I would say that the importance placed on observation contributes to the optimism in this way of thinking. Unlike techniques that prize coming up with a brilliant interpretation, Sullivan's method is plain but within most peoples' capacities. If we try hard enough, we can observe the other person and ourselves. Being alert and noticing details are less mysterious than coming up with unconscious meanings.

The emphasis on health as the ability to profit from new experience reinforces privileging the stimulation of curiosity in both analyst and patient. Curiosity, like so much else, is more human than otherwise, but some life experiences can dampen it. It is central because it increases the chances of having the new experience that is crucial to the treatment process. I think the eager explorer, that was my younger self, felt her strong suits were valuable in this way of working.

Several of my supervisors taught me that, very frequently, change *precedes* insight. It is fascinating to me that the same lesson can be learned from the letters of the poet Rilke, who said: "All of our insights occur after the fact" (Baer, 2005, p. 23). For example, one of my patients avoided most social contact in the years before our work began. As this changed, and she exposed herself to peers, she began to feel the anxiety social contact stimulates in her. This helped her understand why she had avoided socializing in the past. In other words, changing her behavior brought her insight about her old patterns. Once again, I think this approach can evoke hope in both participants, since it is sometimes possible to will a behavioral change more easily than one can will oneself to have an insight.

For Sullivan, clarity in interpersonal communication is a very significant agent of change. He fundamentally believed that with better "equipment for living," in his terms, human beings generally can cope with their lives. This equipment includes the ability to communicate "syntaxically," or without significant distortion. Together with his belief in an inborn "drive toward health," this way of thinking makes it feel like significant change is possible.

Finally, Sullivan taught that "problems in living" are largely the result of selectively inattended (rather than repressed) ways of relating. There is no inaccessible layer, but, rather, experiences that can be noticed with dedicated effort.

Thus, we are all a product of our real experiences, and they can be known, since their traces are observable in our current behavior. Perhaps we emerge sans mystery and sans magic but, on the positive side, are knowable, curable, ultimately reachable.

The potential for misuse of Sullivanian conviction

Generally, I believe that the advantages of every theoretical perspective in psychoanalysis are the other side of its disadvantages. The sharp-edged, confrontational style brings aggression into the open, but it may not provide enough of a warm, empathic atmosphere for some. The attuned, gentle approach may not sufficiently engage aggressive energy.

Sullivan's doggedly determined "expert" may not doubt himself or herself enough. In line with the issues raised at the beginning of this chapter, the clinician may tilt too much toward closed-minded convictions, without sufficiently appreciating his or her inherent subjectivity. I suggest that this may be related to some poor behavior on the part of the clinician. Take, for example, the case material that Sullivan (1956) himself said he did "not cite as an instance of particularly good treatment" (p. 259). The patient was an obsessive man with a fear of committing suicide. His fear drove him to avoid staircases by working from home, but, eventually, he had to go to a hospital. Sullivan was convinced that this patient was enjoying considerable secondary gains from controlling his environment. He believed that the patient would be forced to change if avoiding staircases became less convenient. It is also important to say that Sullivan admitted that this patient "pulverized" him. It sounds to me as though they were locked in a power struggle that neither could escape. In any event, Sullivan told the patient:

> I am transferring you to the second floor now, and issuing orders that you will not be served a tray. And so, I don't know; maybe you will die by flinging yourself over the stairs; I doubt it. Maybe you will starve to death, I doubt that too. But we'll have to see.
>
> (p. 259)

Shortly after that, the patient was discharged. In other words, Sullivan's confidence in taking this rather bold position was rewarded with a kind of success. But it is easy to speculate that his conviction that he knew the direction of health for the patient served to justify a rather cavalier enactment of his countertransferential frustration. I think that the feeling the patient is "getting away with something" can easily contribute to enactments, most especially if we can find a way to rationalize them with a theory about how our actions are in the patient's best interests.

Frieda Fromm-Reichmann's passionate convictions

Perhaps more than anyone else, Frieda Fromm-Reichmann epitomizes the power and the difficulties of practicing with unswerving certainty about the work she was doing. Even in her own time, Frieda was not without detractors (Hornstein, 2000). I can certainly see how her steely conviction that she was fighting on the side of the angels could lead her to overestimate her vision of health for the patient. With that degree of certainty, an analyst could easily mistake her subjective reactions for objective realities. The potential for harmful enactments is clear.

In our time, I believe that our emphasis on our awareness of our subjectivity can certainly make her thinking sound completely out of date. As I have already suggested, at conferences and in print, we tend to valorize our uncertainties. We don't want to appear self-satisfied, pompous, or elitist in any sense. So we emphasize what we *don't* know and the qualities we have in common with our patients. We make sure to show that we are aware that we each have an unconscious and see the world through a subjectively colored lens.

While these trends have provided a needed corrective to some of the over-generalizations and presumptions of the past, I suggest that this turn has made it more difficult to avoid burnout. Without a powerful sense of purpose, without unshakable belief in what we are doing, it is extremely hard to keep committed to a painful process, session after session and year after year. Especially in intensive work with challenging patients whose progress can be glacial, at best, especially when loneliness, stress, and sorrow weigh us down, it can be hard to keep going, without conviction and an abiding sense of purpose. More than anyone else, Frieda Fromm-Reichmann represents the ballast of solidly inhabited values. I have already referred (Chapter 1) to Joanne Greenberg's (1954) classic book, *I Never Promised You a Rose Garden*, but here I make reference to some passages that express the sense of conviction that can sustain a tremendously challenging treatment. While Greenberg's book was billed as fiction, it surely captured the essence of their work, so a careful reading of it can give us insight into the spirit of Frieda's treatment style. I see the treatment described by Greenberg as a vivid depiction of how Frieda's understanding of emotional health infused her clinical work with spirit, as explicitly articulated in *Principles of Intensive Psychotherapy* (1950) and *Psychoanalysis and Psychotherapy: Selected Papers* (1959).

Durability

What allows Dr. Fried (who represents Frieda Fromm-Reichmann in Joanne Greenberg's account) to persevere in the enormously arduous treatment of Deborah (who represents the author/patient)? I think one factor is the analyst's semi-permeable boundary between herself and the patient, which allows the doctor to embody both durable strength *and* empathic sensitivity. One without the other would not have been enough. Elsewhere (Buechler, 2008), I discuss the need for the clinician to be "semi-permeable." It must be possible to get through to us, yet not possible to destroy us. We must show we are porous, that our emotional skin can be penetrated. But we don't lose our own shape. I think of the clinician as a transitional object. That is, like the child's teddy bear, we maintain our own contours, but our feel is partially a product of the patient's projections. While being deeply affected, we don't lose centeredness. Dr. Fried is penetrable and steady as a rock. This allows Deborah to unleash her rage, voice her despair, whisper her terror.

Inspiring hope

It would be hard to imagine a more despairing human being than Deborah at the beginning of this treatment. Her experience is of a drab, colorless world. This is true for her on a literal as well as a figurative level. She feels permanently relegated to a position outside the human race. She will always be "other." So when Dr. Fried declares that she will not betray Deborah, the patient challenges her to prove it. Deborah has heard too many promises that turn out to be meaningless. Dr. Fried is undaunted, answering that time will show Deborah that she is trustworthy. I believe that the hope that is kindled in the patient begins as a belief in Dr. Fried's absolute integrity. Whatever this clinician promises will be delivered. She doesn't promise "rose gardens." But she does promise effort. And she means it.

In a number of books and chapters, I have thought about what inspires hope in clinicians and our patients. Elsewhere (Buechler, 2004), I suggest that in treatment the most crucial hope is not a mere cognitive expectation but, rather, an active, propelling emotion. Hope can be a gift one person gives another as, I believe, is true in this case. Many gifts change hands in the story of Deborah and her therapist, and hope is essential to them all.

Initially, it is the clinician's task to maintain hope about the work, since it is often impossible for the patient to hope. But in order to be strong and contagious, hope has to be realistic, grounded in self-knowledge. Dr. Fried can hope because she knows she will do whatever this treatment takes.

In this treatment, the patient's hopefulness is a hard-won but awe-inspiring achievement. Dr. Fried is encouraging, declaring her own hopefulness without exaggerating. For example, she tells Deborah that the process won't be easy, but with patience and hard work they will make it. Her integrity shines so bright that it is impossible to disbelieve her. Against her great resistance, Deborah's hope (which never completely died) is kindled and grows.

Absolute allegiance to truth

Dr. Fried doesn't lie and expects the same from her patient. At one point, she registers her belief that they have that in common. With a wry wit, Dr. Fried declares that, since Deborah is allergic to lies, her therapist must try not to tell them.

I believe that telling inconvenient truths is vital to the work. It is crucial for both participants to become able and willing to voice their subjective truths, even when they know they are saying something the other may not want to hear, or something they, themselves, are loath to admit.

The first encounter between this patient and clinician is representative. Deborah expects phony evasions. She asks whether she is sick and whether she belongs in the mental hospital. With stunning directness and candor, Dr. Fried answers both questions in the affirmative. Pat, polite hedging will not do. Dr. Fried gives Deborah the unvarnished truth, as she sees it, though not without compassion. Deborah expects outright lies and subtle window dressing and is startled, and, ultimately, deeply affected by getting something else that is difficult to hear but is profoundly healing.

Stubborn perseverance

Deborah certainly starts out with the potential to withstand a great deal, but I believe it is Dr. Fried's unflagging perseverance that calls out something similar in her patient. By the end, Deborah feels proud of her own strength as she battles to achieve a high-school diploma. Against a backdrop of scathing self-criticisms, she now has the experience of being someone with some sterling qualities. Her positive self-reflections are not empty praise, but accurate, hard-won achievements, modeled by her devotedly, dependably persistent clinician.

Belief in the patient's life force

At first, and at many times throughout this treatment, it was certainly hard to discern the life force in Deborah. After every insight or bit of progress, the patient's self-destructive tendencies held sway, and she would cut or burn herself and end up in ice packs. And yet, there was something alive and kicking, and Dr. Fried never forgets it and takes every opportunity to point it out. For example, after one of Deborah's extremely bloody self-destructive rage attacks, Dr. Fried points out that Deborah made sure to time it for when she would be most likely to be rescued by her favorite nurse. While recognizing the tremendous suicidal force in Deborah, Dr. Fried never loses sight of the self-protective side. She communicates her belief that, at some point, Deborah's will to live will be the stronger motive. I see this unshakeable belief in Deborah's healthier side as part of Dr. Fried's ability to inspire her patient's hope.

Humility and willingness to learn

Dr. Fried is always open to learning from her patient. For example, when Deborah challenges her by saying that, since the doctor has never been a mental patient, she doesn't understand her experience, Dr. Fried reacts with humility rather than defensiveness. She admits that she can only guess at what it is like and asks Deborah to be patient with her and explain everything fully. Without being self-effacing, Dr. Fried shows her willingness to be taught and her recognition that empathy only goes so far. I think she is showing respect for her patient, as well as modeling prioritizing truth over pride. Clearly the treatment (and Deborah) mean more to Dr. Fried than looking like she is always the expert.

Empathy

Elsewhere (Buechler, 1999, 2008), I have explored the notion of empathy in treatment. I would say that in this encounter, Dr. Fried exemplifies empathy, as I understand it. Briefly, I think that empathy often requires us to feel what the other is feeling, but that is just the first step in an empathic interaction. For example, when a child is having a tantrum, it is not empathic for a parent to simply join in and tantrum too. A moment of resonating with the tantrum may be a necessary first step, so as to truly understand the child's experience, but empathy doesn't stop there. It goes on to supply something the child needs. The parent uses his or her ego strengths to modify the anger enough to transform it, and then (re)presents it to the child in a form that helps the child find constructive outlets.

In some exchanges, I see Dr. Fried as at first reverberating with Deborah's rage. But then the doctor's rage becomes her own version of rage, which includes a strong, assertive push. Dr. Fried has felt Deborah's anger (in what can be called projective identification), but then the anger is *transformed* inside Dr. Fried. It is no longer merely a copy of Deborah's anger. We each bring to the clinical situation our own history with each of the basic emotions. No one can put "their" anger into me, without it being *shaped by my life experience*. I have a history of Sandra feeling anger, Sandra feeling fear, Sandra feeling joy, and so on. Similarly, Dr. Fried had a history of using anger to forge strength before she met Deborah, and she brought that to her work with this patient.

The greatness and limitations of Erich Fromm's passionate legacy

One of Erich Fromm's (1980) books is entitled *Greatness and Limitations of Freud's Thought*. A theory's strengths and limitations can be intricately linked. I think Fromm's passion has left us with an extremely valuable but also potentially problematic legacy. Of course, all theories impose patterns, and therein often lay their strengths and inherent problems. Erich Fromm epitomizes the strengths and potential pitfalls of fervently championing one's personal vision of health. Just as he deftly summarized the greatness and limitations of Freud's thought, his own approach had its invaluable benefits and some problems for adherents. Elsewhere (Buechler, 2004), I discuss the effects on the clinician of practicing with Fromm in mind. Briefly, there I suggested that, for the clinician, Fromm

> gives us a strong sense of purpose, hope, courage, and integrity. We feel we are fighting the good fight, on the side of the angels. On the positive side this can contribute to our stamina, holding us steady during periods of treatment stasis or regression. It may help us tolerate the patient's confusion, doubt, skepticism, even contempt. We have conviction in our mission. We can feel centered and whole.
>
> (p. 169)

But there is another side. His passionate stance can sometimes obscure nuance and ambiguity. We can become too convinced we know what is good for people and promote a way of life that is colored by our own biases. We can think we know more than it is possible for one human being to decide about how another should live.

Here I focus on one aspect of Fromm's legacy: his stirring conviction that he understood the requirements for leading a healthy life, and that he and his adherents could promote it in treatment, as well as in the wider public arena. Every time I reread Fromm, his passion stuns me. Can anyone read his insistent prose without feeling profoundly affected? Here is just a brief sample of Fromm's statements about emotional health and the analytic task.

1   Fromm was absolutely clear about the goals of treatment: "The aim of the analytic process is to help a patient grasp his hidden total experience" (Fromm, 2009a, p. 20). In this, I believe he didn't fundamentally differ from other analysts, but his vision of what is "hidden," or dissociated, was somewhat broader. It includes becoming aware of the "filter" that comes with membership in a particular culture. As I discuss more fully below, Fromm sees the "hidden" as (mostly) dissociated, rather than repressed, meaning that it includes what has been in awareness previously *and* what was never in awareness. Thus, for Fromm, health includes an awareness of how society has affected our perceptions.

2   Health also includes an awareness that "everything is inside us—there is no experience of another human being, which is not also an experience we are capable of having" (p. 22). I see this as similar to Sullivan's (1953) one genus postulate, that "everyone is much more simply human than otherwise . . ." (p. 32). It is a profoundly humanistic statement.

3   The analyst forms a conception of who the patient was meant to be if he or she were not distorted by life experiences and resulting defensiveness. In other words, armed with a theoretical vision of healthy human experience, we can imagine a healthier version of the patient we have before us.

4   Essentially, as I understand it, according to Fromm, we help people by relating to them in a very direct way, so that they feel less isolated, and by avoiding intellectualization: "the task of analysis is that the patient *experiences* something and not that he *thinks* more" (Fromm, 2009a, p. 34). We should not withhold what we see out of concern that the patient isn't ready to hear it, because that would not fully reach him. In Fromm's words, when you think you see something, you have to "stick your neck out" (p. 36) and say it. My way to describe a similar idea (Buechler, 2004, 2008) has been that the analyst has to have the courage to voice inconvenient truths. Training (including one's personal analysis and supervision) should enable us to become radical truth-tellers. Ideally, the patient leaves the session with an exhilarated feeling of increased vitality.

Other aspects of Fromm's vision of health:

1   Fromm ardently championed the value of knowing the truth. For example, "this is the hope for the human race, that in fact truth makes us free, as the New Testament says (John 8:32)" (Fromm, 2009a, p. 8).

2   We must fight against alienation, as individuals and as a society. Here is how Fromm defined alienation:

> By alienation I project an experience, which is potentially in me, to an object outside of me. I alienate myself from my own human experience and project this experience onto something or somebody outside, and then try to get in touch with my own human being, by being in touch with the object to which I have projected my humanity.
>
> (p. 12)

For Fromm, health is a relative absence of dissociation, as I have already mentioned. He preferred to use the term *dissociation*, rather than *repression*, for what is not conscious. In his paper "Being Centrally Related to the Patient," Fromm (2009a) explains that the repressed refers to what was conscious and now is not. In contrast, the dissociated can refer to what was conscious and what was never conscious, like the filter each society imposes on our experience. Thus, it is a more inclusive term.

Health includes the capacity to embrace life's contradictions, for example, that we are, and, in another sense, we are not, responsible for others.

Fromm has a permanent place in my own "internal chorus." That is, he is a kind of professional ego ideal. Particularly when my stamina wavers, thinking of him lifts me.

What my internalized Fromm can do, more than any other theoretician, is inspire me to engage in treatment passionately. Could an author have this powerful effect without such firmly held (and sometimes closed-minded) convictions? Could someone with less certainty about his vision of health nevertheless profoundly move, ballast, deeply inspire? Speaking for myself, I doubt it. And yet, as I argue below, the passion itself opens me to serious dangers. Once again, while ardent conviction, open-mindedness, and curiosity *can* co-exist, depending on the functions the conviction serves, in practice I think it is very hard to maintain all three.

In his paper "Factors Leading to Patient's Change in Analytic Treatment," Fromm (2009b) tells the story of his work with a Mexican woman whose "symptoms" included homosexuality. The patient seems to be locked in a relationship where she is intimidated and copes by drinking. Her history includes being used by her mother to get money from the father and being sent as a prostitute to other men. At 15, sent to school in the USA, she meets another girl and starts a sexual relationship. Other relationships with women follow. She returns to Mexico and gets involved with the woman who intimidates her and, at that point, enters treatment with Fromm. Fromm concludes that the patient was not genuinely homosexual, but was behaving out of fear of life. He sees the treatment as successful, since the patient left the homosexual relationship, was alone for a while, and eventually met and married a man. Fromm concludes that the patient "develops into a perfectly normal girl, with normal reactions" (p. 45).

Despite Fromm's avowed belief that we clinicians must become aware of our own societal filters, it is hard to read this case material without concluding that Fromm had some bias against homosexuality. Of course, other factors are also present. I have no doubt that Fromm's assessment of the patient as fearful and traumatized was accurate. After all, the patient, herself, came to the treatment disturbed by the relationship she was in. However, Fromm's statement of her "cure" comes perilously close to saying she was cured of homosexuality, as though that were pathological. Even seen in the context of the time period, it seems to me that Fromm is vulnerable to bias precisely because he believes he can know how to define health for another person. It is one of life's ironies that the man who passionately argued for clinicians to make every effort to be self-aware was not immune to the influences of his own cultural and personal biases.

But my question is whether we can share his passionate commitment *without* falling prey to his vulnerabilities. Others have persuasively presented some of the pitfalls of Fromm's approach. On this subject, I am particularly moved by the writing of Michael Maccoby (1996). Maccoby was in treatment with Fromm and also served as his collaborator (*Social Character in a Mexican Village*, Fromm & Maccoby, 1970). Maccoby identified two voices in Fromm, the prophetic and the analytic. Unfortunately, in Maccoby's treatment, sometimes the prophet spoke louder than the analyst.

> Fromm became like a religious master who unmasks illusions and thus expands the limits of the social filter, dissolving resistances. By experiencing and confessing to one's unconscious impulses, the patient would gain the energy and strength to change his or her life, and to develop human capabilities for love and reason to the fullest. This is an unproved theory, and in practice Fromm's technique sometimes resulted in a very different outcome.
>
> (p. 75)

Is it possible to truly inspire and treat patients with passionate conviction, without imposing our own values about health? Throughout this book, it is assumed that many people vitally need help leading lives with a strong enough sense of purpose to bear their inevitable hardships. Within the analytic field, as well as outside it, many people are reaching toward spirituality (rather than psychoanalysis) to find meaning that much of society seems to have bartered away. To me, this underscores the analyst's need for strong convictions. Without firm beliefs about our goals and the value of achieving them, I don't think we can inspire people to carve out their own senses of what their lives are about.

Human beings share a capacity to respond to the world with wonder and joy, as well as the potential to be overtaken by fear, anger, shame, or guilt. What constitutes successful coping with this legacy? In short, what are some conceptions of health that could inspire a life-enhancing treatment, while respectfully facilitating each human being's process of *self-discovery* and *invention* of a personally fulfilling way of life?

The blessing and curse of conviction

> My god, how magnificent life is precisely owing to its unforseeability and to the often so strangely certain steps of our blindness. Life has been created quite truthfully in order to surprise us (where it does not terrify us altogether).
>
> (Rilke, in Baer, 2005, p. 10)

> How is it possible to live since the elements of this life remain entirely beyond our grasp? If we are continually inadequate in love, insecure in making decisions, and incapable in our relation to death, how is it possible to exist?
>
> (p. 18)

> All of our insights occur after the fact.
>
> (p. 23)

> The wish to alter and improve another person's situation means to offer him in lieu of the difficulties in which he has practice and experience other difficulties that might find him even more baffled.
>
> (p. 40)

Rilke has always been a sobering influence on my efforts to attain clarity. My training (and, before that, my personal experiences and character) instilled strong convictions. My clinical (and life) experience continues to help me question them, as well as cherish them.

Aside from being among the first Interpersonal psychoanalysts and founders of the W. A. White Institute in New York, what do Fromm-Reichmann, Fromm, and Sullivan have in common? Like many others in their era, they had the power of believing they understood emotional health and pathology. The wider culture had its heroes and villains, and the rest of us could confidently tell them apart. A war was waged and won, and the good guys triumphed. American "can-do" fostered plucky determination. Growing up in that era, I was profoundly affected by its values. More than I realized at the time, I was primed to be inspired by the legacy of these three great clinicians. Many of their students were fiercely committed to an Interpersonal tradition. With religious fervor, they sought to spread the word.

My contention is that these convictions can lend strength to the clinician but also have their dangers. "Knowing" what health is can operate like a compass. The analyst's sure sense of direction inspires the patient's faith in the process. Clearly, the resulting power can be misused, and our field's history is littered with examples. Of course, this is just as true of orientations other than the Interpersonal.

Is it possible to retain the strengths of Sullivan's, Fromm-Reichmann's, and Fromm's convictions but join them with open-minded curiosity and the knowledge of our subjectivity that permeates the analytic (and the wider) culture today? I return to this question in the last chapter of the book.

For now, I conclude with two beautiful expressions of the benefits of remaining capable of wide eyed, open-minded uncertainty. One of my favorite poets, Emily Dickinson (1960), declares that "The Soul should always stand ajar . . ." ready for its next "accomplished guest" (p. 481). And another great poet, Wallace Stevens (2016) issues a firm challenge to reason when he states that "The only emperor is the emperor of ice-cream" (p. 119). In Seiden's discussion of this poem, he cites Keats' concept of "negative capability," which suggests that being capable of remaining in a state of unmoored uncertainty is a great artistic accomplishment.

Seiden considers this strength just as essential for the analyst as it is for the poet, since "Who more than we should value the capacity to be in 'uncertainties, mysteries, doubts, without any irritable reaching after fact and reason?' You could say our method depends on it" (p. 120).

References

Alexander, F. (1961). *The scope of psychoanalysis, 1921–1961*. New York: Basic Books.

Altman, N. (1995). *The analyst in the inner city: Race, class, and culture through a psychoanalytic lens*. Hillsdale, NJ: Analytic Press.

Baer, U. (2005). *The poet's guide to the wisdom of Rilke*. New York: Modern Library.

Buechler, S. (1999). Searching for a passionate neutrality. *Contemporary Psychoanalysis*, *35*, 213–227.

Buechler, S. (2004). *Clinical values: Emotions that guide psychoanalytic treatment*. Hillsdale, NJ: Analytic Press.

Buechler, S. (2008). *Making a difference in patients' lives*. New York: Routledge.

Buechler, S. (2012). *Still practicing: The heartaches and joys of a clinical career*. New York: Routledge.

Buechler, S. (2015). *Understanding and treating patients in clinical psychoanalysis: Lessons from literature*. New York: Routledge.

Dickinson, E. (1960). Poem 1055. In T. H. Johnson (Ed.), *The complete poems of Emily Dickinson* (p. 481). Boston: Little, Brown, & Company.

Freud, A. (1936). *The ego and the mechanisms of defense*. New York: International Universities Press.

Friedman, T. L. (2017, 21 June). Where did "we the people" go? *New York Times*, p. A23.

Fromm, E. (1941). *Escape from freedom*. New York: Farrar & Rinehart.

Fromm, E. (1950). *Psychoanalysis and religion*. New York: Bantam.

Fromm, E. (1956). *The art of loving*. New York: Harper & Row.

Fromm, E. (1976). *To have or to be?* (R. N. Anshen, Ed.). New York: Harper and Row.

Fromm, E. (1980). *Greatness and limitations of Freud's thought*. New York: Harper and Row.

Fromm, E. (2009a). Being centrally related to the patient. In R. Funk (Ed.), *The clinical Erich Fromm* (p. 7–38). New York: Rodopi Press.

Fromm, E. (2009b). Factors leading to patient's change in analytic treatment. In R. Funk (Ed.), *The clinical Erich Fromm* (pp. 39–59). New York: Rodopi Press.

Fromm, E., & Maccoby, M. (1970). *Social character in a Mexican village*. Englewood Cliffs, NJ: Prentice Hall.

Fromm-Reichmann, F. (1950). *Principles of intensive psychotherapy*. Chicago, IL: University of Chicago Press.

Fromm-Reichmann, F. (1959). *Psychoanalyis and psychotherapy: Selected papers of Frieda Fromm-Reichmann* (D. Bullard, Ed.). Chicago, IL: University of Chicago Press.

Greenberg, J. (1954). *I never promised you a rose garden*. New York: New American Library.

Hornstein, G. A. (2000). *To redeem one person is to redeem the world: The life of Frieda Fromm- Reichmann*. New York: Free Press.

Hoffman, I. Z. (1998). *Ritual and spontaneity in the psychoanalytic process: A dialectical-constructivist view*. Hillsdale, NJ: Analytic Press.

Levenson, E. A. (1978). Psychoanalysis: Cure or persuasion? In D. B. Stern & I. Hirsch (Eds.), *The interpersonal perspective in psychoanalysis, 1960s–1990s* (pp. 75–94). New York: Routledge.

Levenson, E. A. (1991). *The purloined self: Interpersonal perspectives in psychoanalysis.* New York: Contemporary Psychoanalysis Books.

Maccoby, M. (1996). The two voices of Eric Fromm: The prophetic and the analytic. In M. Cortina & M. Maccoby (Eds.), *A prophetic analyst: Erich Fromm's contributions to psychoanalysis* (pp. 61–93). Northvale, NJ: Jason Aronson.

May, R. (1953). *Man's search for himself.* New York: W. W. Norton & Company, Inc.

Mitchell, S. A. (1993). *Hope and dread in psychoanalysis.* New York: Basic Books.

Mitchell, S. A. (1997). *Influence and autonomy in psychoanalysis.* Hillsdale, NJ: Analytic Press.

Morris, W. (Ed.). (1978). *The American heritage dictionary of the English language.* Boston: Houghton Mifflin Company.

Orange, D. (2017). *Climate crisis, psychoanalysis, and radical ethics.* New York: Routledge.

Phillips, A. (2005). *Going sane: Maps of happiness.* New York: HarperCollins.

Schoen, S. (2017). Commitment fears: Why the analyst avoids analysis. In J. Petrucelli & S. Schoen (Eds.), *Unknowable, unspeakable, and unsprung: Psychoanalytic perspectives on truth, scandal, secrets, and lies* (pp. 103–113). New York: Routledge.

Singer, E. (1977). The fiction of analytic anonymity. In D. B. Stern & I. Hirsch (Eds.), *The interpersonal perspective in psychoanalysis, 1960s–1990s* (pp. 60–75). New York: Routledge.

Slochower, J. (2017). Going too far: Relational heroines and relational excess. *Psychoanalytic Dialogues, 27,* 282–300.

Stern, D. B. (2017). Introduction: Interpersonal psychoanalysis: History and current status. In D. B. Stern & I. Hirsch (Eds.), *The interpersonal perspective in psychoanalysis, 1960s–1990s* (pp. 1–28). New York: Routledge.

Stevens, W. (2016). The emperor of ice cream. In H. M. Seiden (Ed.), *The motive for metaphor* (pp. 118–121). London: Karnac.

Sullivan, H. S. (1953). *The interpersonal theory of psychiatry.* New York: W. W. Norton.

Sullivan, H. S. (1954). *The psychiatric interview.* New York: W. W. Norton.

Sullivan, H. S. (1956). *Clinical studies in psychiatry.* New York: W. W. Norton.

Wolstein, B. (1975/2017). Countertransference: The psychoanalyst's shared experience and inquiry with his patient. In D. B. Stern & I. Hirsch (Eds.), *The interpersonal perspective in psychoanalysis, 1960s–1990s* (pp. 45–60). New York: Routledge.

Chapter 6

Finding meaningful work and nourishing interests

In sessions with patients, what do we communicate about our own relationship to work? What do we express, advertently and inadvertently, in our demeanor? For example, regardless of our theoretical allegiances, theories about therapeutic action, and preferred techniques, we can listen with varying degrees of intensity. Whatever our beliefs about the proper stance of the analyst, we can palpably work hard. Effort can be visible in what the analyst remembers from previous sessions, from the patient's history, from the patient's current life, and from dreams the patient has reported.

During a session, working hard can take many forms, including a laser-sharp focus or a more free-floating attention. It can be manifested in the frame, in the analyst's attitudes about missed sessions, lateness, and "small talk." I am not advocating any particular approach to frame setting, but I am making the point that patients may (consciously or unconsciously) read our behavior as reflecting our own work ethic, among many other interpretations. As Singer (1977) and others have suggested, the patient is busy reading the analyst, at the same time as the analyst is reading the patient. Patients are interested in who we are and, often, try to glean our motives from our actions. Some trust their conclusions from our actions more than they trust our words.

Analysts differ in how consistently we maintain a certain style. Do we prioritize steadily working in our own characteristic way or adapting to shifting relational signals? What does this say about the values we bring to work? More generally, in our behavior with the patient, what do we express about mutual adaptation, partnering, conforming to (professional) standards and social conventions, taking interpersonal risks, and bringing our whole selves to our work? How does our conduct in sessions comment on the role of sublimation in our own work lives? Does our behavior suggest that, for us, psychoanalysis is a calling? In our tone, silence, pace, and the content of what we say, do we seem to be looking at work as an important source of our self-esteem? Do we value working playfully?

I don't think there is any ideal message we should strive to communicate in sessions, other than a clear intention to hear the patient. Beyond that, some of us emphasize empathic listening, while others lean toward interpreting, or active interventions. While we differ on these stylistic points, each of us brings a personal orientation about work itself to our professional task. I don't believe that this orientation can (or should) be "scrubbed away" by our training. I do think training should help the analyst become better able to work effectively but not necessarily more or less vigorously. However, it seems significant to me that we raise our consciousness of the attitudes about work, itself, that we communicate.

In this chapter, I explore some of the psychic functions of work, as I understand them. I then describe some ways we "show" patients (advertently and inadvertently) what work means to each of us. I hope I can be clear that I don't intend to prescribe any particular attitude about work as better therapeutically. I do believe that enhancing our awareness of the work ethic we communicate will improve our ability to engage the patient's conflicts about work, should they arise.

The psychic functions of work

Work as self-realization

> But yield who will to their separation,
> My object in living is to unite
> My avocation and my vocation
> As my two eyes make one in sight.
> Only when love and need are one,
> And the work is play for mortal stakes,
> Is the deed every really done
> For Heaven, and the future's sakes.
> (Frost, 1946, pp. 113–114)

The protagonist in this poem ("Two Tramps in Mud Time"), who, presumably, represents the poet, is happily splitting wood, when two poor vagabonds appear. They make it clear that they need work and want his job. He loves what he is doing but isn't in their impoverished position. Who should be entitled to do the job: the one who loves it, or the one who needs it? Frost acknowledges that

> My right might be love, but theirs was need.
> And where the two exist in twain
> Theirs was the better right – agreed.
> (pp. 113–114)

However, Frost decides, he won't give them his job, for he believes that unless we do what we love and love what we do, we don't really accomplish anything. (I find this remarkably similar in spirit to Rilke's statement that "We have to mix our work with ourselves at such a deep level that workdays turn into holidays all by themselves, into our actual holidays"; Baer, 2005, p. 45). Frost is unequivocal in the conclusion he comes to. The dilemma we so often face, as human beings, is that, despite a burning passion to be a poet, or an actor, or a painter, we have to feed our families and pay our rent. Frost does not tell us how to resolve this conflict as, of course, no one can. But he offers us inspiring advice: Keep looking for something you can need and also love to do. Integrity is living your whole self every minute you can. Frost may be read as offering a point of view about a healthy relationship to work. In his commentary on this poem, Tim Kendall (2012) suggests that Frost merged love and need, heaven and the future, and the poet's visibility and invisibility as the subject of the poem. Frost saw integrating love and need as a means for saving the soul, though, according to Kendall, Frost believed we never completely accomplish this.

As clinicians, do we agree? What does this imply about the way we understand health? An answer was provided by Erikson (1962). In his description of identity formation in the adolescent, he says that "each youth must forge for himself some central perspective and direction, some working unity, out of the effective remnants of his childhood and the hopes of his anticipated adulthood" (p. 4). Commenting on Erikson's thinking, Marcus (2017) suggests that "Erikson's identity theory thus puts forward the powerful claim that the career one chooses reflects the individual's deepest needs, wishes and values. It's an important way that a youth deploys and instantiates his identity" (p. 35). This way of thinking suggests to me that career choice can both reflect and further identity formation. Choosing a particular career is an opportunity to consolidate who we have been and who we want to become.

I see Frost's view as not unlike the writing of Erikson and Erich Fromm, who also emphasized striving for self-expression and full self-realization in every sphere of life, including work. Elsewhere (Buechler, 1996), I have described how Fromm saw the failure to fully use oneself as linked to the development of depression. Here are a few of Fromm's countless statements about what human beings need in order to fully realize ourselves.

> The dynamism of human nature inasmuch as it is human is primarily rooted in this need of man to express his faculties in relation to the world rather than in his need to use the world as a means for the satisfaction of his physiological necessities. This means: because I have eyes, I have the need to see; because I have ears, I have the need to hear; because I have a mind, I have the need to think; and because I have a heart, I have the need to feel. In short, because I am a man, I am in need of man and of the world.
>
> (1968, p. 72)

> [T]here are also certain psychological qualities inherent in man that need to be satisfied and that result in certain reactions if they are frustrated. What are these qualities? The most important seems to be the tendency to grow, to develop and realize potentialities which man has developed in the course of history-as, for instance, the faculty of creative and critical thinking and of having differentiated emotional and sensuous experiences.
>
> (1941, p. 5)

[In the sane society] no man is a means toward another's ends but always and without exception an end in himself; where nobody is used, nor uses himself, for purposes which are not those of the unfolding of his own human powers; where man is the center, and where all economic and political activities are subordinated to the goal of his growth.

(Funk, 1982, p. 78)

In *The Sane Society*, quoting from C. W. Mills, Fromm (1955) uses the thirteenth- and fourteenth-century craftsman as an example of a healthy work life:

The craftsman is thus able to learn from his work; and to use and develop his capacities and skills in its prosecution. There is no split of work and play, or work and culture. The craftsman's way of livelihood determines and infuses his entire mode of living.

(p. 178)

In another expression of our need to avoid compartmentalizing in *The Sane Society*, Fromm says: "One cannot separate work activity from political activity, from the use of leisure time and from personal life. If work were to become interesting without the other spheres of life becoming human, no real change would occur" (p. 326). In what I hear as a similar spirit, Rilke declares that seeing "leisure" as the opposite of work is a misunderstanding, since "work cannot have an opposite just as the world cannot have one, or god, or any living soul. For it is *everything*, and what *it is not* is nothing and nowhere" (Baer, 2005, p. 46).

Elsewhere (Buechler, 1996), I have written that the ultimate example of compartmentalization of work and non-work is the Dickensian industrial-era sweatshop. In such a setting, most of oneself is irrelevant, forcing the individual to split the "real" self from the "work" self. I suggested that chronic despair is a likely result:

To survive, one would probably become furtive, stealing morsels of pleasure, in secret moments of escape from duty. One would define one's real self, one's real life, as taking place outside work. Thus, there would be two selves—a passive, masked, lifeless work-self, and a pressured, intense 'real' self".

(p. 408)

How far have we come from the Dickensian sweatshop? Barbara Garson (1994) suggests that the computer facilitates an electronic supervision that exceeds anything possible in the old-fashioned factory, so that technology enables employers to exert ever greater control over workers. She cites some innovations, in the name of increased efficiency, that reduce jobs to meaningless routines. There is no place in them for the individual worker's expression of initiative, imagination, or creativity. Surely, the more these qualities can't be expressed at work, the more likely we are to become deadened and dispirited. What are the values that currently inform the way we, as a society and as individuals, integrate work with the rest of our lives, and how can we become better able to facilitate this process?

In a bitter complaint about society's values, Fromm (2005) declared: "Man is dead, long live the thing!" (p. 27). In this disturbing cry, we can hear Fromm's antipathy to materialism, consumerism, and the loss of soul satisfactions in work and elsewhere in society. We have become slaves to our escalating consumerism and lost track of an emotionally healthy life. Similarly, in a succinct phrase, Elburt Hubbard summed up the ideal of work as self-actualization: "We work to become, not to acquire" (Fitzhenry, 1987, p. 379).

While Fromm had great respect for the impact of culture, ideas about human emotional health that *transcend* any specific time and place are embedded in his thinking. Fromm wrote a piece for the Milan evening newspaper, which Rainer Funk (2005) included in his collection *On Being Human*. In this essay, originally published in 1972, Fromm describes "What I Do Not Like in Contemporary Society." Fromm decried that fewer and fewer people could be trusted since, "[b]eing for sale, how can one be trusted to be the same tomorrow as one is today?" (p. 39). Fromm goes on to relate this to the problem that "ever fewer people have convictions. By conviction I mean an opinion rooted in the person's character, in the total personality, and which therefore motivates action" (p. 39). I believe that Fromm is championing integrity as having significance that transcends time and place. Elsewhere (Buechler, 2003, 2004), I have discussed human integrity as a state in which our motives, beliefs, and actions form a seamless whole. This seemingly straightforward concept raises complicated issues about the nature of the self, multiple self-states and, in a profound sense, our understanding of what it means to be human. If work is an arena for self-realization and integration, what is the nature of the self we must aim to realize? Clearly, these philosophical and psychological questions are beyond the scope of this chapter, but I will touch on them again shortly.

Michael Maccoby has spent a good deal of his long career applying Fromm's concepts to workplaces and other organizational settings. Fromm was his teacher, analyst, and colleague from 1960 to 1970. Studying leadership and work, and guided by Fromm's concepts, much of Maccoby's research and extensive experience as a consultant explores how work can be shaped to further human development. I read a challenging message from his report on the successes and failures of his mission (Maccoby, 2017). At many points, he is openly critical of the values that currently guide business decisions and politics in the United States. Here are a few excerpts from this cogent statement.

- "The challenge for the United States is the humanization of capitalism, attacking inequality, and putting people before profits" (p. 534).
- "Good organizations produce products and services that improve the quality of life. But a product of work is the people who work in these organizations. The best organizations I have studied develop the social character. They encourage individuation, collaboration, and respect for life, rather than conformity and exploitation of employees and the environment" (p. 535).

- Finally, in a statement that shows us Fromm's relevance to our own times, Maccoby states that Fromm believed that "human survival depends on developing the social character to be more life-loving and collaborative, but this requires changing the culture" (pp. 535–536).

Work as social adaptation

Work benefits society, as well as the individual. How does our acculturation foster adapting to society's necessities?

In his concept of "social character," Fromm (1941) gave us one answer. He wrote of our individual character, a product of personal experiences, and our social character, which is created by experiences shared by a social group. Both of these are internalized. Conflict can occur between the dictates of conscious versus unconscious individual character, or conscious versus unconscious social character. Conflict can also develop between the dictates of the individual versus the social character. Thus, if from our culture we internalize values that radically oppose the values we learn from our individual interpersonal experiences, profound conflicts will develop. In other words, if our society inculcates, let's say, prejudices that we internalize, but, in personal relationships, we internalize values that are diametrically opposed to prejudice, we will be in conflict with ourselves. To me, this means that the analyst can't afford to look aside from the dictates of society, since they are likely to be a significant aspect of our patients' conflicts.

Most especially in his widely read book, *Escape from Freedom*, Fromm (1941) strove to further differentiate social character from other concepts:

> that part of their character structure that is common to most members of the group. We can call this character the social character . . . if we want to understand how human energy is channeled and operates as a productive force in a given social order, then the social character deserves our main interest . . . the subjective function of character for the normal person is to lead him to act according to what is necessary for him from a practical standpoint and also to give him satisfaction from his activity psychologically . . . by adapting himself to social conditions man develops those traits that make him desire to act as he has to act . . ."
>
> (pp. 1–3)

The contrast between Fromm's concept of social character and Sullivan's concept of sublimation is extremely interesting to me. Both describe ways that society influences our motives and shapes our behavior. Although Sullivan groups sublimation in the category of defenses, he is clearly describing a necessary piece of our equipment for living. Sullivan's (1956) definition of sublimation is "unwitting substitution of a partial satisfaction with social approval for the pursuit of a direct satisfaction which would be contrary to one's ideals or to the judgment of the social censors and other important people who surround one" (p. 14). Fromm's social character is also an inevitability but with significant differences. Sullivan is saying that sublimation won't work if it is made conscious. It is as though if we were aware of the bargain we were making, we would not make it. But I think Fromm's message is different. He very much wants us to know about the bargains that society has influenced us to make. He warns us against too ready an adaptation to society's influence. Elsewhere (Buechler, 1996), I concluded that

> it is consonant with Fromm's spirit that we keep a watchful eye on the changes in our current work climate, careful of any assumption that so-called progress is always for the good. A team may be no more life-enhancing than a patriarchal employer, if the individual's true voice is still unwelcome. In fact, I wonder if an illusion of team cooperation, company concern, and openness to difference might be especially spirit-shattering. The employee must then act as though he can freely speak, hiding wariness in his heart.
>
> (p. 411)

It is very interesting to me to contrast Fromm's and Sullivan's views with Freud's (1930) more conflict-driven model, at least in his *Civilization and Its Discontents*. Freud did give credence to the idea that work, and especially professional activities, can provide opportunities for healthful sublimations, particularly if it "makes possible the use of existing inclinations, of persisting or constitutionally reinforced instinctual impulses" (p. 80 fn). However, in the same footnote, he declares that:

> as a path to happiness, work is not highly prized by men. They do not strive after it as they do after other possibilities of satisfaction. The great majority of people only work under the stress of necessity, and this natural human aversion to work raises most difficult social problems.
>
> (p. 80 fn)

It may be factually true that the majority of people only work under the stress of necessity. I don't know. But I think this doesn't give full recognition to how much we may actually come to *want* to do what society needs us to do or to how much curiosity is a powerful, inborn motive, as is evidenced by countless studies of infant behavior.

Is it our *nature* to avoid the effortful? Watching infants' robust play activities always makes me question this conception. Rilke put it beautifully when he said:

> Don't you think a little sapling would have an easier time by staying in the soil? . . . Life itself is heavy and difficult. And you do actually want to live? Then you are mistaken in calling it your *duty* to take on difficulties. It is your survival instinct that pushes you to do it. So what is duty, then? It is duty to love what is difficult . . . You have to be there when it needs you.
>
> (Baer, 2005, p. 46)

In my own language, both sublimation and social character may operate to reduce our obsessive conflicts between what we are supposed to do and what we want to do. The classic expression of this conflict is something like: "I should do my homework but I want to play baseball. I don't know what to do." I think much energy can go into deciding whether to go to the right or the left, in countless variations of this dilemma. Both sublimation and social character, it seems to me, give us a way to conform to society's needs without feeling we are sacrificing our own. But I think Fromm worries more about the blind adaptation that can result. Perhaps another way to say this is that Sullivan sees conformity in a more positive light than Fromm does. His work with schizophrenics and others who couldn't fit into society may play a role in this attitude.

But society doesn't always succeed in getting us to "desire to act" as we have to act. If it did, we wouldn't so frequently develop the draining obsessive conflicts that I illustrated in my 2015 book and described above (in the example about homework versus baseball). Since this issue is nearly ubiquitous in adults as well as children, it seems clear that society's capacity to shape us is far from perfect. As Robert Benchley put it: "Anyone can do any amount of work provided it isn't the work he is supposed to be doing at that moment" (Fitzhenry, 1987, p. 382). Nevertheless, most of us adapt to society's work ethic to some degree.

Elsewhere (Buechler, 2015), I wrote about what can happen to the outliers, like Bartleby in Melville's (1994) great story, "Bartleby the Scrivener." Bartleby suffers from frustrations that are typical in obsessive conflicts: He can't *want* to do what he knows he *should* do. We have probably all navigated a similar conflict. Our work assignment stares us in the face, as we long to relax. Or we know we should shut the lights and go to sleep, but we want to watch one more television show, or play one more video game, or read one more page. Or when we get on the scale we vow to diet until, confronted by a piece of cheesecake, we give in to the temptation we know we "should" withstand.

But Bartleby takes the conflict further than most of us would. When asked by his employer to do some work, he responds: "I would prefer not to" (p. 142). His employer, a lawyer, is astonished, speechless. Recovering, he asks Bartleby the reason for his refusal. Bartleby merely repeats: "I would prefer not to." The lawyer tries to reason with him, explaining why Bartleby should be willing to do the work. But Bartleby doesn't budge. The employer checks with his other employees. Has he the right to ask this of Bartleby? Is there any way to understand the scribe's refusal? All three confirm their boss's viewpoint on the matter. Thus begins a series of verbal duels between Bartleby and his exasperated employer. Gradually, the battle takes on greater meaning, until the lawyer comes to feel that his own manhood is at stake: "For I consider that one, for the time, is sort of unmanned when he tranquilly permits his hired clerk to dictate to him . . ." (p. 148).

At first, it seems that Bartleby is deranged. Why is he willing to lose his life, rather than do his job? But then, is the lawyer any less irrational? Why does he let this stubborn, recalcitrant man take over his office, his mind, his heart and soul? What gives his treatment of Bartleby so much power over his conception of himself?

Bartleby reminds me of Cordelia, King Lear's youngest daughter. Both are foolishly tied to a concrete version of the truth, to their own detriment. Cordelia refuses to flatter her father, despite knowing his craving for it. She insists on telling him that she honors him according to their bond, no more nor less. It is the truth, but a chilling truth, that temporarily estranges father and daughter. Although the stories are different in almost every way, Bartleby has one thing in common with Cordelia. He clings to a concrete version of his "truth." He really would rather not copy legal documents. He will not yield to pressure to comply. Like Cordelia, Bartleby will not go along to get along, as most of the rest of us do, at some points in our lives.

Like Melville's Ahab, Bartleby is single-minded. His quest is to pursue a life absolutely consonant with his real feelings or "true self." By contrast, his employer is much more conflicted and confused. Once he gets immersed in Bartleby's fortunes, he is unable to steer a clear course. He wobbles between trying to negotiate a compromise and issuing firm edicts. When Bartleby begins to refuse orders, the lawyer admits that if anyone else had conducted themselves in this manner, he would have dismissed them but "there was something about Bartleby that not only strangely disarmed me, but, in a wonderful manner, touched and disconcerted me. I began to reason with him" (p. 143). Of course, that didn't work, since Bartleby's behavior is unmoved by reason. We can see Bartleby as heroically or neurotically unwilling or unable to "desire to do what he has to do," in Fromm's terms. What would Sullivan or Fromm have thought of Bartleby? And how would they see Bartleby's employer? It seems fairly clear to me that Sullivan would have seen both as suffering from neurotic conflicts, but, at least in my imagination, Fromm's response is less clear.

Work as a calling

Find out the reason that commands you to write; see whether it has spread its roots into the very depths of your heart; confess to yourself whether you would have to die if you were forbidden to write. This most of all: ask yourself in the most silent hour of your night: must I write? Dig into yourself for a deep answer. And if this answer rings out in assent, if you meet this solemn question with a strong, simple "I must," then build your life in accordance with this necessity . . .

(Rilke, 1934, p. 6)

This is the advice given by the accomplished poet, Rilke, to the "young poet" who asked him whether he should pursue writing as a profession. Clearly, work can't be a passion for everyone, as it was for Rilke. I don't think we can be clear just what is necessary for work to become a calling. Surely one does not have to be a Rilke, or a Mozart, or a Rembrandt to feel implacably drawn toward some endeavor. Priests and nuns often speak of a calling, as might the opera singer, the journalist, the clinician, and many others.

But some struggle their whole lives to feel engaged in their work and capable. A man, well into middle age, still questions his career choice. In sessions with me, he laments his limitations, wonders why he still lacks confidence and why his real achievements don't seem to raise his self-esteem. Sometimes, he focuses on the question of whether anything he does matters, but at other times, his attention shifts to whether he has talent. Occasionally, he is able to lose himself and actually enjoy something, but these are fleeting moments.

While this is a description of a particular person in a particular field, it could apply to many I know. A sense of fraudulence dogs them. They long for an "objective" assessment, but also make sure to avoid getting one. Focused on their "grade," they fail to get truly involved in their work. It is a sad and worsening picture, as aging makes matters more serious. Early career jitters easily slide into middle-aged regrets for time and opportunities squandered. I am left with many questions. Does everyone have the potential to feel a calling? If so, what prevents some from ever having this experience?

Work as a source of self-respect

Otto Rank put the issue succinctly when he said:

> Man works primarily for his own self-respect and not for others or for profit . . . the person who is working for the sake of his own satisfaction, the money he gets in return serves merely as fuel, that is, as a symbol of reward and recognition, in the last analysis, of acceptance by one's fellowman.
>
> (Fitzhenry, 1987, pp. 380–381)

While this can't be universally true (some must work for the sake of the money they need to survive), it does point to the human need to respect ourselves for the work we do.

"The Dilettante," a great short story by Thomas Mann (1997), tells the story of a man who is unable to settle into any career or, indeed, any stable life. Mann gives us a tortured narcissist, replete with the childhood history that helped shape him. He has a mother, perpetually lost in melancholy, whose main companions are melodies. His father, on the other hand, is all action, powerful and proud. A toy theater gives the growing child his own world, where, in fantasy, he can shine every night. The father is unequivocal in his disapproval of his son's preoccupation: "You will never get anywhere in life like this" (p. 40). But his mother responds warmly. Significantly, while he plays the piano, he can never get himself to learn how to read music, which limits the development of his native abilities.

The father is the first to call his son a "dilettante." When he passes his eighteenth birthday, both parents ask him what is to be done with him. Having no idea what he wants to do, he agrees to enter the lumber business. He performs his tasks mechanically, only paying concerted attention to his story books. At this point, he is still able to feel superior to boys from poorer backgrounds, which allows him to be satisfied with his own life. When his parents die, he decides to take his inheritance and travel. There are moments of pure pleasure, especially when he is able to successfully entertain acquaintances he meets on his journeys. But travel becomes more tedious, and he decides to settle and create a contemplative life. While he enjoys setting up his new home, he feels some anxiety, "a faint consciousness of being on the defensive" (p. 47). He suffers from "the slightly depressing thought that I had now for the first time left behind the temporary and provisional and exchanged it for the definite and fixed" (p. 47).

As a clinician, I am familiar with some of the ways this fictitious moment can sound when it is described by a prospective patient in an initial therapy session. Some complain of problems with making commitments or report others' dissatisfactions with their inability to make choices. Like Peter Pan, some seem unwilling to grow up. But, at some point, life refuses to be put on hold. A girlfriend declares that marriage must be now or never. A career opportunity makes a limited appearance. Friends begin to settle into their lives, willingly exchanging the provisional for the permanent. The narcissist becomes uneasy, as he or she realizes that any firm commitment spells limitations of some kind, but failing to commit will result in a different set of limitations. How can someone addicted to fantasy, where what is possible stretches to the furthest reaches of imagination, accept the confines of a limited role? The temporary is endlessly expansive, but the permanent can feel like a depressing, confining Procrustean bed.

Increasingly, it feels that way to our dilettante. He passes his days in leisure, often able to look down on the ordinary pursuits of those around him. But more and more frequently, he feels unhappy in his isolation. Rather than a chosen way of life, it has become a compulsion, for he can no longer introduce himself to strangers, "being insecure myself and unpleasantly aware that I could not make clear even to a drunken painter exactly who and what I was" (p. 49).

Musing, he concludes that there are two kinds of happiness, inward and outward. He needs the outward recognition in order to find inward delight. He deeply craves being a favorite of the gods even though he knows that "the real point is what one thinks of oneself, to what one gives oneself, to what one feels strong enough to give oneself!" (p. 51). But he can't even let himself admit he is unhappy, because then he would lose all self-respect. He thinks of unhappiness as ugly and contemptible.

The dilettante's misery is complete when he meets a beautiful, wealthy young woman, who has no interest in him but shows her love to her male companion. He describes her as having high spirits born of "an inward and unconscious poise" (p. 55) in contrast to his own groundless pride. He makes another, even more painful comparison between the man she admires and himself. The chosen man has real self-respect while he feels himself to be "[s]hut out, unregarded, disqualified, unknown, *hors ligne – déclassé*, pariah, a pitiable object even to myself!" (p. 56). He contrives an encounter with the young woman, as a final test of whether his low opinion of himself is justified. Of course, she continues to have no interest in him. This inflicts a mortal wound.

Since that moment it is all up with me. My last remaining shreds of happiness and self-confidence have been blown to the winds, I can do no more. Yes, I am unhappy; I freely admit it, I seem a lamentable and absurd figure even to myself. And that I cannot bear.

(p. 59)

For the dilettante, at this point, the only choice is suicide. Reflecting on this, he realizes that it is not the loss of the woman that has driven him to self destruction. It is the loss of himself. "One does not die of an unhappy love-affair. One revels in it. It is not such a bad pose. But what is destroying me is that hope has been destroyed with the destruction of all pleasure in myself" (p. 59). He sees that his "love" for the woman is really a form of vanity. He is tormented because she is a prize he cannot have. As he puts it: "Love was the mere pretext, escape, and hope of salvation for my feelings of envy, hatred, and self-contempt" (p. 60).

Looking back on his life, he recognizes a central conflict. He couldn't do without people, because their applause was vital to him. But, unable to forge a self, he was of no use to society, so he had to hide from it. In a line that, I think, presages our current emphasis on the effects of shame, rather than guilt, he suggests that a "bad conscience" is always, really, a "festering vanity" (p. 60). He has become a pitiable and disgusting spectacle in his own eyes. And he concludes that others will no doubt share his low opinion of himself. As a final degradation, he predicts that he won't even be heroic enough to kill himself. "In the end I shall go on living, eating, sleeping; I shall gradually get used to the idea that I am dull, that I cut a wretched and ridiculous figure" (p. 61). This, he decides, is the dilettante's doom.

Mann has isolated one of the greatest problems for the narcissist. Self-esteem is determined by audience reaction. This creates extreme dependence which can, itself, feel shameful. But, even worse, no audience always applauds. The narcissist has no inner "bank account" of solid self-esteem to provide reserves in the absence of applause or in the presence of "boos." Every encounter is significant, every failure is self-defining. It is as though, with each "test" of his quality, the narcissist is meeting himself for the first time and asking the usual questions we use to get acquainted. What do you do for a living? How well have you fared, according to our society's standards of success? How much are you worth?

I have always believed that time is the narcissist's chief enemy. When we are young, investing in temporary relationships and career possibilities seems adventuresome and appropriate. But, often, there is a point when this lifestyle turns sour. I think of it as the point when traveling begins to feel like wandering. The dilettante reached that point and lost hope.

It is easy to see how a narcissistic orientation is likely to slant a work life. But every character style has an impact on the way we work and, most especially, what we want and get from our work. For example, the obsessive need for perfection and control is likely to express itself in one's relationships on the job, work habits, style of presentation, attitudes about expending effort, and capacity to be satisfied by results, regardless of one's chosen occupation.

Work as a source of structure

In a *New York Times* op-ed piece, David Brooks (2017) described a problem of modern life. He sees today's young adults as profoundly unprepared. In his own day, there were a finite number of career ladders to choose from. Now, the choices are infinite, which can create great uncertainty and anxiety. In his view, in the past, society provided more structure to young people who were searching for where they belonged. But now their virtually unlimited choices can leave the young feeling lost and casting about for a life that feels meaningful. Adrift, they are unprepared to confront the existential questions they nevertheless must face. Eventually, they recognize that their lives lack sufficient purpose and direction.

A deeply moving poem by Philip Levine (2016) is titled "What Work Is." It expresses the experience of a man waiting on a line, hoping to get work. Looking at another applicant, the man notes his

> sad slouch, the grin
> that does not hide the stubbornness,
> the sad refusal to give in to
> rain, to the hours wasted waiting,
> to the knowledge that somewhere ahead
> a man is waiting who will say, "No,
> we're not hiring today," for any reason
> he wants . . .
>
> (pp. 79–80)

I see work, in this poem, as a kind of scaffold that promises to give shape to experience. Standing in line narrows life's questions to just one: Will I get work today, or won't I? Forcing oneself to stand on that line is an assertion of the will to go on, despite the despair of knowing the odds against us and the impersonal, uncaring, arbitrary forces that determine our fate. "As flies to wanton boys, are we to th' Gods; / They kill us for their sport" (Shakespeare, 1972, *King Lear*, Act IV, Scene 1, lines 36–37). We look toward work, as toward a holy grail, to rescue us from our emptiness and give our lives substance, but many end up hitting their heads against unmovable walls. Like much else in life, work is not supplied to those who need it most, because of the extent of their need. Sometimes, we wait on a line without any expectation of pity or compassion, asking because we must, rather than because we still have hope.

Work as therapeutic

Many jobs require us to deal with our personal demons. The schizoid must have at least a modicum of contact with coworkers; the narcissist may have to concede that others have talents. The obsessive may be required to bend his or her will to the dictates of the boss, and the phobic person may have to brave a subway ride. If only by highlighting the worker's limitations, work acquaints us with our limitations.

A patient whose compulsions required him to spend several hours a day checking and rechecking every sentence couldn't avoid seeing the extreme price he paid for his defenses. Another patient, struggling with alcoholism, was unable to get up for work in the morning after a binge, and this forced her to face her inability to stop drinking on her own.

Work often confronts us with something we would like to avoid registering. It does not cure us, but may help us look at the extent of our problems. It sometimes acts as a kind of reality check. Freud (1930) makes this clear. "No other technique for the conduct of life attaches the individual so firmly to reality as laying emphasis on work; for his work at least gives him a secure place in a portion of reality, in the human community" (p. 80 fn). Freud goes on to extol the possibility work offers for libidinal displacement onto the work itself and the relationships it affords, as well as its value to society. He singles out professional activity as a potential source of special satisfaction "if it is a freely chosen one . . ." (p. 80 fn). Going further, Galen, a physician, suggested that "[e]mployment is nature's physician, and is essential to human happiness" (Fitzhenry, 1987, p. 380). Thomas Carlyle called work "the grand cure of all maladies and miseries that ever beset mankind" (p. 380). Some would say it brings out the best or, at least, the most forward-moving aspects of our characters. C. Wright Mills stated that "when white collar people get jobs . . . they must practice prompt repression of resentment and aggression" (p. 380). Baudelaire declared: "As a remedy against all ills-poverty, sickness, and melancholy-only one thing is absolutely necessary: a liking for work" (p. 379). Finally, Theodor Reik agreed with Freud that "[w]ork and love—these are the basics. Without them there is neurosis" (p. 383).

Another way to look at work as therapeutic is that it can provide a legitimate canvas for our curiosity. Elsewhere (Buechler, 2004, 2008), I have discussed how curiosity can help us balance painful feelings with more positive emotions. Emotion theory (Buechler, 2008; Izard, 1972, 1977) suggests that our feelings exist in a system, so that an alteration in any feeling affects the whole balance. This means that an increase in my joy will impact my anger, or a rise in fear will affect my curiosity, and so on. We instinctively act on this concept when we show a crying baby a rattle, counting on curiosity to drown out or at least distract from distress. Something similar can happen to adults. For example, I think it is clear that love can often modulate and color all our other affects, as can profound sadness.

For some people, work provides a reliable opportunity to experience curiosity, which can help us cope with the more painful aspects of our lives. Curiosity is seen by emotion theory (Izard, 1977) as an inborn motivating force, distinguishable from any other. Schachtel (1959) described what human beings need, in order to benefit from the positive expression of curiosity.

> Curiosity, the desire for knowledge, the wish to orient oneself in the world one lives in-and finally the posing of man's eternal questions, "Who am I?" "What can I hope for?" "What shall I do?"—all these do not develop under the pressure of relentless need or of fear for one's life. They develop when man can pause to think, when the child is free to wonder and to explore.
>
> (p. 274)

The scientist wondering about the results of an experiment, the teacher experimenting with ways to educate, the poet playing with words—all have frequent chances to exercise curiosity. Wondering is part of their workday and not just a hobby (though, of course, they may have curiosity-inspiring and satisfying hobbies as well). Just like the child throwing a ball in the air for the sole purpose of seeing what happens, they can play with reality. This can bring a healthful balance to a life that may, at the same time, be marked by suffering.

Of course, the clinician's work, which constantly changes hour by hour and which focuses on the endless varieties of human experience, certainly offers us opportunities to experience curiosity. We can imagine (silently or out loud) what would make someone act the way our patient behaves, or why we, ourselves, made the choices we did in the last session. We can be stimulated to follow T. S. Eliot's advice (1943) for the elderly when he says that old men ought to be explorers of their inner worlds since, as we age, other kinds of adventures become less accessible. I discussed this poem at greater length in Chapter 3.

Of course, work doesn't always offer great opportunities to be curious. But, when it does, I think it can contribute to the strength to face hardships. When our work life encourages curious exploration, we do not need to invent excuses to play with reality. In fact, work can become play, and we can follow Rilke's advice when he says: "Get up cheerfully on days you have to work, if you can. And if you can't, what keeps you from doing so?" (Baer, 2005, p. 46).

This accords nicely with Fromm's advice (quoted above) not to compartmentalize work and play.

Manifestations of the analyst's relationship to work

> As Winnicott noted, it is free, non-purposive play, including non-rule governed games, that can be conceived as the equivalent of work in childhood, and for some analysts it is what constitutes psychoanalytic work, that is, psychotherapy at its creative best . . .
>
> (Marcus, 2017, p. 8)

I am sure we have all know analysts for whom play is the soul of their work. Word play is certainly prominent in the clinical writing of Adam Phillips, Christopher Bollas, and Antonino Ferro, for example. I feel sure that this attitude about work and play communicates itself to their patients, whether or not it is ever explicitly articulated in sessions.

I think there are countless ways we manifest our attitudes about work in sessions and, perhaps even more frequently, in the frame. How goal-directed does our work seem to be (regardless of who sets the agenda)? How much evident pleasure do we take from our work or even seem to want? Do our choices in sessions reflect an attitude that work should be a form of self-sacrifice? For example, in scheduling (or rescheduling) sessions, do we try to be infinitely available?

The analyst's work-related attitudes reflect his or her human values in a broader sense. Elsewhere (Buechler, 2004), I have written about how our behavior in sessions inevitably communicates our own curiosity, hopefulness, kindness, courage, integrity, sense of purpose, capacity to mourn, and emotional balance. Of course, who we are as workers is related to who we are in other contexts. If I am a courageous analyst, I am more likely to be a courageous friend. I think it is this that makes our work-related attitudes so important to our patients. They know that, regardless of our beliefs about the merits of the blank screen, they will be influenced by who we are as workers and, more generally, who we are as human beings.

We could read some of Hoffman's (1998) classic *Ritual and Spontaneity in the Psychoanalytic Process* as a study in the analyst's attitudes about adapting to his or her profession's rules. How do we judge when to play by the rules, as we understand them, and when to allow ourselves to express a spontaneous response? This is a fascinating study of the analyst's moment-by-moment process. It seems to me that it also points to the treatment's (advertent and inadvertent) messages about adaptation to rules in general and, specifically, in work settings. What do we communicate about our own values when we extend the session of a patient who arrived late or when we end on time? What do we "say" (consciously and unconsciously) in how we deal with the frame, boundaries, self-disclosure, confidentiality, and the myriad of other rules of our profession? How strictly do we follow insurance company billing requirements?

Patients can read so much about our own work-related values from our conduct. Do we seem to be limping through, or dutifully fulfilling our obligations, or having a good time? More can be gleaned from our writing, websites, and the professional "ratings" of us that are easily available on the internet. Much can be read from levels of emotional intensity we bring to our work life, from the schedules we keep, the vacations we take, the conferences we attend, and our teaching and other professional activities. Does work seem to take up most of our waking hours? Our attitudes about our own work are pretty much public knowledge for those interested in discerning them. Much is also evident in the atmosphere we create in our offices. Are they fastidious, highly organized spaces? How much do they reflect our personal interests and outside lives? Do we display pictures that, silently, tell patients our values about integrating the realms of our own lives?

Most often, our values are implicit, and open to many different interpretations by the patient. Hoffman (1998) says that "even the start of the hour and its conclusion leave much latitude for the analyst to convey a range of personal attitudes and moods. Is the analyst smiling, or frowning, or neither?" (p. 221). Whatever mood we express can be understood in many ways. If I am smiling at the start of the hour, does my patient imagine I am happy to see them, in particular? Or do they understand my smile as an expression of my enjoyment of my work in general? Or in some other way? Similarly, if I seem sad at the session's end, what meaning does the patient ascribe to this? We could simply think of these questions as aspects of transference and countertransference. Indeed, they are. But they may also reveal, and be read, as reflections of our own relationship to our work.

Elsewhere (Buechler, 2008), I have written about the joy the analyst can experience in the course of a workday. "Analysis can provide chances to nurture, experience, and witness leaps forward, self-transcendence, immersion in a creative process, exhilarating movement, miraculous second chances, healing understanding, profound acceptance, self-discovery, and generativity. Each of these can be associated with joy" (p. 121). While our days are not filled with rapture, I do believe that our work often affords us opportunities to experience self-realization and self-respect. It can certainly provide structure and the chance for therapeutic benefits for ourselves. Returning to the beginning of this chapter, where I outlined some of the psychic functions of work, I believe that *our own work can fulfill many of these functions*. In other words, the patient participates in the occupational life of a professional who derives a sense of his or her meaningfulness from work. As I have already suggested, patients are watching us as much as we are observing them. The patient will wonder (consciously or unconsciously) whether what we manifest is consonant with the relationship to work they are developing for themselves. Do we seem to do what we love, and love what we do, as the poet Robert Frost recommended? How much do we *integrate* our work lives and our lives as daughters and sons, parents, readers, and the rest of our walks of life? On the issue of adaptation to society, have we found a personally resonant degree to which to adapt to the rules of our own profession? Does our own work appear to be a calling? Does our work life seem sufficiently structured and organized without being overly rigid? Do we relate to it as a source of curiosity about ourselves, as well as others? Do we follow T. S. Eliot's advice for old men and explore our own inner world?

In several previous publications (Buechler, 2002, 2005, 2008), I have suggested that experiences of joy often result from times when we feel connected with all that lives, as well as from times when we encounter our own unique identities. In other words, at moments when I recognize that I am "simply human" (Sullivan's phrase), I may feel joy. For example, in a group therapy setting, when someone pours out their heart and others resonate with similar feelings, members may feel the joy of being part of a vast human family. But it is equally true that seeing myself being quintessentially me may also bring a smile to my lips. Erich Fromm once said that a goal of treatment is to help the patient become more nearly himself. But this accomplishment is available for the clinician, as well. With every treatment we do, we have another chance to become more nearly ourselves.

Personally, I don't believe there could be another profession that affords more chances to participate in leaps forward, in inner (and outer) worlds explored, in selves (re)discovered, in fears conquered, in sorrows accompanied, in intimacies shared, in loneliness assuaged, in curiosity stimulated, in meaning created, in love kindled.

References

Baer, U. (2005). *The poet's guide to the wisdom of Rilke*. New York: Modern Library.

Brooks, D. (2017, 23 June). Mis-educating the young. *New York Times*, p. A27.

Buechler, S. (1996). A commentary. In M. Cortina & M. Maccoby (Eds.), *A prophetic analyst: Erich Fromm's contribution to psychoanalysis* (pp. 402–412). Northvale, NJ: Jason Aronson, Inc.

Buechler, S. (2002). Joy in the analytic encounter: A response to Biancoli. *Contemporary Psychoanalysis, 38*, 613–622.

Buechler, S. (2003). Analytic integrity: A review of "Affect intolerance in patient and analyst." *Contemporary Psychoanalysis, 39*, 323–326.

Buechler, S. (2004). *Clinical values: Emotions that guide psychoanalytic treatment.* Hillsdale, NJ: Analytic Press.

Buechler, S. (2005). Secret pleasures: A discussion of Maroda's "Legitimate gratification of the analyst's needs." *Contemporary Psychoanalysis, 41*, 389–395.

Buechler, S. (2008). *Making a difference in patients' lives*. New York: Routledge.

Buechler, S. (2015). *Understanding and treating patients in clinical psychoanalysis: Lessons from literature*. New York: Routledge.

Eliot, T. S. (1943). East coker. In *Four quartets* (pp. 23–32). New York: Harcourt, Inc.

Erikson, E. (1962). *Young man Luther: A study in psychoanalysis and history*. New York: W. W. Norton.

Fitzhenry, R. I. (Ed.) (1987). *Barnes and Noble book of quotations*. New York: Barnes and Noble Books.

Freud, S. (1930). Civilization and its discontents. In J. Strachey (Ed. & Trans.), *The standard edition of the complete psychological works of Sigmund Freud* (Vol. 21, pp. 59–147). London: Hogarth Press.

Fromm, E. (1941). *Escape from freedom*. New York: Farrar & Rinehart.

Fromm, E. (1955). *The sane society*. New York: Rinehart & Winston.

Fromm, E. (1968). *The revolution of hope*. New York: Harper & Row.

Fromm, E. (2005). What I do not like in contemporary society. In R. Funk (Ed.), *On being human* (pp. 38–50). New York: Continuum.

Frost, R. (1946). *The complete poems of Robert Frost*. New York: Holt, Rinehart, & Winston.

Funk, R. (1982). *Erich Fromm: The courage to be human*. New York: Continuum.

Funk, R. (2005). *On being human*. New York: Continuum.

Garson, B. (1994). *All the livelong day*. New York: Penguin.

Hoffman, I. Z. (1998). *Ritual and spontaneity in the psychoanalytic process: A dialectical-constructivist view*. Hillsdale, NJ: Analytic Press.

Izard, C. (1972). *Patterns of emotion*. New York: Academic Press.

Izard, C. (1977). *Human emotions*. New York: Plenum Press.

Kendall, T. (2012). *The art of Robert Frost*. New Haven, CT: Yale University Press.

Levine, P. (2016). What work is. In H. Seiden (Ed.), *The motive for metaphor* (pp. 79–80). London: Karnac.

Maccoby, M. (2017). Learning and doing: Working with Fromm and applying what I learned. *The Psychoanalytic Review, 104*, 523–539.

Mann, T. (1997). The dilettante. In *Little Herr Friedman and other stories* (pp. 36–62). London: Minerva.

Marcus, P. (2017). *The psychoanalysis of career choice, job performance, and satisfaction.* New York: Routledge.

Melville, H. (1994). Bartleby the scrivener. In A. Walton Litz (Ed.), *Major American short stories* (pp. 135–167). New York: Oxford University Press.

Rilke, R. M. (1934). *Letters to a young poet.* New York: W. W. Norton.

Schachtel, E. (1959). *Metamorphosis: On the development of affect, perception, attention, and memory.* New York: Basic Books.

Shakespeare, W. (1972). *King Lear.* In *The Arden edition of the works of William Shakespeare* (pp. 1–206). London: Methuen Drama.

Singer, E. (1977). The fiction of analytic anonymity. In D. B. Stern & I. Hirsch (Eds.), *The interpersonal perspective in psychoanalysis, 1960s–1990s* (pp. 60–75). New York: Routledge.

Sullivan, H. S. (1956). *Clinical studies in psychiatry.* New York: W. W. Norton.

Chapter 7

Transcending pride, shame, and guilt

Some sources of feelings of insufficiency

She is a highly experienced, talented, creative, married educator. We have worked together in analysis for many years, with her on the couch. Agitated depression frequently disrupts her sleep and pervades our sessions. When she is tense, her edgy, impatient, jumpy staccato can unsettle me.

I usually know in the first few moments whether this will be one of our more unnerving hours. An example comes to mind. She started talking rapidly before her head hit the couch. It took me a while to unravel the story she spilled out, which involved a provocative student who was challenging her authority. In a tone of utterly righteous indignation, she described him as a no good, disrespectful, disruptive, budding psychopath. He makes jokes, talks out of turn, fidgets, and demands attention from her and from his classmates. How dare he challenge *her* authority! What right has he to undermine her? That no-good brat represents everything wrong with some kids nowadays. No respect, no diligence, no discipline! Furthermore, the administration doesn't back her as much as they should, some of the other teachers spoil the kids by being too lax, and some parents don't take their children's education seriously enough.

As my stomach tightens, I wonder whether, when, and how to break into this diatribe. I try to get a word in, but she talks over me. I have an image of being flattened under the wheels of a car. I am frustrated.

I believe that my patient experiences herself as unjustly insulted and disrespected. I will list some aspects of her feelings that emerged as we explored them and some speculations about their roots.

1   My patient experiences this child's response as though it will be seen by other students as a measure of her worth as a professional and, more generally, as a human being.
2   Her tension mounts as she feels she is losing the group's attention permanently. That is, once they are distracted, she believes she will not be able to re-engage them. This belief is largely unformulated (in D. B. Stern's [1997] sense of the word), but she is aware of it once I point it out.
3   My patient knows her outrage is disproportionate to what the child has done. She feels she can barely contain it and must control herself by reminding herself that if she loses her temper in front of the class, things are likely to get worse.

In this section, I will mention only one possible early root of my patient's intense indignation. Generally, what happens when a child can't get a parent's *full* and *joyful* attention? What message is conveyed? I suggest that often the child swallows whole a feeling of unworthiness and unimportance. Furthermore, a pattern coalesces of judging one's worth based on another's attentiveness and responsiveness.

Briefly, my patient was literally abandoned for long periods of time, left with relatives and other temporary caretakers, by a distracted, depressed mother and a self-involved father. Even when they were physically present, my patient could sense that their minds were elsewhere. She frantically tried to capture her mother's focus, only to withdraw into a lifelong, hurt, lonely, angry sulk.

As I see it, aspects of our current culture may make this dynamic more and more prevalent. I believe a central challenge today is the effect of technology on our ability to give our children our undivided attention. Clearly, this is not an entirely new problem. Parents have had difficulty fully attending to children in previous eras, as I think my patient demonstrates. But, more and more, our focus is fractured. As our cell phones vibrate and our emails collect; as we are texted, Facebooked, and Twittered, we lose the ability to concentrate solely and soulfully on each other. As soon as we glance at our children, offering them our eyes and minds, something distracts us. They lose us, perhaps for the tenth time that morning. Our children, themselves, are similarly fractured in their ability to focus. As our attention spans shorten, how will this affect our children's sense of self-worth? Can a child feel seen, wanted, held in mind by a parent scrolling computer screens and eying a cell phone? When that child grows up, will she have a strong, centered sense of self, or will she feel unable to really matter?

A child who didn't feel her presence captivated her own parents, a child who rarely elicited excited joy and never felt she fascinated anyone, will likely live with a hunger to know how she counts. It may be impossible or, at least, extremely difficult to truly fill that hunger. I believe that mattering becomes the subtext, and often the text, of her treatment.

In this context, I can only suggest the vital role of the analyst's passionate engagement in this enterprise. To capture the analyst's emotional involvement, to fill her mind, to be able to break her heart and sometimes elicit her joy, are necessary for the patient to heal from the traumatic sense of insufficiency created when children repeatedly feel that they can find no way to earn their parents' undivided attention. But, as can be surmised from the vignette that opens this chapter, my patient and I sometimes interact in ways that leave us both unsatisfied and profoundly alone. What could happen in this treatment that might alter my patient's haughty, prideful, and deeply insecure sense of self?

Humility as transcendence in treatment and beyond

Jewish mysticism provides one possibility: "In Jewish mysticism, humility is seen as the only true remedy to narcissistic imbalances, for when we truly stand before God in awe and wonder, we cannot be haughty. The two experiences are mutually exclusive" (Frankel, 2003, p. 87).

This leads me to ask why an awareness of our limitations sometimes engenders vicious, violent rage, while at other times it seems to inspire a healing humility. I would also like to ask how, as analysts, we may best embody and inspire humility. It seems clear to me that as clinicians we rely on our empathy to take us where shame, humiliation, and intense guilt live, and, hopefully, we dwell there long enough to inspire a transformation. But how do we develop the capacity to last long enough for this to come about?

This challenge reminds me of the sinking sensation I felt, many years ago, sitting with one of my patients, a woman who was confined to a wheelchair. (I have written about my work with this woman in a previous [Buechler, 2000/2017] publication). Her rage at me knew no bounds. Why, she would ask me, does Sandra Buechler deserve two good legs and the chance to have whatever and whoever she wanted? In one particular session, overcome by the realization that she could not even storm out of the room without asking for my help with her wheelchair, she got hold of the tissue box and, one by one, shredded every single tissue onto the carpet. It was an act of defiance that did not require my cooperation! She hoped I would have a taste of helplessness, calling me a "TAB," which I later learned was a term used by some handicapped people to designate the "temporarily able bodied." She accented the word *temporarily*, expressing the wish that, someday, I would understand her humiliating position from my own experience of it.

While I imagine intense hate can come from many sources, I understand it as easily stemming from utter, unfair humiliation. While shame and humiliation are related, they differ in some vitally important respects, and I think that the feeling of being humiliated is the more likely trigger of violence. Differentiating shame from humiliation, the psychiatrist Aaron Lazare (1987) has suggested that humiliation differs from shame in that it is not so much an exposure of the self as a lowering, debasement, or degrading of the self by another. I think it is not infrequent that the human response to feeling deliberately humiliated can be a blind, fierce rage that sweeps through us, single-minded and unopposed. The total absence of compunction may, perhaps, be understood by a concept Freud introduced in his 1916 paper on "the exceptions." Freud believed that when we feel unfairly limited or disadvantaged, we may demand the right to be beyond usual strictures, entitled to break rules with impunity. Freud gave these claims a vivid voice and suggested that they are universal: "We all think we have reason to reproach Nature and our destiny for congenital and infantile disadvantages; we all demand reparation for early wounds to our narcissism, our self-love" (1916, p. 315).

However illogical it is for us all to be exceptions, in some sense, we may each feel entitled to a special tribunal, with allowances made for life's unfair blows. Self-reflection has sometimes led me to place some of the blame on our elementary-school system for deluding us into thinking that life would be fair, and for doling out gold stars when we are good and try hard. In contrast, as analysts, we inevitably come to realize that the path to hell is often laid with good therapeutic intentions. Meaning well toward the patient does not at all ensure doing well, in sessions as in other walks of life. But perhaps it is I who has been unfair in my allocation of blame to the influence of primary school. Maybe even without school, childhood would require an initial period of blind belief in the triumph of goodness. As D. W. Winnicott (1971) suggests, maybe we need absolute trust before we can bear gradual disillusion.

Freud hardly ever refers to shame or humiliation, yet his writing is filled with the issue of the consequences of feeling belittled. Interestingly, Sullivan, too, writes extensively about such feelings but most often names them as a form of anxiety. Whatever name we give them, I think it is crucial for us—as clinicians, as citizens, as human beings—to make every effort to understand the psychological relationship between feeling undeserved disrespect and wreaking violent revenge. For example, James Gilligan (1996) has suggested that experiencing some form of shame is the most frequent cause of violence. Feeling our culture, ethnic group, religion, personal appearance, or any other aspect of us has been "dissed" can so easily, and so dangerously, unleash a violent response. The cartoon that makes light of a belief at our core can evoke unlimited wrath. The ubiquity and human significance of this pattern cannot escape our notice.

Why do some belittling experiences engender violence? My bet would be that the best way to understand this is to look at the whole array of emotions the aggrieved, humiliated individual feels and, perhaps even more significantly, the modulating emotions such a person may *not* deeply feel. Since I see emotions as most often serving vital functions in human behavior, I would conjecture *that emotions that are missing*, as often as emotions that are present, elicit and permit violence to occur. In my patient's violent tissue shredding (described above), there was no modulating guilt, anxiety, joy, or love. Curiosity did not lend her that leavening perspective that can lead us to pause and ask: "I wonder why I feel like shredding those tissues?"

Humiliation wildly seeking revenge comes to vivid life in Shakespeare's (2000) play, *Richard III*. In the title character, Shakespeare challenges us to understand a man so embittered by his physical and amorous disadvantages that no cruelty seems enough to satisfy his thirst for vengeance. Listening to these lines from the opening soliloquy, I have the sense I am about to witness the violence that lifelong humiliation can engender:

> I that am not shaped for sportive tricks
> Nor made to court an amorous looking glass,
> I that am rudely stamped . . .
> . . .since I cannot prove a lover
> To entertain these fair well-spoken days,
> I am determined to prove a villain,
> And hate the idle pleasures of these days.
>   (Act 1, scene 1, lines 16–31)

I would like to highlight a difference I see between the roles of the *presence* of shame and the *absence* of guilt, at least in my tissue-shredding patient's behavior.

I think her shame over feeling unfairly handicapped maddened her. The humiliated shame whipped up the violent rage. Freud's concept of the freedoms we may permit ourselves as exceptions can help us understand why she *allowed herself* to act on her feelings. I think she felt her unfair disadvantages earned her the *right* to act out against me without guilt. Thus, shame and humiliation instigated her urge toward violence, but the *absence of guilt* permitted her to allow herself to act it out.

In his illuminating and vivid book *Humiliation*, Koestenbaum (2011) differentiates it from shame: In his view, humiliation arises externally, although it registers internally. Humiliation involves an observable lowering of status and position. On the other hand, shame can arise internally, without any reference to outer circumstances. Reading Koestenbaum's descriptions of humiliating moments he has heard about, observed, and participated in makes it clear how much humiliation is woven into the fabric of our lives and how important it is to consider the part it plays in our intimate relationships, schools, politics, media, courts, prisons, military, hospitals, and psychotherapeutic encounters.

As I reflect on my countertransference with the wheelchair-bound patient, I remember how I often dreaded the approach of her sessions. Personally, it is hard for me to feel hated. Her violent, jealous, humiliated, and humiliating rage was terrible, but also riveting. I stared in disbelief, and a kind of wonder, as the torn tissues spread over the carpet. I was amazed that she could want to do this but, I think, even more amazed that she could let herself do it. I felt that, at least at that moment, I was not a human being to her, deserving consideration, but merely a symbol of lucky people who were blessed with two good legs. I think I also represented a withholding Mother Nature, who didn't care enough about her to give her a fair chance at having a good life. Like Richard III, she felt "cheated of feature," "deformed," and unlikely to become anyone's lover. Cruelty toward me was just retribution for the suffering I had caused her, in her view.

In the ensuing years of the treatment, I think we achieved a kind of spiritual reversal of the earlier roles. That is, I became the one who was cut off at the knees, not in a literal, physical sense, of course, but in a psychological sense. Countless times, this patient watched me stumble for words, falter in my ability to find a way to be with her, and reveal my own uncertainties. Eventually, she realized that although I had feet, they were obviously made of clay. As the playing field leveled, I think it grew harder for her to hate me in the pure way she could initially. That is, at times she could still hate me, but she couldn't *just* hate me. She never again shredded the tissues. The intense sorrow we both felt that she would never have legs gave the tissue box other functions.

Shame versus guilt

Countless times I have been asked how I differentiate shame from guilt. I explain the difference with a story. Suppose you get a failing grade on an exam. If you didn't study and you believe one should, you might feel guilt for not living up to your own standards. But if you studied and got a failing grade, you might feel shame for being "insufficient" to achieve a passing grade. The distinction is not always clear-cut. Nevertheless, I think it can pay to try to differentiate them. Making these distinctions can clarify our experience and help us understand ourselves and each other.

A poet, Richard Wilbur (2009), attempts to clarify the differences between shame and guilt. At an advanced age, he decides to reflect on his "sins" and calls to mind all the memories capable of evoking his regret. What he remembers are moments of embarrassment, where he felt exposed. Some foolishness, something unworthy, was revealed to others, who were shocked to see it. Chagrined, he asks himself how to understand the pain that accompanies these memories. What does his acute discomfort say about him? Wilbur concludes that the discomfort itself speaks volumes. It signals his excessive pride.

I think the poet is making a subtle psychological point. He suggests that embarrassment is not weighty enough to be a sin. Therefore, we can't atone for it. But the pride that *causes* us embarrassment is worthy of atonement. In a sense, I think he is saying that sin resides in one's *character*. It takes a great deal of pride to expect outstanding performances of ourselves, and when we are embarrassed by falling short of the mark, the sin is in having set our standards so high, rather than in failing to meet them. Looking at it this way can inspire us, in that it enables us to define our task (in treatment and elsewhere) as working on character functioning.

Some of my own writing conveys a more somber opinion about shame. I have seen it as potentially extremely problematic, and even deadly:

> In a sense, people die of shame every day. They are willing to kill or die themselves because someone insulted their family, or their country, or their religion. They commit suicide rather than face the shame of bankruptcy, or failure in school, or work, or love. They kill themselves when a bully threatens to expose their shameful secrets. Some of us take our time dying of shame, spreading it out over a lifetime, while others exit abruptly, but dying of shame is as old as humankind.
>
> (Buechler, 2015, p. 45)

I have often thought that one of the goals of treatment can be facilitating the patient's ability to value life over pride. In this way of thinking, who we are is more important than how we look. The quality of our relationships and the meaningfulness of our legacies should matter more than the way we look in others' eyes. I am drawn to these values, but, as I will shortly describe, I have come to understand some problems they can pose.

Transcending overwhelming guilt can be just as clinically crucial as transcending shame. A harsh, overly demanding, guilt-inducing superego can stultify. In fact, for some, the constant barrage of self-blame plays a role in impeding having the strength to make any change. I have found that guilt is even more adept than shame at shape-shifting. A guilt-prone son or daughter may not fulfill potentials that they sense could evoke a parent's envy. Sometimes, the offspring presents as too "lazy" to work hard, which expresses guilt's self-loathing and also explains underachievement. But often, an accompanying depression suggests that much more than "laziness" is involved. More generally, I have sometimes thought of the early phases of many treatments as requiring an alteration in the harshness with which the self is judged. I think this plays out frequently, regardless of the theoretical allegiances of the analyst.

Both guilt and shame short-circuit self-worth. I think their expressions often have somewhat different flavors, with shame showing itself in feelings of insufficiency whereas the guilty person feels "bad." Schecter (1979) lucidly described guilt and shame and their frequent combinations in human experience:

> In contrast to shame, in which one's whole identity is brought into question, guilt feelings can be more localized in connection with the act of transgression . . . In reality the feelings of shame, guilt, and self-esteem are all closely related to one another, the experience being an amalgam of these feelings.
>
> (p. 372)

Guilt can so easily stem from imaginings. Personally, I think it is hard to treat; for some of the same reasons an eating disorder is particularly challenging. One can't stop eating, but, at least theoretically, one can live without alcohol, drugs, or gambling. Similarly, guilt or, at least, the threat of guilt is too vital to surrender entirely. For example, we stop ourselves from harming others partly because we fear the guilt that would ensue. I have heard similar arguments about the civilizing functions of shame.

Countless stories exemplify how compassion can leaven shame and guilt. I think the clinician's compassion toward their own and the patient's limitations can be transformative. Here is one such story quoted in Estelle Frankel's (2003) book *Sacred Therapy*:

> A young man once came to Rabbi Yisrael of Rizhin seeking counsel as to how he might break or overcome his "evil inclination" (sexual impulse or desire). The rabbi's eyes laughed as he looked compassionately at the young man and replied, "You want to break your impulses? You can break your back or hip, but you will never break an impulse no matter how hard you try. However, if you pray and study and serve God with love and sincerity, the evil *in* your impulses will vanish of itself. In its place will remain a passion that is pure and holy. With this passion you will be able to serve God in truth."
>
> (p. 153)

I feel this story tells us how compassion potentially transforms. The rabbi understands what the young man can and can't will. He can't will his impulses away, but he can focus on his love for God. By giving him an assignment he can achieve, the rabbi treats him with compassion. Like a good analyst, the rabbi is *modeling the content* of his message in *the process* of delivering it. His compassion shines as much in what he does as in what he says. This is what can make the message powerful.

From my point of view, the classical analyst's "holy grail" is structural change. I understand that as most often accomplished through a moderating of the way the patient's superego functions. That is, our conscience, our shame and guilt, need to become more helpful than hurtful. At their best, they offer useful guidance that prevents pain in us and others. In this story, the compassion is expressed in the rabbi's stance of acceptance, recognition of the good intentions in the young man, and that all-important laughter in the rabbi's eyes. I imagine the laughter puts the situation in perspective, implicitly suggesting that this moment will pass and is not so very grave.

I see many therapeutic inclinations as efforts to transform intense shame and/or guilt. Why is confession good for the soul? Perhaps, at least partially, because the confessor doesn't shriek in horror when we have told our story, so we take in that moderating response. Why do so many current clinicians lean towards self-revelation? Maybe because it is a way to implicitly communicate that we are all "more simply human than otherwise," as Sullivan (1953) famously suggested. Why does telling one's story in a group setting help many suffering with addictions, traumas, difficulties parenting, and other human dilemmas? I think the mutative power of each of these approaches has, at its base, a potential for leavening shame and guilt.

One more wise note from Frankel (2003) will have to suffice, although her work contains much that is relevant to this topic: "At first God thought to create the world through the quality of judgment (*din*), but realizing that the world could not endure at this level, God added on the quality of compassion (*rachamim*)" (p. 182).

Elsewhere (Buechler, 2004), I have discussed the importance of kindness in treatment. Here, I am emphasizing its role in superego transformations, that is, in modulating intense shame and guilt. We have countless opportunities to show compassion for the patient and for ourselves. This serves as more than just a model, although I take very seriously the role of modeling in treatment. But, as a powerful emotional experience, it can give the patient a sense of mattering, being valued, despite whatever is evoking shame and/or guilt. In fact, as stated above, the patient may be helped to genuinely admire the courage with which they are facing their shortcomings. In general, it seems to me that an important part of the clinician's task is to inspire the feeling that one deserves credit for looking in the mirror (no matter how much shame one feels for what one sees reflected there).

Much of the process of training, and the professional experiences beyond, can be seen as an opportunity for the clinician to improve his or her superego functioning. I discuss training more fully in another chapter of this book. Briefly, elsewhere (Buechler, 2004, 2008, 2012) I have developed the concept of the "internal chorus," an array of voices we internalize from our mentors, supervisors, analysts, and others. Hopefully these voices offer us ballast in troubled (professional and personal) moments. For example, if a patient accuses us of having nothing to offer, our internal chorus may lend us the strength for a very complicated reaction. At one and the same time, we take in the criticism, think (and feel) what it may mean, but maintain enough of a sense of worth to keep going. Training is an especially propitious time for internalizing a chorus that can carry us through rough times. We hear some solos (echoes of those, in our training and beyond, who have most influenced us), but other voices blend together. All have had the opportunity to help us modify our experiences of shame and guilt so that they contribute to a loving superego. This would be useful for anyone, but it is a professional as well as a personal requirement for the clinician, since we spend all our careers in challenging interpersonal interactions, many of which have the potential to signal our inadequacies.

But opportunities for intense shame and guilt don't end on the day we receive our professional licenses or degrees. They abound in countless moments when we fall short of what is needed. In my 2012 book, I suggested that these moments subject the clinician to potential burnout. But they also give us a chance to transform shame and guilt by using the information they contain about ourselves and our patients. Using any painful feeling to grow, in insight or in any other way, can be transformative. We are (implicitly) showing ourselves (and others) that pain can be more than just pain and that the meaning of any event is, to some degree, a construction.

As an example, I have noticed a change in my countertransference toward injured narcissism when I encounter it. A patient tells me how she unleashed her fury when a colleague attempted to disrespectfully ignore her advice. "How must he see me, if he believes he can act like this! Who must he think I am, and who must he think he is!" Not for the first time, I pointed out that the patient is experiencing her colleague's behavior as a bad report card. That is, the patient feels her worth is defined by how she is being treated. Some time back, I believe I would have gotten more agitated in response to this story. Inwardly, I might have justified myself with thoughts of how wasteful of life injured narcissism can be. But lately, I see this agitated countertransference as a form of self-righteous narcissism *in me*. As analysts, I think it can be easy to slide into a prideful prophet's fury as we encounter obstacles. We can experience the patient's character or defenses as though they were personal enemies. We can feel something like: "If only the patient felt less easily wounded, what wonderful results would be possible!" In a similar vein, I remember an indignant Leslie Farber calling hysteria life's opponent, and Fromm's campaign speeches against necrophilia, and Sullivan's diatribes against stutterers. As I stare into my own, personal, characterological mirror, my rage at wasted life melts into sorrow about the limitations of time. Sometimes, I still feel my old agitation, but I am more aware of the subjectivity of my idea of what constitutes waste.

Whenever I feel I need a reminder that what is considered "waste" is in the eye of the beholder, I reread Shakespeare's *King Lear* (Shakespeare, 1972). For me, this play is the ultimate expression of the wages of the sin of pride but, also, the best antidote to my becoming judgmental about it. Perhaps it is more accurate to say that reading the play helps me add compassion to my reactions. At first, Lear's vision of his daughters is shaped by their ability to flatter him. Pride rules Lear and guides his rule of others. He trusts his fortunes to his two eldest daughters, who win his favor by fawning. His youngest, Cordelia, unable/unwilling to comply, is stripped of all inheritance and banished.

In a moving soliloquy, Lear tries and fails to touch his eldest daughter's heart. She has mercilessly cut his retinue, arguing that he has no need of it. But to Lear, his retinue represents the honor to which he still feels entitled. While the old king fails to reach his daughter, he certainly moves me.

> O reason not the need! Our basest beggars
> Are in the poorest thing superfluous;
> Allow not nature more than nature needs,
> Man's life is cheap as beast's. Thou art a lady;
> If only to go warm were gorgeous,
> Why, nature needs nor what thou gorgeous wear'st,
> Which scarcely keeps thee warm.
>   (Act 2, scene 2, pp. 255–256)

Harold Bloom (2008) calls the play "an encyclopedia of egotism and desire" (p. 14). While Lear sputters and roars in his injured pride, he has no way to see beyond his desperation for outward signs of grandeur. Though he has reached old age, by his own account Lear "but slenderly knows himself." Foolishly, he has traded in real power and majesty for fake tokens of loyalty and love. Eventually, he is undone by his own grief, rage, and wounded pride. Though at times he behaves with autocratic cruelty, he evokes tender concern in many of the other characters. As I think about my response to him, I realize that, from early in the play, I have seen him as trapped by his own limitations. He can't help needing what he needs and being unable to see beyond his misperceived self-interest. Lear reminds me of so many lives, driven and, eventually, truncated by pride. A patient, turning to alcohol to drown out feelings of failure, spirals down into further degradation. Another, devoted to his own image, increasingly senses that he has wasted his life. Hurt pride and fear of further shame diminish all our lives at some points and some lives at almost all points.

Probably, I will always want outraged pride to cost us all less. I will look around and inside myself and feel that each time we avenge pride's wounds we could be better occupied. When we are gone, doesn't the score-card of tributes and indignities also disappear? Shouldn't we, at least, try to pay more attention to that which endures?

Attitudes about pride and self-love

The differences between pride and self-love, and the question of their co-existence with love for others, have preoccupied human beings throughout time and can only be touched on here. For an extensive and extremely evocative point of view, I recommend Paul Zweig's (1968) beautiful book *The Heresy of Self-Love*. Philosophers, psychologists, portrait painters, biographers, self-help gurus, and so many others have commented on these topics. In brief, how can we integrate empowering self-love, healthy pride in our strengths and accomplishments, with a capacity for genuine, loving investment in the lives of others?

As I have already implied, some consider health to require us to tame our pride, while others see pride as an important component of health. The philosopher Richard Taylor (2002) goes so far as to say that it is better to die than to live without pride. In her book *Fasting Girl*, Michelle Stacey (2003) tells us that our problem stems from what our society teaches us to have pride about (denial of appetite), rather than pride itself. On the other hand, the Bible tells us that pride goeth before a fall and that pride is one of the seven deadly sins. Frankel (2003) warns that "love can easily be hijacked by pride when we take ourselves too seriously" (p. 84).

Similarly, Paul Zweig (1968) traces the theme of pride in Milton's *Paradise Lost*. Zweig states emphatically that "[t]he world we encounter in *Paradise Lost* has been flawed by the adventures of pride" (p. 109). Poetically, he writes: "Man, we learn, contains side by side the upward aspiration toward God and the deflected energy of self-love which turns him back into himself" (p. 115). Eve succumbs to the serpent because it corresponds to her fatal flaw, her narcissistic self-love. Adam, too, can't resist temptation because of his "unruly egotism" (p. 117). As a result, paradise, a world of love, is replaced by a world of constraint, laws, force, and power.

Sullivan (1956) declared: "It has seemed to me that people are always proud, in this specific psychiatric sense, of things which are not so. In other words, pride seems to be the presenting aspect of an elaborate self-deception" (p. 117). And yet, a few lines later, he states: "I do not mean that what one is 'proud of' in a more general sense is necessarily not there" (p. 117). These statements have always puzzled me. To the extent that I understand them, I think Sullivan is saying that pride is a defensive maneuver to compensate for an inadequacy that may be *either* real or imagined.

Referring to himself, Fromm said that his narcissism was a malignant tumor blocking his ability to love (Maccoby, 2017). In *The Art of Loving*, Fromm (1956) states of the lover that "[b]y loving, he has left the prison cell of aloneness and isolation which was constituted by the state of narcissism and self-centeredness" (p. 37). Fromm points to differences between genuinely loving oneself versus being self-centered or narcissistic. For Fromm, the capacity to truly love allows us to love ourselves *and* others.

Working with intense pride, shame, and guilt

In my view, analysts have neglected (and sometimes disparaged) the role of modeling in treatment. While we are certainly not paragons of virtue or mental health, sometimes there is something valuable that we can communicate in how we conduct ourselves in sessions. From watching us, patients may learn who they would like to be or, at times, who they would not like to be. At the least, how we conduct ourselves can bring certain aspects of the human condition into focus, like, for example, the human vulnerability to shame and guilt. One way this is played out is in the analyst's handling of his or her own potentially shame-inducing moments. In sessions, how do I react to my factual mistakes? What do I do with my own slips of the tongue? When the patient accuses me of not helping, questions the value of our work or, more generally, of psychoanalysis, do I respond defensively? Must I uphold my own image at all costs? Must I look smart, right, well-intentioned, intuitive, emotionally responsive, self-contained? Am I willing to take interpersonal risks in the name of the treatment? Will I say what can sound foolish if I think it is right and risk the patient's scorn, dismissal, contempt? On a more subtle level, how much do I need credit for the treatment's accomplishments and/or for the patient's accomplishments? When do I eagerly make "points," without any obvious regard for their effect on the patient? When do I seem to be serving or protecting my own self-esteem? How easily can I allow myself to cry in front of the patient or ask potentially foolish sounding questions? Can I be "childishly" eager, openly curious? Can I need help? In areas where the patient is more expert, can I ask for information? What is the feel of moments when I am the one who asks, or needs, or is more emotional?

Basically, what I am suggesting is that we can sometimes have a positive effect by dealing transparently with potential triggers of shame and guilt in ourselves. This is not (just) a matter of modeling or teaching. It can facilitate insight and interpretation of the patient's self-esteem difficulties. By bringing the ever-present human potential for shame and guilt into focus, we are helping the patient examine his or her experience in this area. For example, on occasion, I have mistakenly ended a session too early or too late. There are many possibilities for what follows. Do I wait until the next session to say anything? Do I say nothing at any point unless the patient brings it up? Do I apologize? Offer to make up the time if I cut the session short? Charge less for that session? Speculate aloud about why it may have happened at this point?

The patient is likely to try to make sense of whatever we do, that is, to try to fit it into their picture of who we are, what our values are, what we stand for, and what they think is going on between us. If it is highly discrepant with who we have been in the past, it may be disturbing (though this is likely to occur on a less than formulated level). As we know, both patient and analyst can be occupied in trying to figure each other out. I think one of the most important aspects of this question for the patient is: "What are my analyst's values? What guides her own behavior in sessions and in the rest of her life?" This can be anxiety-provoking for both participants, especially if the patient feels highly vulnerable to our influence and/or if we feel extremely uncomfortable with having an influence. My experience is that, regardless of what analysts from various schools believe about neutrality, *patients* don't really believe in it. By and large, they believe we have opinions about what generally constitutes health, a good life, and a good treatment outcome, and they think we have more specific ideas about what progress would entail for them. They may wish we would share our opinions more openly, and they may hope to be influenced or dread being influenced. But most are deeply curious about who we are, at the very least. Of course, my experience (and my patients' experience) is colored by how I work and who I am. Maybe your patients are more curious about who you are, or less so. But I will wager they have some curiosity, and they interpret your values from your behavior in sessions. They form a more clear or less clear picture of their analyst's self-esteem needs. They watch us deal with potentially shaming or guilt-inducing moments and compare today's observations with their previous picture of us. All of this may occur on less than conscious levels. But I strongly believe it occurs, if not with all patients and analysts, certainly with most.

For example, it often seems to me, when analysts credit self-disclosure as having helped a patient, that what helped was *not* the disclosure itself but the *values* expressed in the act of *choosing* to disclose. The analyst is saying, in effect: "I am willing to give you information you could use to shame me. I am willing to do whatever it takes to reach you." The analyst is behaviorally expressing valuing the treatment more than her own pride and, more generally, life more than image. I view the treatment of empathic failures similarly. What I believe the patient often derives from this work has mainly to do with how the analyst relates to their own self-esteem. I see the value of work on empathic failures as deriving from their providing an opportunity for the analyst to fail, acknowledge the shortcoming, react without undue shame, guilt, or denial, and move on. But however the analyst behaves, an empathic failure highlights issues of shame, guilt, and the preservation of self-esteem.

One potentially useful insight both participants might gain when the self-esteem of either is challenged is that, paradoxically, honest self-confrontation can enhance one's sense of self. That is, if we are willing to brave the narcissistic injuries inherent in seeing ourselves clearly, we can develop self-respect. It takes courage to face one's cowardice or other shortcomings. As I mentioned earlier, the analyst must help the patient learn to respect herself for facing herself, regardless of what she sees when she looks in the mirror.

Elsewhere (Buechler, 2004), I have distinguished the analyst's sense of purpose from any particular therapeutic goals. The sense of purpose is an expectation that the work will be meaningful in the life of the patient. I think it is especially important in our work with (narcissistic) patients whose self-esteem is vulnerable. Without inspiration from the analyst's sense of purpose, the narcissistic patient will not feel sufficiently called upon to deal with the crucial issue of time. Time is narcissism's enemy, since it pressures us to accept reality's limitations. But unless life has purpose, how does the passage of time matter? Unless it is important to have a life, what difference does it make if the narcissist lets his only chance at life go by? Without purpose, it doesn't matter if life is squandered in the hope that someday a truly impressive role will come along. The narcissist's analyst must capitalize on the pressure of time, but that can only happen if life has purpose.

In the treatment of narcissism, we encounter our deepest priorities as human beings. What really matters? When am I willing to be a fool for love? Each of us has to come to our own conclusion about what we will fight for. Somehow, we must embrace the paradoxes essential to our role. We need the humility born of recognizing our limitations, but also passion born of fierce conviction. I must know that I can only see subjectively, yet I must believe in my vision with all my heart. In her book *Sacred Therapy* (discussed above), Estelle Frankel (2003) quotes a Hasidic master, Reb Zusia, who once told a disciple: "I'm not worried that I'll be asked why I wasn't Moses when I die and enter the heavenly realm, but why I wasn't Zusia" (p. 85). Remarkably similarly, Erich Fromm (1976) said that "[j]oy, then, is what we experience in the process of growing nearer to the goal of becoming ourselves" (p. 106). We are always trying to rise to the challenge of being ourselves with our patients, but, I suggest, narcissism in ourselves and our patients makes this task especially daunting.

To close, what does it take to transcend shame, guilt, humiliation, and the other emotions we may feel in response to life's inevitable blows? Is "transcendence" dependent on a strong sense of purpose about one's life? Does it require sufficient positive emotions to adequately modulate the intensity of the suffering? Must pain be formulated, verbalized, witnessed? In order to "heal," must we adapt to our vulnerability to self-esteem injury? Is accepting shame or guilt as inescapable human experiences "better" for us than fighting it? I feel daunted by these questions (in other words, perhaps, I feel insufficient!). But when I think about specific instances, I come back to the curative power of love. All of the factors I just named may play roles in "transcendence." But I think the most frequent rescuer is love. As far as I know, being mirrored by loving eyes softens shame, guilt, and humiliation more powerfully than any other force. For one thing, it improves our image of how we believe we are seen by others, which may also enhance how we see ourselves.

Returning to the play *King Lear*, I find the end almost unbearably sad but also uplifting. Bloom (2008) calls it "the most remarkable instance of a representation of human transformation anywhere in imaginative literature" (p. 306). Lear, maddened by grief, wanders in a windy storm that seems a perfect expression of his state of mind. His suffering teaches him what it means to be human, totally exposed, meeting the elements in the "unaccommodated" state in which we are born.

> Poor naked wretches, whereso'er you are,
> That bide the pelting of this pitiless storm,
> How shall your houseless heads and unfed sides,
> Your loop'd and windowed raggedness, defend you
> From seasons such as these? O! I have ta'en
> Too little care of this. Take physic, Pomp;
> Expose thyself to feel what wretches feel,
> That thou mayst shake the superflux to them
> And show the heavens more just.
> (Act 3, scene 4, lines 27–36)

In an essay entitled "The 'Lear' Universe," G. Wilson Knight (2008) called *King Lear* a play of "creative suffering" (p. 185), which I find a particularly felicitous phrase. Knight sees Lear as working to free himself from self-deceptions, facing truths, however painful, until, at last, "[h]e wins his purgatorial reward in finding that which is most real to him, his love for Cordelia" (p. 191). Love for suffering humanity, love for his wise "fool," love for his ever-loyal servant Kent, and the ultimate love for his tender, forgiving daughter, Cordelia, at last makes Lear *truly* every inch a king.

References

Bloom, H. (2008). *Bloom's Shakespeare through the ages: King Lear*. New York: Checkmark Books.

Buechler, S. (2000/2017). Necessary and unnecessary losses: The analyst's mourning. *Contemporary Psychoanalysis, 36*, 77–90.

Buechler, S. (2004). *Clinical values: Emotions that guide psychoanalytic treatment*. Hillsdale, NJ: Analytic Press.

Buechler, S. (2008). *Making a difference in patients' lives*. New York: Routledge.

Buechler, S. (2012). *Still practicing: The heartaches and joys of a clinical career*. New York: Routledge.

Buechler, S. (2015). *Understanding and treating patients in clinical psychoanalysis: Lessons from literature*. New York: Routledge.

Frankel, E. (2003). *Sacred therapy*. Boston: Shambhala.

Freud, S. (1916). Some character types met with in psychoanalytic work. In J. Strachey (Ed. & Trans.), *The standard edition of the complete psychological works of Sigmund Freud* (Vol. 14, pp. 311–333). London: Hogarth Press.

Fromm, E. (1956). *The art of loving*. New York: Harper & Row.

Fromm, E. (1976). *To have or to be?* (R. N. Anshen, Ed.). New York: Harper and Row.

Gilligan, J. (1996). *Violence: Our deadly epidemic and its causes*. New York: Putnam Publishing Group.

Knight, G. W. (2008). The "Lear" universe. In H. Bloom (Ed.), *Shakespeare through the ages* (pp. 169–195). New York: Checkmark Books.

Koestenbaum, W. (2011). *Humiliation*. New York: Picador.

Lazare, A. (1987). Shame and humiliation in the medical encounter. *Archives of Internal Medicine, 147*, 1653–1658.

Maccoby, M. (2017). Learning and doing: Working with Fromm and applying what I learned. *The Psychoanalytic Review, 104*, 523–539.

Schecter, D. (1979). The loving and persecuting superego. *Contemporary Psychoanalysis, 15*, 361–379.

Shakespeare, W. (1972). *King Lear*. In *The Arden edition of the works of William Shakespeare* (pp. 1–206). London: Methuen Drama.

Shakespeare, W. (2000). *The Oxford Shakespeare Richard III* (J. Jowett, Ed.). New York: Oxford University Press.

Stacey, M. (2003). *The fasting girl*. New York: Penguin.

Stern, D. B. (1997). *Unformulated experience: From dissociation to imagination in psychoanalysis*. Hillsdale, NJ: The Analytic Press.

Sullivan, H. S. (1953). *The interpersonal theory of psychiatry*. New York: W. W. Norton.

Sullivan, H. S. (1956). *Clinical studies in psychiatry*. New York: W. W. Norton.

Taylor, R. (2002). *Virtue ethics*. New York: Prometheus Books.

Wilbur, R. (2009, 31 August). A reckoning. *The New Yorker*, p. 55.

Winnicott, D. W. (1971). *Playing and reality*. London: Tavistock.

Zweig, P. (1968). *The heresy of self-love*. Princeton, NJ: Princeton University Press.

Chapter 8

Forgiving

Personally, I have always liked the idea that to love is always, really, to "love anyway." Whether it is a particular person or life itself that we love, loving requires us to be able to love despite myriad reasons for not loving. We all have valid complaints about what life has taken from us and gripes of other kinds. What does it take to love (ultimately to love life) anyway?

At times, we all want what we can't have. We all bear profound disappointments. Yet, ultimately, we need to say "yes" to life, with all its humiliations, indignities, piercing sorrows. If we can forgive life, perhaps our grief can become *just* grief and not grief potently mixed with rage, guilt, and regret. Whatever life gives it also takes away. Should we forgive life for that? Should we love it anyway?

This reminds me of one of the essential meanings of the Oedipus saga, from my perspective. It centers on the issue of how, as human beings, we bear unrequited desire. What happens when we want the (m)other that we can't have? What messages about bearing this inevitability do we (advertently and inadvertently) send patients? For example, do we communicate (in our own actions and attitudes) that unfulfilled desire of the other is inherently shaming? Do we (perhaps inadvertently) signal that it is healthiest to move past resentments, and that forgiving is a vehicle toward that end? More generally, what are our own attitudes about harboring or letting go of strong feelings?

Though I remain convinced that, ultimately, we each must find a way to forgive life, I am less clear about other acts of forgiveness. For me, the topic of forgiveness raises issues that have been threads throughout this book. What is health in relation to forgiveness? Is it "healthier" to forgive, regardless of the situation? Is forgiveness another name for "adaptation," "adjustment," and the kind of acquiescence we have met in other chapters in considering attitudes toward aging, mourning, and other of life's inherent difficulties? Do we value "moving on," whether we are referring to mourning or resentment or any of life's blows? Is health a matter of freeing oneself from pain by "getting it out of our system," the way we might deal with pus if we suffered an infection? How do these attitudes affect our beliefs about what constitutes progress in treatment and, more generally, in life? What is most significant to me, is how we signal our own attitudes about forgiveness in *unspoken* and often *unrecognized* ways in sessions that are ostensibly about other issues. More specifically, in the following pages I explore how our values about forgiveness get played out in sessions, and how they relate to our attitudes about health, adjustment, intense emotionality, and the value of verbalized, as opposed to non-verbalized insight.

Terms and conditions

Before we look at arguments that link forgiving and health, I think it is important to clarify what we mean by forgiveness and who it is for. Forgiving does not, necessarily, entail forgetting, excusing, or reconciling, although it can be linked with any or all of these actions. Safer (1999) makes the case for, and the case against, "forgiving and forgetting" as enhancing each other. One can argue, as many have with regard to the Holocaust, that we should never forget what happened as a safeguard against recurrences. On the other hand, for some, forgetting is a sign of forgiveness and, sometimes, a necessary concomitant. That is, for some, it can be hard to imagine forgiving without forgetting. To some people remembering inevitably brings a resentful, revengeful, unwillingness to forgive. Whether we see this state as inherently unhealthy seems to me to be in the eye (and mind) of the beholder.

Another very significant issue is who forgiving is seen as benefitting. If it is understood as for the sake of the forgiven, then the question of whether or not it is deserved becomes relevant. But if forgiving is seen as a precondition of health for the person who has been wronged, this issue may not pertain. For whose sake do we forgive? Perhaps, as analysts, we might consider whether forgiving the other allows us to look more closely at our own contribution to the situation and learn all we can about ourselves. Seen in this light, forgiving is warranted whether or not the forgiven deserves it. Another argument along the same lines is that only by forgiving do we release energy for better uses than ongoing resentment. For example, in his paper "Grudge and the Hysteric," Masud Khan (1975) spells out the unhappy fate of those who cannot forgive and create of their lives what he might call a cemetery of refusals.

Arguments for forgiving as inherently healthy

Basically, the argument that forgiving is inherently healthy rests on hierarchical beliefs about our emotions. That is, it presumes that some emotional states are healthier than others. As with mourning (Chapter 2), it assumes that people may need to "go through" some painful feelings in order to emerge from them and enter a more emotionally positive state. Some may view forgiveness as a value in itself, while others center on it as a vehicle. In other words, for those who see forgiveness as healthy, what do they view as its healing aspect? Is there something healthy about the *act* of forgiving, or is health a consequence of where forgiving allows us to go, emotionally? If the latter, what makes that emotional state a desirable outcome?

More broadly, what is the basis for seeing some emotional states as more desirable than others? Furthermore, in order to arrive at these desired ends, must forgiveness be put into words or can it be unspoken and even, perhaps, unconscious? In this chapter, I suggest that clinicians are often unaware of our biases about forgiveness and, more generally, about which emotional states are more conducive to health than others. But I believe that no matter how much effort we exert to be "neutral," our biases are still expressed in our actions in a session. As clinicians, and as members of society, we are affected by values prevalent in our community and in our families. No matter how hard we try to be guided by the *patient's* goals and values, it is inevitable that our work will, to some extent, reflect our own. At the end of this chapter, I illustrate this point with clinical vignettes.

Jeanne Safer (1999) cites vivid illustrations of the common belief that to forgive promotes health. For example, "on *Good Morning America*: A rabbi asserts that 'forgiving is like taking a poison out of your body,' and a priest agrees that, otherwise, 'evil is recycled'" (p. 1). But Safer makes the point that "[t]hough it is a cornerstone of the Judeo-Christian tradition, forgiveness is not 'natural,' or religion and society would not have to lobby so hard to get people to do it . . ." (p. 3).

Religiously, forgiveness has been a value for centuries. In works of great literature, to err is human, to forgive divine. Shakespeare's (1972) King Lear seeks forgiveness several times. For example, poignantly, he asks for (his previously banished daughter) Cordelia's forgiveness:

> Come, let's away to prison;
> We two alone will sing like birds i'th' cage:
> When thou dost ask me blessing, I'll kneel down,
> And ask of thee forgiveness: so we'll live,
> And pray, and sing, and tell old tales, and laugh
> At gilded butterflies . . .
> (Act 5, scene 3, lines 8–13)

It seems as though Lear sees forgiveness as part of a healing conversation or a ritual, made ordinary by repetition. His fantasy is to create an enclosed, safe space with his newly rediscovered loyal youngest daughter. Mutual forgiveness will allow them to separate from the false but glittering outside world. Through forgiveness they become one, in a poetic expression of "at-one-ment" or atonement.

Shakespeare had a great deal to say in favor of forgiveness, for both the forgiver and the forgiven. Rosenbaum (2006) suggests that in almost every one of his plays, one can find some examination of the quality of mercy. Rosenbaum mentions *Henry V, The Tempest*, and *The Winter's Tale*, among other instances. He writes of the power of forgiveness to transform a character's nature, which he sees as the source of the most pleasurable instances of forgiveness. Perhaps the most unforgettable lines belong to Portia in *The Merchant of Venice* (Shakespeare, 2000):

> The quality of mercy is not strained;
> It droppeth as the gentle rain from heaven
> Upon the place beneath. It is twice blessed;
> It blesseth him that gives and him that takes.
> (Act 4, scene 1, lines 182–185)

It is as though mercy envelopes forgiver and forgiven in a healing mist. And in the last lines of *The Tempest* (Shakespeare, 2011) we hear another quality of mercy.

> As you from crimes would pardon'd be
> Let your indulgence set me free.
> (Act 5, epilogue, lines 19–20)

Being merciful to another creates a world where we, ourselves, can imagine being forgiven for our own "crimes." In other words, forgiving enacts the Bible's Golden Rule.

On the general subject of forgiving life for its blows, rather than forgiving an individual, a case can be made that forgiving is healthy because it speaks of acceptance that one is not entitled to be an exception, in Freud's (1916) sense of the term, as discussed in his paper, "Some Character Types Met with in Psychoanalytic Work," to which I referred in the previous chapter. In the first part, "The Exceptions," Freud investigates the reasons why some make the claim that they should be spared from life's demands.

> [I]n the cases I investigated I succeeded in discovering a common peculiarity in the earlier experiences of these patients' lives. Their neuroses were connected with some experience or suffering to which they had been subjected in their earliest childhood, one in respect of which they knew themselves to be guiltless, and which they could look upon as an unjust disadvantage imposed upon them. The privileges that they claimed as a result of this injustice, and the rebelliousness it engendered, had contributed not a little to intensifying the conflicts leading to the outbreak of their neurosis.
>
> (p. 313)

In other words, those who feel they were never sufficiently nurtured may feel entitled to be exempt from life's rules. Today, these "exceptions" might well be diagnosed as narcissistic characters. Health, then, could be understood as an acceptance of the "cards" life has dealt us, with a resulting acquiescence to aging and the rest of life's constraints.

An interesting example of negative responses to claiming the right to be an exception occurs in a Jewish tradition. At the Passover Seder, the youngest child asks why this night is different from all other nights. With the telling of the story of the emergence of the Jews from Egypt, it is said that the "evil" child asks what this history has to do with him. In other words, the evil child claims to be outside the story of his people. That defines him as evil. Here, the child who will not equate himself with the group is morally bad, rather than pathologically problematic, but it may not be all that different. In both, health is acceptance of one's membership, with all the consequences it entails.

Margaret E. Bruner's (1996) poem "Plea for Tolerance" could have been written by a psychoanalyst.

> If we but knew what forces helped to mold
> the lives of others from their earliest years –
> Knew something of their background, joys and tears,
> And whether or not their youth was drear and cold,
> Or if some dark belief had taken hold
> And kept them shackled, torn with doubts and fears
> So long it crushed the force that perseveres
> And made their hearts grow prematurely old, –
> Then we might judge with wiser, kindlier sight,
> And learn to put aside our pride and scorn . . .
> Perhaps no one can ever quite undo
> His faults or wholly banish some past blight –
> The tolerant mind is purified, reborn,
> And lifted upward to a saner view.
>
> (p. 32)

The poet makes it clear that since none of us can entirely overcome childhood hurts, the healthiest approach is to forgive their inevitable consequences. I find the wording of the poem interesting. The poet suggests that tolerating behavior that results from a troubled childhood is "saner" and purifies the one who forgives.

There is a fascinating passage in Primo Levi's (1988) book *The Drowned and the Saved*, where he makes a similar argument about the executioners in the concentration camp.

> [W]e are asked by the young who our "torturers" were, of what cloth were they made. The term torturers alludes to our ex-guardians, the SS, and is in my opinion inappropriate: it brings to mind twisted individuals, ill-born sadists, afflicted by an original flaw. Instead, they were made of the same cloth as we, they were average human beings, averagely intelligent, averagely wicked: save the exceptions, they were not monsters, they had our faces, but they had been reared badly. They were, for the greater part, diligent followers and functionaries, some fanatically convinced of the Nazi doctrine, many indifferent, or fearful of punishment, or desirous of a good career, or too obedient.
>
> (p. 202)

Clearly, I can't comment on the voluminous literature on these issues, except to ask myself and other practitioners to be as aware as possible of how much we believe that the "tolerant mind" that forgives those who have been "reared badly" is "purified, reborn, and lifted upward to a saner view," in Margaret Bruner's words. Of course, a great deal depends on what must be forgiven, but, I still suggest, we each can have unformulated biases about the value of forgiving and they can shape how we hear our patients, what we ask them, what we don't ask about because we take it for granted, how we understand therapeutic progress, what we register as defensive, and so much else. My belief is that no matter how much a clinician is determined to keep personal attitudes from shaping their responses to patients, our views on this subject will inevitably affect our focus in some sessions, especially when the content includes some form of abuse.

Elsewhere (Buechler, 2008), I have written about an issue that comes up in treating some victims of abuse that I called the regret for the loss of the unharmed self. This refers to a psychological attachment with a fantasized version of the self. This healthier "self" is the person the abuse victim feels she could have been, had the trauma not occurred. The regret this "double" of oneself does not exist in reality can be exquisitely painful. It can be argued that an unwillingness to forgive a perpetrator expresses a form of attachment to the fantasy of being restored to the unharmed self. If the clinician implicitly (or explicitly) holds that forgiving the perpetrator is desirable, it is possible to see this fantasy as hindering the recovery process.

Arguments against forgiveness as inherently healthy

One argument against considering forgiving as always essential to health is the belief that sometimes the forgiveness would not be real. Rather, it would be an act of compliance with an authority that encourages it in some way. As I see it, there are several issues that are hard to tease apart. One is whether being unwilling to forgive always involves vengeance of some kind. Another is whether vengeance is always unhealthy. And, aside from the motive for forgiving or not forgiving, there is the emotional result each has. How does it affect an individual emotionally to decide not to forgive? Can the psychological benefits of not forgiving outweigh its costs? As already noted above, some try to forgive out of a belief that holding onto unforgiving is inherently poisonous and forgiveness is the only route toward expunging the poison. But is that true?

Safer (1999) sees our culture as biased on this issue. "Americans demonize not forgiving as much as they idealize forgiving. False forgiveness, the quick fix of easy peace, and the emotional inauthenticity that springs from them have proliferated as a result" (p. 143). Safer cites many instances where the decision not to forgive was a hard-won assertion.

Perhaps the most extreme test of these ideas can be found in the literature about responses to the Holocaust. An interesting discussion appeared in a book *Fed with Tears—Poisoned with Milk* by H. Shmuel Erlich, Mira Erlich-Ginor, and Hermann Beland (2009). In a series of conferences, German and Israeli psychoanalysts met with Tavistock-trained group leaders to explore how feelings and fantasies about

"German-ness" and ""Israeli-ness/Jewish-ness" influenced the ways they related to each other. This book emerged out of their experiences. It is a collage of expressions of what the meetings meant to some of the individual participants.

Among the challenges this book explores, is the question of the extent, and the limits, of individual responsibility. Is forgiveness relevant when, for example, we are relating to the children of Nazis who committed no atrocities themselves? More generally, in our hearts, do we hold ourselves and each other accountable for only our own actions and inactions? I think most would agree that a German person born after the war should not be held responsible for the crimes committed during the Holocaust. Similarly, it is relatively easy to consciously assert that an Israeli is not responsible for upholding his or her parents' attitudes toward the German people. But sometimes strong feelings override rational assertions. We can understand this, when, for example, we listen to the report by Ursula Kreuzer-Haustein that she heard of an Israeli conference participant whose mother implored him not to travel with a friend in Germany, saying, "Don't do that, don't trust them, they killed your grandparents!" (p. 126). At another juncture, a German analyst asks whether or not forgiveness makes any sense in this context and is told that the *wish* to be forgiven can be registered, but that is all. Some things can't be forgiven. Some of the conference participants felt powerful shame and guilt and a sense of being a betrayer merely because they *went* to these meetings. Nevertheless, some overcame external pressures and internal barriers and attended. Is merely attending such a meeting a statement that forgiveness is a goal to be pursued? Is refusing to attend a pledge to avoid false forgiveness regardless of the cost?

Apart from one's position on these issues, there is something especially valuable to the Interpersonal analyst in this book. It explores the need for the presence of an "other" in the process of trying to formulate one's stance about forgiving. In the foreword to the book, Archbishop Desmond M. Tutu draws a parallel between these conferences and the work of his own Truth and Reconciliation Commission. He suggests that "each group can face its own most deeply held prejudices, assumptions, and beliefs *in the presence of the other group*" (p. 13, original emphasis).

Interestingly, in the meetings between the German and Israeli analysts, the "other" necessary for personal exploration was not at all a neutral party. Many participants expressed the feeling that they couldn't have learned as much about themselves without the other group. But some emphasized that this wasn't so much about dialogue as it was about working on oneself in the presence of the other. In the words of H. Shmuel Erlich: "Dialogue implies the prior recognition of the other's otherness and right to be what he is. This cannot be a direct goal; it can only emerge as the byproduct of a process which in itself need not be, and is not yet dialogic" (p. 181). In other words, by being there, each participant provides a necessary backdrop for the other's self-understanding. That is, in the company of the other we are more likely to discover our own, previously unrecognized, fundamental interpersonal assumptions. Contrast is a powerful teacher. Contrast teaches us who we have always expected others to be.

I take from this that, perhaps, the only way one can ascertain whether forgiveness would be genuine or false is in a dialogue with another, who is not attempting to be neutral. This is a point to which I return. But, regardless of one's beliefs about how we can get to know our position about forgiveness, it is affected by our attitudes about whether hatred is an inescapable human feeling. Is hatred ever useful? Can it be healthy to hate?

Writing about the German-Israeli conference, one member made this comment:

> Empathy for their suffering began to emerge in the Israeli group and the question remained what to do with our hatred. Is it useful or is it just a poison to our minds and to the minds of our children? With no hatred, how do we remember or prevent it from happening again?

(p. 91)

It seems to me that analysts should have something to say about the nature of emotional health and whether or not hatred can play any part in it. I have elsewhere (Buechler, 2008) considered the roles of anger and hatred in providing cohesion in the face of potential self-obliteration. When the existence of the self is profoundly threatened, perhaps by extreme anxiety, mourning, or depression, some turn toward anger and hatred to provide a center that can hold. Sullivan (1953) considered anger a defense (against anxiety) that we learn early in our lives from watching our parents use it. Perhaps this approach to self-cohesion is partially a product of limited choices. If other ways to hold the center are not available, might we need to rely on anger and hatred?

Fed with Tears—Poisoned with Milk has much to say about the idea that a *fear* of "false reconciliation" can result in a deadly, stuck stasis. While many expressed a wish for reconciliation, there was also a fear that the conference would promote a pretense of "forgiveness" that was not real. Perhaps the fear of looking like they were reconciling made some of the Israelis stand further apart from the Germans than they otherwise might. I think we can easily recognize clinical versions of this phenomenon. Anyone who has worked with couples (or been in a relationship themselves!) will probably resonate with how a stubborn unwillingness to let the other off the hook can stymie us. Patients and analysts can be similarly trapped.

Forgiveness and atonement in the clinical context

I think it is inevitable that our own positions about forgiveness play a role in how we focus in sessions, even if they are never overtly expressed. Safer (1999) definitively asserts that "members of the profession tend to be passionate propagandists for forgiveness, especially of patients' parents" (p. 160). I would modify this statement in two ways. First, I think that early in treatment we may (subtly or more directly) hope that the patient will see the negative aspects of his or her parents' behaviors. But I agree that somewhere down the line we frequently associate forgiving them with progress in treatment. Also, in contrast to Safer's comment, I believe that our bias generally expresses itself less in outright advocacy and more often in what we question, notice, remember, and other subtle behaviors. But I agree with Safer that patients often understand that our underlying assumption is that forgiving is "healthier."

We frequently "vote" in favor of atonement and forgiveness as healthy in how we behave toward our own errors and limitations. When we, personally, use doing treatment as an opportunity to atone for our own interpersonal "misdeeds," we are (perhaps unwittingly) endorsing atonement. Clinical work provides unceasing opportunities to atone. Each of us probably has personal sources of the need to overcome guilt, regret, and secret shame. Doctoring these wounds can be seen as healing a breach. Through our work, we have a chance to feel ourselves becoming more whole, at peace, at one.

Aside from the personal guilt each of us brings to our task, I would suggest that clinical work, itself, can inspire an added need to atone. Along the way, we may feel responsible for many injuries to our patients. We assert a frame that serves important therapeutic purposes but often creates significant frustrations for both participants. Elsewhere (Buechler, 2012), I have explored some of the fantasies the frame disconfirms. Briefly, these include the fantasy of having a perfect soul mate, the fantasy of being able to dispense with self-interest, the fantasy of words being unnecessary, the fantasy of all needs being met by one person, the fantasy of perfect agreement, and the fantasy of unlimited availability, among many others. While generally we are quite aware of the necessity for the frame, we may sometimes feel responsible for the pain it engenders.

Interestingly, at least for me, it is a Shakespearean scholar who most movingly described the clinician's inevitable trespasses. Ron Rosenbaum (2006), writing about *Dream*, Peter Brook's version of Shakespeare's *A Midsummer Night's Dream*, says of the actors at the end:

> It was as if they were asking for forgiveness for the inevitable separation from us, one that the clasped hands would postpone. For the inevitable separation of reality and dream, reality and the realm of higher reality they'd briefly ascended to like Bottom. Taking us with them and then waking us and forcing us to abandon the dream.
>
> (p. 537)

Some moments clinically feel similar in spirit, at least to me.

I have already described some of the ways doing clinical work can capitalize on our need to atone (Buechler, 2008). Briefly, whatever we regret can motivate us to modulate unrecognized harmful impulses in ourselves and develop greater wholeness or integrity. Every clinical hour is an opportunity to make up for something, to own up to something, to "make good."

I think the wish to atone can enhance the clinical will. In other words, profoundly wishing to compensate for something potentially strengthens the determination to help people. Supervisors are prone to frown upon this motive in clinicians.

I remember one who advised young clinicians that it is fine to *want* to help but problematic to *have* to help.

This sounds sensible, and yet, can we really tell the difference? I think it is often impossible. But it seems to me that a genuine longing to atone can contribute to the clinician's non-narcissistic investment in the work. Of course, it could also motivate a narcissistic wish to appear saintly. But I think it can also spur us on to deeply want to render real service, regardless of the form it takes. In Gail Hornstein's (2000) fine biography of Frieda Fromm-Reichmann, she quoted from Joanne Greenberg's descriptions of the noted analyst. Greenberg said that Fromm-Reichmann "would have swung from the chandelier like Tarzan if she thought it would help" (p. 39) her patient get better. I can't help but wonder whether Frieda was trying to atone for something, though I wouldn't want to speculate about what it might be. But I am sure that such dedication can help analysts atone, no matter what we might be atoning for. The chance to atone can be counted as one of the blessings that the profession offers.

Frankel (2003) provides another way to describe this blessing.

> *Teshuvah* actually comes from the Hebrew root *shav*, to return. The implication is that we all have within us a reference point for wholeness to which we can return—a spiritual essence encoded within our souls that enables us to remember who we truly are. *Teshuvah* is not something one does for once and for all; rather, it is a lifelong journey, a journey of spiritual homecoming.
>
> (p. 129)

Since one of the benefits of being a clinician is the chance to atone, I think those attracted to the profession may be biased in favor of forgiveness/atonement and may, perhaps unwittingly, promote these values in our patients. Safer (1999) warns:

> Therapists must take care not to foist forgiveness (or anger, or anything else) on their patients, but rather to assist them in reaching their own conclusions. Patients intuitively know what their therapists expect, even if it is not explicitly stated, and comply without realizing it; this cuts off the exploration and grieving process essential for real resolution, and leads to compliance, false forgiveness, and secret despair.
>
> (pp. 5–6)

Opportunities to explore these issues make frequent appearances in treatment. For example, when I forgot a make-up session with a patient, would it have been sufficient to apologize and offer to make up the time? I don't think so. It would have said that I am responsible and want to be fair. But as an analyst, I believe I should focus on the *meaning* of my behavior, rather than merely accept responsibility. Wondering why I forgot is as essential as apologizing. Being genuinely curious is as important as showing sufficient contrition. In using the moment as an opportunity, I transform it (to some degree). There are times, then, when we can *intentionally* bolster the spirit of analytic inquiry. This goes beyond my personal need for forgiveness.

The concept of atonement has been understood (Bokser, 1978) as, literally, being "at one," that is, integrating oneself internally as well as joining others to form a community of selves. Yom Kippur, or the Day of Atonement, prescribes rites that symbolize the oneness of the Jewish people. For example, as Frankel (2003) describes, on that holiest of days the high priests perform an incense offering, which is called the "ketoret." The tradition is that the ketoret is made of eleven different spices, one of which is, by itself, foul-smelling. Its inclusion symbolizes unity and the interconnectedness of all of us. We must welcome the vulnerable, as well as our own personal weaknesses, so that we don't fragment ourselves as a people or our own, inner selves. What we reject or deny becomes an adversarial force, which will take away from our strength. Frankel concludes that, "[d]espite whatever has been broken or shattered through our own mistakes or fate itself, Yom Kippur, the day of at-one-ment, gives us a chance to heal and be whole once more" (p. 163). Thus, according to this way of thinking, *personal atonement is integration of the "foul" in ourselves, and interpersonal atonement is inclusion of the weakest members into the human community.* This clearly defines health as a kind of wholeness that can be achieved by seeking forgiveness for oneself. I would assume that in this way of thinking forgiving others is also considered healthy, since it fosters the embrace of everyone into the human fold.

Compromises with the concept of neutrality: My own odyssey

In order to come to terms with the clinical impact of my attitudes about forgiveness, I have had to grapple with the issue of neutrality. To what degree is it (still) considered desirable in the analyst, despite the rise of Interpersonal and relational orientations? Are my own attitudes about atonement and forgiveness merely countertransferential potentialities? Can/should I aim to correct for their tilts, so that the *patient's* attitudes can emerge clearly, regardless of whether or not they coincide with mine?

I can chart the development of my own analytic voice by looking at the stages in the evolution of my beliefs about the feasibility of analytic neutrality. I always had doubts about my own capacity to be neutral, but I also felt clear that my own values may not coincide with the patient's, and analytic work should help the patient, in Fromm's (2009) sense, to become more fully himself. This created a dilemma for me, and, in my teaching and supervisory work, I have come to believe that many clinicians struggle with feeling we fall short in this area.

For a time, I told myself (and candidates) that, while I don't know whether a patient should live in Westchester, get married, have children, and so on, I can recognize paranoid functioning, obsessive defenses, and other problematic patterns I have studied. Thus, I felt I could be neutral about lifestyle decisions but knowledgeable about character patterns and defenses. This satisfied me, for a portion of my career. Then, in 1999, I wrote a paper titled "Searching for a Passionate Neutrality" (1999), in which I grappled with the concept again. Briefly, the paper examines a consultation with a patient whose severe eating disorder threatened her life. I asked myself what neutrality required of me in this clinical situation. I was aware of having strong countertransferential feelings that pulled me toward wanting the patient to be willing to change her bulimic patterns, but she expressed her unwillingness to give them up, stating that they were all she had. I had to confront the strength of my feelings and a vague sense that I actually needed them in order to work with sufficient intensity to have any impact. But, then, how could I reconcile this with an equally strong belief that pitting myself against her eating patterns would inevitably result in an enactment of a power struggle that would actually stand in the way of her treatment? Here is my attempt to resolve my conflict.

> Passionate engagement in treatment is a genuine investment in life itself. It is communicated in the "music" of the treatment—in the analyst's tone, manner, directness, allegiance to the truth, and the deeply felt conviction about the meaningfulness of the work. *The passion is felt; the neutrality is spoken.* The analyst's *words* invite the patient to express all that is within him, even the most self-destructive and sadistic pulls. But, without consciously shaping it, the analyst's *manner* conveys an abiding commitment to life and growth.
>
> (p. 226)

For a time, this felt like a reasonable compromise. But working on my first book (Buechler, 2004) led me to question the feasibility of this stance. Could my words really be neutral, in any meaningful sense? And, if my words did not correspond to my manner, wasn't I in danger of mystifying the patient? Might the contradiction, itself, recreate her parents' problematic communications that have confused the patient in the past?

In *Clinical Values*, I evolved the belief that, in treatment as well as supervision, integrity is vital. Clinical integrity means to me that our words, actions, and manner should reflect the same principles. Over time, I came to see that the requirements of integrity conflicted with my stance about neutrality. I began to realize that my values pervade my words, as well as all other expressions, so that my attempt to "speak neutrally" while conveying passion in my manner was doomed to failure. Other problems presented themselves as I worked on this book. The intense sense of purpose that seemed vital to treatment seemed hard to maintain alongside neutrality. As I put it: "The ideal of neutrality made it difficult to face yearnings we bring to our work, to express them with patients and with each other, and to confront the value the profession places on having a sense of purpose" (p. 86).

Writing *Clinical Values* reacquainted me with the work of Erich Fromm. Although I had studied Fromm in undergraduate, graduate, and analytic training, it took time for me to fully appreciate the implications of his thinking for the practicing analyst. Reading Fromm taught me that the clinician can't separate beliefs about societal problems from analytic practice. One's vision of society informs clinical work, and clinical work has impact on one's vision of a healthy society. Fromm took me further along the path of feeling that my values had to have a place in my work with patients.

But at this point, the values I was considering were limited to what I called "clinical values," that is, the hope, curiosity, kindness, courage, sense of purpose, emotional balance, ability to bear loss, and integrity that I thought of as essential to clinical functioning. I had not yet gone beyond these to inquire about the place of other values, such as forgiving.

During the time I wrote my next book, *Making a Difference in Patients' Lives* (2008), I began to be fascinated by the concept of atonement and, most especially, the analyst's need to atone. I wrote a paper on atonement (Buechler, 2009), citing some personal experiences and discussing their history. I looked at how unmet needs to atone can contribute to burnout. Here is how I focused on regret and repentance, in patients as well as clinicians: "The regret that continues to sap our strength, I would suggest, is the sorrow and guilt that is not balanced by atonement . . . if it were more fully repented, atoned, and integrated it could add, rather than detract, from our strength . . ." (p. 97).

In my next book, *Still Practicing* (2012), I explored some of the sources of the need for forgiveness in clinicians in general and in myself in particular. This book traces the arc of an analyst's career, from training, through early clinical experiences, later career development, and the end phase of terminations and retirement. I studied some of the sources of shame, guilt, and feelings of loss that are inherent in the clinical enterprise with its many limitations. More than anything else I have written, this book faced me with my own demons. It is meaningful to me that I titled one chapter (Chapter 8) "Ordinary Tragedies of an Analytic Life." Writing this book, I actively searched for sources of resilience. What can keep me going in difficult long-term treatments and, more generally, in a career that acquaints me with all the ways human beings suffer? When, for example, I have had to face a patient committing suicide minutes after I interviewed him, or, in less dramatic examples, treatments that seem to be going nowhere or even seem to be harmful to both participants, how do I go on? This is a subject I return to in many chapters of the present book.

Emotion theory has shaped an answer that has been of some help to me. It tells me that:

1 Emotional intensity can foster, as well as hinder "adjustment." Emotions are our most powerful motivators and, most often, serve as information and communication.
2 Each emotion we feel has the potential to impact all the others. So, for example, access to joy, curiosity, and love can mitigate depression, regret, guilt, and shame.
3 Along similar lines, anger and anger-related emotions can rescue us from unending sorrow, shame, guilt, regret, anxiety, and other disturbing states.

These basic beliefs incline me toward looking for help with the pain of my work from access to other strong emotions. With regard to forgiveness, this means to me that if I seek to atone, it is not necessarily to escape the intensity of my (guilty, ashamed, sorrowful) feelings, but it could be for the purpose of having them fully, learning from them, and perhaps transforming them into an emotional state that strengthens me.

A marvelous example of the transformative power of emotions can be found in Tolstoy's (1886) masterpiece, "The Death of Ivan Ilych." I have written about this story in my 2017 book and mentioned it in other chapters of the present volume as well. Briefly, Ivan Ilych is an examining magistrate in a small town. He lives a personal and professional life filled with petty power struggles and routine official business. Nothing really happens until he "stumbles" while arranging furniture. Life continues around him, but he has now stumbled into a private hell from which he somehow knows he will never emerge. Something is terribly wrong with him. He longs for someone to understand it and explain it to him. The horrible, unbearable thought that creeps up is that he didn't live as he should have. At first, he fights against this crushing insight, but, very gradually, he accepts that he is dying from the false, mechanical way he lived his life. Ilych has to face the way he has wasted his life and live through the self-accusations, the guilt and grief of it, in order to eventually transform the experience. He has to fully inhabit his failure, and all the emotions it elicits, to find his way toward self-forgiveness.

> "Maybe I did not live as I ought to have done," it suddenly occurred to him. "But how could that be, when I did everything properly?" he replied, and immediately dismissed from his mind this, the sole solution of all the riddles of life and death, as something quite impossible.
>
> (p. 273)

Ivan Ilych fights to avoid this awareness, but, eventually, he gives in to it. Each night, he reviews his life, and in the morning, he sees his own falseness mirrored in the lifeless attention to form of his doctor and his wife.

> In them he saw himself—all that for which he had lived—and saw clearly that it was not real at all, but a terrible huge deception which had hidden both life and death. This consciousness intensified his physical suffering tenfold.
>
> (pp. 276–277)

Tolstoy ends his story on a note of hope. Much as might happen in a good treatment, Ivan Ilych is transformed by an insight that is deeply felt as well as profoundly comprehended. At last, he understands that he can *transform* his death into a final gift to those he cares about. He feels sorry for his family and sees his death as their release. Once that happens, he becomes matter of fact about his pain, and "sought his former accustomed fear of death and did not find it. 'Where is it? What death?' There was no fear because there was no death. In place of death there was light" (p. 279).

As I would hope to do with my own self-accusations, Ilych has lived his pain fully enough to transform it into something else deeply felt. His atonement is not a delimiting of feeling but, rather, an inhabiting it enough to find its transformative possibilities. Elsewhere (Buechler, 2000), I have written about a similar process in which I felt I was able to experience my grief for a patient who died thoroughly enough to fully grasp loss and other aspects of being a human being. The pain became something to learn from, a human experience that could help me reach others. *Feeling it enough* was the first step toward transforming it. This may be similar to the insight of B. J. Miller (Mooallem, 2017), quoted in Chapter 4, who said of his loss of both legs and part of one arm in an accident, that he tried to get *into* his injuries rather than *over* them, as he was encouraged to do by some of his doctors.

Attitudes about forgiveness in the clinical context

It is my belief that how I relate to forgiveness is a significant factor in my behavior in sessions, whether or not I value a neutral stance. The clinician's attitudes about forgiveness and atonement color her noticing, her remembering, her affect, and other aspects of her behavior in a session.

Many moments in sessions come to mind. I think that once we are willing to see how ubiquitous they are, we can recognize them. A patient speaks about his difficulties dealing with his ex-wife as they negotiate the roles they will each play in raising their children. He feels bitterly resentful about his ex-wife's impact on his own life and his children's experiences. His stated goal is to "resolve" his feelings so he can "move on." What attitudes do I bring to this situation? Some analysts might say that my own attitudes are not relevant as long as I am well-analyzed and trained. What matters is that the patient comes to his own conclusions about the direction of "health" for him. But I no longer believe that this is possible. I can't hear him with "evenly hovering attention," as Anna Freud (1936) recommended in her famous definition of neutrality. If I personally agree that his bitter resentment is problematic (for himself and everyone else in the situation), certain phrases he uses will catch my attention. But, on the other hand, if I hear his resentment as an accomplishment (perhaps an expression of therapeutic progress), I will hear differently. For example, the phrases that I selectively attend to (Sullivan, 1953) might be those that reflect his *use* of his resentment to guide his behavior as a parent. Or, I might hear, remember, and smile about his clarity and assertiveness after long years of flailing in confusion. Do I imagine resentment fueling his progress or impeding it? Just what does "progress" in this context mean to me and to him?

Another patient, a wife and mother, enters treatment wanting to "work on" her feelings that her husband is more invested in their son than in her. A third patient is passionately determined to keep her husband from getting away with thinking himself a good person, when, in her view, he has subtly undermined her for decades. She feels triumphant that she is able to "call him" on his behavior at long last. Two sisters, well into their older years, come to treatment asking to be helped to forgive each other so they might end their lives in greater harmony. Another woman, married for many years, wonders whether she should continue to live with her husband after finding out he has been engaging in a long-term affair. Should she forgive him and continue the life they have built together? Finally, a middle-aged woman recalls her sexual abuse when she was a very young child and directly asks me whether it would serve her health to forgive her (long-dead) father.

I don't believe I can hear these requests without, at times, tilting toward or away from forgiveness as in the patient's best interests. Because of this tilt, I might focus on some aspects of the material more than others (and I am likely to remain unaware of this selectivity during the session). I bring a lifetime of my own experience of forgiving, not forgiving, and trying to atone. I am a particular person, with a history, with emotional strengths and vulnerabilities, with defenses that limit my hearing, seeing, remembering, and understanding. At times, I can use my subjective responses to enliven my work, support a strong sense of purpose, and nurture my own resilience. My feelings in a session sometimes teach me, sometimes offer me and my patient a contrast with theirs, sometimes suggest ways pain can be transformed. Of course, they don't always enlighten, and they may incline me in one direction or another outside my awareness, especially when I am in the presence of highly evocative clinical material. But, I believe, I am a better clinical instrument if I make every effort to acknowledge their impact and stay open to their transformative potential.

References

Bokser, B. B. (1978). *Abraham Isaac Kook*. Mahwah, NJ: Paulist Press.

Bruner, M. E. (1996). A plea for tolerance. In S. A. Stuart (Ed.), *A treasury of poems* (p. 32). New York: BBS Publishing Corporation.

Buechler, S. (1999). Searching for a passionate neutrality. *Contemporary Psychoanalysis, 35*, 213–227.

Buechler, S. (2000). Necessary and unnecessary losses: The analyst's mourning. *Contemporary Psychoanalysis, 36*, 77–90.

Buechler, S. (2004). *Clinical values: Emotions that guide psychoanalytic treatment*. Hillsdale, NJ: Analytic Press.

Buechler, S. (2008). *Making a difference in patients' lives*. New York: Routledge.

Buechler, S. (2009). The analyst's search for atonement. *Psychoanalytic Inquiry, 29*, 426–437.

Buechler, S. (2012). *Still practicing: The heartaches and joys of a clinical career*. New York: Routledge.

Buechler, S. (2017). *Psychoanalytic reflections: Training and practice*. New York: IPbooks.

Erlich, H. S., Erlich-Ginor, M., and Beland, H. (2009). *Fed with tears—poisoned with milk*. Giessen, Germany: Psychosozial-Verlag.

Frankel, E. (2003). *Sacred therapy*. Boston: Shambhala.

Freud, A. (1936). *The ego and the mechanisms of defense*. New York: International Universities Press.

Freud, S. (1916). Some character types met with in psychoanalytic work. In J. Strachey (Ed. & Trans.), *The standard edition of the complete psychological works of Sigmund Freud* (Vol. 14, pp. 311–333). London: Hogarth Press.

Fromm, E. (2009). Being centrally related to the patient. In R. Funk (Ed.), *The clinical Erich Fromm* (pp. 7–39). New York: Rodopi Press.

Hornstein, G. A. (2000). *To redeem one person is to redeem the world: The life of Frieda Fromm- Reichmann*. New York: Free Press.

Khan, M. (1975). Grudge and the hysteric. *International Journal of Psychotherapy, 4*, 349–357.

Levi, P. (1988). *The drowned and the saved* (R. Rosenthal, Trans.). New York: Summit Books.

Mooallem, J. (2017, 8 January). The house at the end of the world. *New York Times Magazine*, pp. 39–45.

Rosenbaum, R. (2006). *The Shakespeare wars*. New York: Random House.

Safer, J. (1999). *Forgiving and not forgiving: Why sometimes it's better not to forgive*. New York: HarperCollins Publishers.

Shakespeare, W. (1972). *King Lear*. In *The Arden edition of the works of William Shakespeare* (pp. 1–206). London: Methuen Drama.

Shakespeare, W. (2000). *The merchant of Venice*. In A. R. Braunmuller (Ed.), *The Pelican Shakespeare* (pp.1–208). New York: Penguin.

Shakespeare, W. (2011). *The tempest*. In V. M. Vaughan & A. T. Vaughan (Eds.), *Arden Shakespeare* (pp. 161–308). London: A & C Black.

Sullivan, H. S. (1953). *The interpersonal theory of psychiatry*. New York: W. W. Norton.

Tolstoy, L. (1886/1982). The death of Ivan Ilych. In A. Maude & L. Maude (Trans.), *The raid and other stories* (pp. 228–280). New York: Oxford University Press.

Chapter 9

Societal and personal attitudes about suffering

Conclusions and speculations

When I was growing up, there was a television show called *Queen for a Day*. As I recall, people would talk about their misfortunes and get rewarded with prizes. I found it strange. For one thing, I wondered just what was being rewarded. It seemed incongruous to me. My grade-school mentality assumed that rewards came to those who did something well. What had they done well? I also couldn't understand why people would choose to tell these stories in front of strangers. Given my more current bewilderment about the popularity of Facebook, and my startled reaction every time strangers shout their life stories into cell phones on the street, I guess that I have not changed much.

As I see it, our society has confusing attitudes about the suffering of others. Silent suffering, endured in uncomplaining solitude, is seen as noble. It is a sign of strong, independent, self-sufficient character. We admire the hero who dies without revealing years of intractable pain. We revere the ability to quietly contain misery, but we also reward those who tell all. Nothing sells books, films, theater and opera tickets like vividly depicted outright misery. Pictures of torture sell newspapers, and war movies and video games offer endless images of terrible deaths. Becker's (1973) bestseller *The Denial of Death* still resonates, but we are also attracted to watching people (and action figures, cartoon characters, and so on) suffer. Drivers slow down to get a glimpse of the accident, yet people look away from the burn victim's face. Why do we look away? We act as though we don't want to notice the burns and cause shame. But why would someone feel shame about the evidence of pain endured? A fine essay in the *New York Times* by Ross Douthat (2017), entitled "The Misery Filter," makes it clear that we frequently behave as though suffering is something to be ashamed of. Douthat suggests that we avoid registering the misery of others, just as we tend to avoid encountering those who disagree with us politically. As he sees it, we are unavoidably aware of the misery of others when misfortune first occurs or when the consequences of serious diagnosis, addiction, scandal, or other afflictions are impossible to ignore. But otherwise, we tend to look away from misery, because we can't work it into our public narratives.

Douthat is explicit about the problems this causes, for both the healthy and those who are ill. The healthy are misled about the likelihood that they will someday suffer. Those who are already afflicted are left feeling alone. It is as though being healthy is equivalent to being normal, so that the ill have failed, in some sense. Suffering puts a person in a vague category of outsiders or even freaks. In America, we are taught to strive for success, but we are not taught how to bear suffering. We avoid the topic of suffering, even though finding a way to endure it remains our hardest challenge and one that each one of us will have to face.

In turning away from sufferers, we commit what Donna Orange (2016) calls, "the scandalous shame of every instance in which we turn away from the suffering of the other. Therefore, the evil of all suffering is the evil of failing to respond to the other's pain" (p. 136).

I think the issue of shame, and fear of shame, are tremendously significant in our attitudes about suffering. We can feel shame because we suffer, because we want to see the suffering of the other, or because we want to turn away. While Douthat (above) doesn't use the word *shame*, I believe it is sometimes shame—or, even more often, the fear of shame—that silences us when we, ourselves, are suffering, as though expressing it would reveal us as weaklings or failures. In clinical work, I think shame poses some unique difficulties for both participants. It counters the impulse to express any other emotion. If we are ashamed of our sorrow, or our anger, or fear, or anxiety, or positive feelings such as joy or curiosity, we are less likely to express it. In a sense, shame is the emotion that can oppose work on all the others. Furthermore, it is the only negative feeling that tends to get more extreme when noticed. We become ashamed of our shame, if someone sees it. Of course, this poses challenges for the talking cure. I will return to this point.

Oddly, our culture can also spawn shame about having recovered from a debilitating problem, such as addiction. Laura Hilgers (2017), a freelance journalist, wrote an opinion piece about the shaming of people formerly addicted to alcohol and other substances. Hilgers interviewed Ms. Zenoff, who is recovering from addictions to alcohol and drugs but had been too ashamed to admit she was in recovery. Zenoff says she felt so much shame about her past behavior that she was unable to reveal that she was in recovery, even to her family and friends. It took three years for her to admit to friends that she was in recovery and another three years to speak about it publicly. Now, she is director of the Center for Open Recovery in the Bay Area. She sees the problem of covering up recovery as highly significant. She believes that there are people dying who wouldn't need to die if it were safe to say they were in recovery. If that were so, more could express their need for help. As it is, we don't ask for help when we need it, and we don't fund addiction programs sufficiently, because, although we may publicize the numbers of those suffering from addictions, we are too afraid of shame to attach our own human faces to the problem.

Openly admitting to suffering depression can also evoke shame. A remarkable book, *Unholy Ghost* (Casey, 2001), chronicles reactions to depression in the depressed person and those in significant relationships with that person. The book was edited by Nell Casey, who, herself, has a sister who has suffered from significant periods of depression. The chapters make clear that those who are depressed often feel great shame, as though depression is a failure to figure out how to live well, or to try hard enough, or to be of good character.

Shame about aging is the subject of another chapter in this book (Chapter 3), so I will not discuss that topic here. But, for me, it raises interesting questions (personally and theoretically). If one reason we are ashamed of having been addicted or depressed is that society assumes these problems result from a failure of character, what about growing older? And, once again, what about the person whose face was burned? Is aging, or burning, also seen as a sign of bad character?

Of course, other attitudes are also evident, and, as I suggested above, the culture also prizes and dwells on stories of human suffering. Sometimes, it is as though our eyes seek them and then are repelled by them. When we look away, what might we be avoiding? Shaming the "other" whose difficulties brand them as inferior beings? Or shaming ourselves for our curiosity, for actually wanting to look, just as much as we also want to look away?

In a previous publication (Buechler, 2010), I identified three attitudes about suffering that I think are prevalent in professional as well as non-professional circles. Briefly, the first is that, primarily, suffering is a symptom, and its reduction or elimination is a pivotal aim in treatment, as well as in the rest of life. Therefore, any method that might delimit emotional pain, such as medication, should be employed. The second attitude is that, for the most part, suffering is a human inevitability. According to this point of view, an important goal of psychological treatment is to facilitate both participants' efforts to become better able to accept suffering as a part of the human condition, endure it courageously and with dignity. A third approach sees suffering as the royal road toward some form of enlightenment, wisdom, or personal identity. In other words, suffering is *the* path toward redemption and self-knowledge. It follows, then, that psychological treatment should further the participants' capacities to learn from their suffering.

No doubt there are countless other ways to look at suffering, but these point out some ways our society's and our profession's attitudes about pain profoundly affect our clinical work. Our personal and professional stance about suffering will have an impact on how we understand treatment's goals, as well as, more generally, our goals as human beings. How do we view denial? Is it an obstacle to be overcome or a useful part of our essential equipment for living? Similarly, if obsessive defenses distract a patient from abject suffering, are these defenses to be *cultivated* in treatment? Do we see this differently if the patient is going through a particularly painful crisis or if the patient is nearing the end of life? In a subsequent section, I return to the role of defenses in bearing suffering.

In this chapter, I refer to three issues that recur, in different forms, in other chapters of this book.

1   How do we view efforts to adjust to whatever life brings, whether it is physical and/or emotional suffering, adversity, aging, loss, aloneness, and, eventually, death?
2   How do we see intensity of emotion as related to health? That is, are emotional responses to acute suffering healthier if they are less intense? Or does it depend on the predominant emotion, so that, for example, extreme anxiety when suffering physically is less healthy than extreme frustration?

3   How do we understand the power of words to affect the experience of suffering? In treatment and beyond, how much should we rely on words to help people bear life's inevitable pain?

Each of these topics deserves more attention than I will give it. A vast accumulation of volumes, from a wide variety of disciplines, pertains to these questions. I can only suggest some ideas that have occurred to me through my reading, living my own personal life, and working clinically.

Attitudes about adaptation to suffering

In various contexts, including my own life, I have come across the issue of whether it is best for human beings to try to adapt to whatever life brings or to fight for betterment. Some inspiring stories suggest that the strong person, undaunted by adversity, can conquer it by refusing to merely adapt. This attitude clearly empowers some to fight for health, for themselves and others. But it seems just as clear that it can also lead to a sense of shame when, for example, cancer wins.

Around the time I was diagnosed with breast cancer, I opened my *New York Times* and read a debate about whether those who have been successfully treated should be called "cancer survivors." Would that objectify us, defining us on one dimension but leaving out the rest of who we are as human beings?

My concern centers on those who fight but are clearly losing a battle with cancer. Will they feel they have been insufficiently motivated or too weak? And yet, I have often been moved by accounts of everyday warriors who persist, against all odds, to fight for their own lives. Sometimes strength (and health) seems to come in the form of unstoppable persistence, but sometimes yielding, accepting a new reality without a fight, seems most wise. As I have suggested many times (Buechler, 2004, 2008), I don't think it is enough to claim we follow the patient's lead on these issues. That is a crucial professional requirement but also impossible, from my point of view. I think it is inevitable that our own tendencies to fight or adapt will be reflected in our focus in sessions. And this, in turn, will have an impact on the patient and the treatment, whether the participants are aware of it or not. It is, to me, both contradictory and true that we must uphold the value of a patient-guided treatment, of the right of the patient to determine his or her path in life, but it is equally true that it is impossible to function entirely neutrally. Our values (often outside our awareness) affect what we focus on, answer, remember, interpret, and so on.

I am reminded of an extremely moving short story (also referred to in Chapter 2), "The Management of Grief" by Bharati Mukherjee (1992), which addresses the issue of "normal" emotionality in the face of an extremely painful loss. Shaila's husband, Vikram, and their two sons are returning from a trip to India when their plane is bombed and splits in half, just a short distance from Heathrow Airport. Shaila is taken to Ireland to identify photographs of the victims. She refuses to see her own outward calm as superior to the more intense emotional expressions of the others. Shaila believes that each person must suffer in their own way. By some standards, she is the one who is behaving oddly and badly. Conforming to one society's expectations about the proper "management" of grief is not necessarily the healthiest approach.

An important factor in how much we fight versus quietly adapt or accept pain is the state of our feelings of hope. In his extremely poignant memoir *When Breath Becomes Air*, Paul Kalanithi (2016) considers his own hopes as he begins to battle the cancer that eventually would cut off his young life, just as he was completing his training as a neurosurgeon and months after the birth of his daughter. He was diagnosed at the age of 36 and began an all-out struggle for life, for time to put his training to use and leave his child with some memories of her father. He fought to hang on to hope, musing about its usual combination of confidence and desire, and ruefully commenting that what he desired was life, but what he was confident of was death. Should he try to keep working at all cost, bearing the searing back pain, trying to shut his mind to thoughts of what lay in the (immediate and long-term) future? Or should he let go of his former plans, hopes, and dreams, stop fighting and start relaxing into the pain? In a very moving epilogue, Paul's wife, Lucy, tells us that Paul "remained vigorous, open, full of hope not for an unlikely cure but for days that were full of purpose and meaning" (p. 219). This book, which Paul was so determined to finish before he died, is a testament to the truth of her words.

An intriguing book that deals with another type of adaptation, *Swamplands of the Soul: New Life in Dismal Places* (Hollis, 1996), declares that "[t]o align oneself with those forces within rather than reflexively adjusting always to the powers without, thereby furthering our self-alienation, is to feel grounded in some deep truth, the nature of our nature" (p. 11). This is the cry of much of the existential philosophic and analytic literature, and it is a position powerfully elucidated by the psychoanalysts Erich Fromm and Rollo May, both of whom wrote extensively about the price we pay for "adjusting" to the values of our society. Whereas H. S. Sullivan, another of my analytic ancestors, was much less focused on the potentially negative effects of society on the individual and the dangers of the need for external approval, Fromm and May espoused values that are universal and supersede those of any particular society. Given the times they lived in, including the rise of Nazi Germany, it may not surprise us that both Fromm and May explicitly warned that adaptation to one's society was a dangerous approach to life. Fromm was highly critical of what he called the empty "marketing character," whose motto is "I am as you desire me." In what I hear as a similar tone, May (1953) described "other-directedness" as typical of many in modern Western culture whose drive for approval can make them into "hollow" people, lacking in inner, guiding, orienting values and strong convictions. The issue of when to adapt to society's unspoken rules about suffering may be seen as a subset of the more general rules about emotional behavior. I wonder whether lifelong "adapters" face mortal illnesses any differently from those who generally have taken a different approach to life. And do those who have always privileged adaptation more readily "downsize" as they undergo aging and changing financial and physical circumstances? Burack-Weiss (2015) comments that she had a more positive view of downsizing before she, herself, became an older woman. She asks how, in the midst of downsizing, she, and others are supposed to

... meet the increasing losses of people, places and things that are now our lot? How are we to face our own declining attractiveness, health, and ability to function day to day? How are we to face our own death that no longer hovers in the distant future but is now too close for comfort?

(p. 20)

Is it wisest to bow to the forces favoring cutting down?

The author and prolific playwright Sam Shepard asked himself whether or not he should just "give in" to the increasingly incapacitating symptoms of ALS (amyotrophic lateral sclerosis, also known as motor neurone disease.) In his last book, *Spy of the First Person*, Shepard (2017) makes his helplessness heartbreakingly clear. "Nothing seems to be working now. Hands. Arms. Legs. Nothing. I just lie here. Waiting for someone to find me" (p. 18). It may well sound absurd, but I am asking what "health" means in this situation. Shepard later comments that wise people have told him to stay in the present, but his mind keeps taking him back to the past. Perhaps the advice was meant to keep him from comparing the present with the past. It is true that those comparisons could be beyond belief and yet all too palpably true. "At one point in the past—at some point in the past—everything was alright. There was no desperation. Everything worked" (p. 50). Putting his experience into the third person (perhaps to find some bearable distance), he comments:

You notice how different. You don't want to believe it. You notice, for instance, his breathing, the lack of breath. You notice for instance the reach of his arms, the lack of coordination between his brain and his hands. Who is it this time?

(p. 63)

Too much of Shepard was lost for him to remain Shepard. I imagine we each may have a somewhat different point at which we no longer feel like ourselves. Each time a devastating change or loss registers, we, along with Shepard, ask: "Who is it this time?"

Challenges to identity

The challenges to Shepard's identity are clear. What he had taken for granted about his body was no longer true. Even to become aware of the necessity for brain and hand to coordinate is foreign. An arm that won't move is not my arm, as I have known it.

In Chapter 3, where I discuss healthy aging, I referred to the question "Will I Still Be Me?" We can ask the same question here. Are there physical, cognitive, emotional, and interpersonal changes that invariably challenge the sense of self? Of course, this is a highly personal question. But I believe it is worth considering whether there are some losses of previous capacities that are more likely to disrupt the ongoing sense of being oneself.

One obvious factor is how we are treated. I remember that when I was undergoing radiation for breast cancer, I was determined not to become "the tumor in Room C." At least to myself, I wanted to remain Sandra. I have known other cancer patients who decorated their chemotherapy cubicles with family photographs for similar reasons. It can be helpful to be reminded of who we still are, besides the tumor in Room C.

A beautiful short story by Alice Munro (1991), "Mrs. Cross and Mrs. Kidd," makes this clear. I have already referred to it in Chapter 3, so I will just mention an aspect of it here. Briefly, the two eponymous women knew each other in kindergarten and meet again, 80 years later, in a nursing home. Their very different characters affect how they adapt to their new circumstances, and their relationship with each other bolsters their ability to cope. Mrs. Kidd is very determined to remain her outgoing, caring self and finds an outlet for these impulses when a new resident, Jack, comes to live at the home. Jack is a relatively young man, who has suffered a devastating stroke. Jack was a journalist, but now he can't speak, write, hold himself straight, or move the left side of his body. It becomes Mrs. Kidd's mission to restore some of Jack's former identity, by reminding him of his previous life. After many failed experiments, she succeeds in guessing the name of the woman he has always loved. We watch as a part of Jack's identity is, in a sense, restored to him, and in the process, an aspect of Mrs. Kidd's sense of self also gains life.

In describing the more debilitated residents, Munro skillfully delineates the progress from being seen as a particular person to being objectified as a "symptom picture." For example, one woman has developed a huge tongue that comes to define her. She is no longer a specific person with accomplishments and idiosyncrasies but, rather, "the tongue" in room 103. I think Munro has depicted the process by which a person can gradually lose individuality, and even humanity, to herself and others.

Do losses of memory affect the sense of self similarly to losses of physical function? And what about emotional and interpersonal losses? In Chapter 2, I discuss how I lose an aspect of myself when someone dies. If my cousin Charlie appreciated my humor in a special way, when Charlie dies, that aspect of me will never live in quite the same way. It may not entirely disappear, but it is not the same. Those who lose a child know this in a particularly poignant way. They may become (or already be) parents to another child, but they will never again be the *particular* parent they were to the child who died.

Frequently, we (inadvertently) exacerbate our own feelings of loss of ourselves through our defenses. We may be trying to distance from unbearable sorrow and helplessness, but as a result we distance from our own experience. A heart-wrenching short story illustrates this. In Thom Jones' (1999) aptly titled "I Want to Live," Mrs. Wilson struggles to bear the effects of wildly proliferating cancer. At first, she grabs precious moments of forgetting about her pain and terror by playing with her little granddaughter. She is momentarily grateful that "[a]fter a year of sheer hell, in which all of the good stuff added up to less than an hour and four minutes total, there was a way to forget" (p. 678). But this gives her less and less respite. Then, through conversations with her son-in-law, she discovers Schopenhauer. Mrs. Wilson is cheered by the resonance between the philosopher's words and her own experience. Finally, here is someone willing to be honest. Facing toward, and not away, from exquisite pain helps Mrs. Wilson bear it. Efforts to escape momentarily may have prevented her from finding this solace earlier.

More generally, how does our previous pattern of defenses affect our ability to cope with extreme challenges to our very identity? The price tag of certain defensive patterns may be higher at these times. A clear example is those who have relied on feeling in control, using obsessive defenses. When control slips away, who are they to themselves? I wonder whether certain patterns of defense make some suffering even worse than it otherwise would be. For those who have heavily relied on careful, deliberate, highly detailed planning, what is it like to lose memory? For those who have battled against being immobilized by depression, what is it like to be trapped in a *physically* immobilized state? I think there are some situations where our customary defenses make it probable that we will deeply suffer from a loss of identity and self-esteem. For example, we may have operated (outside awareness) on an assumption that we are exempt from certain aspects of the human condition. Those vulnerabilities are relegated to the "other" and not to "me." So what happens when such a person is forced to see that, in fact, now they *do* have those very vulnerabilities? Who we were before a crisis, in terms of our character structure and defensive patterns, must have a major impact on how we suffer.

This is beautifully portrayed in a poem by Elizabeth Bishop (2016) titled "In the Waiting Room." In this poem, it is 1918, and seven-year-old Elizabeth (presumably the poet as a child) is at the dentist's office, waiting for her aunt to emerge from treatment. Elizabeth hears her aunt cry out in pain. For the child, this confirmed what she thought she already knew: that her aunt was a foolish, timid woman. But something else did surprise Elizabeth. All at once, she feels that the cries of pain are coming from her own mouth. Elizabeth tries to ground herself in her own reality but is profoundly shaken. Even in her confusion, she intuits that nothing stranger than this moment would ever happen to her.

For me, this poem captures many essential truths. Wherever we are, we are all in the waiting room, in some senses. When suffering strikes, lines may be crossed and identities may blur. In Joan Didion's (2005) moving portrayal of her emotional and cognitive state after the loss of her husband, she knows he is dead, yet she keeps thinking he might still come home and need his shoes. Suffering can blur the lines between wish and reality, self and other, past and present, and so on. From infancy on, we spend a good deal of effort distinguishing self from other, and yet in regard to life's tragedies we are told to ask not for whom the bell tolls. In fact, for Donna Orange (2016), who has written so poignantly about suffering and about the pain of witnessing the suffering of others, "[a] compassionate attitude says to every patient: your suffering is human suffering, and when the bell tolls for you, it also tolls for me" (p. 57). So, on the one hand, it can be considered psychotic to misidentify where voices are coming from, and early in development it is an achievement to *distinguish* mine from yours. But, on the other hand, when suffering strikes, it can feel *so* cruel and arbitrary that it struck one person and not the other. The sufferer asks, why me? And why now? We learn to distinguish self from other early in life in order to function, but then we need to be able to identify ourselves with the other in order to empathize. So much art, opera, and therapeutic and other relationships is predicated on the magical ability to jump the gaps between self and other, then and now, fantasy and reality. Winnicott's (1971) transitional space is a malleable land where we don't have to distinguish one from the other, and it can be such a relief.

Elsewhere (Buechler, 2008), I have written about my treatment of a woman who was confined to a wheelchair. Envying my ability to walk unaided, she frequently reminded me that I was only "temporarily able bodied," and, someday, I too would suffer from limited mobility. She wanted me to feel what it was like to be her and to know that only timing differentiated us. She wanted me to be struck, as was seven-year-old Elizabeth, with the knowledge that *I* was (only temporarily) in the waiting room.

I have already referred (above) to the belief, held by some, that suffering can ennoble us or, at least, educate us about the human condition and connect us with each other. Suffering brings a mother and son closer together in a beautiful story, "In the Gloaming," by Alice Elliott Dark (1994). Janet is taking care of her son Laird, who, at the age of 33, is dying from an HIV-related illness. Martin, Janet's husband and Laird's father, absents himself from his family as much as possible, which has been his approach to life in general but is more notable now. Every evening, Janet and Laird enter into intimate conversations that are much different from their previous exchanges. Of course, they have always spoken with each other, but now they really talk about life, love, yearning. They talk directly, openly, as they have never talked before. Janet comes to cherish this new intimacy with her son. At times, their frank discussions evoke Janet's self-reproaches and feelings of guilt and inadequacy. She confesses to Laird that her children are the only extraordinary things about her. She struggles not to cry in front of him, telling herself there will be plenty of time to cry. She has impulses to flee but fights them off. The words they exchange bring Janet new and startling revelations about herself. For example, "[s]uddenly she realized: Laird had been the love of her life" (p. 697). The author makes it clear that frank words are the only medium through which mother and son can bear their pain.

Laird and Janet let their suffering change them and profoundly alter their relationship. But another attitude about healthy suffering is that we should aim for it to change us as little as possible. This is akin to the belief (articulated in Chapter 3) that we should make it a goal to change as little as possible when we age. Implicitly, I think this suggests that our pre-suffering (or pre-aging) selves were better. The earlier self was our true, pristine identity. Holding on to it is a victory.

The helpful and harmful power of words

Does finding words to express suffering actually improve the experience? Can it also have a detrimental effect? Our analytic culture prizes finding words for what we feel, and it and the wider culture often assume "sharing" it is healthy. Are there times when putting suffering into words augments pain?

One way of thinking about the positive impact of being capable of finding fitting words is that perhaps it balances the helplessness of suffering with a sense of competence. Analysts may be particularly likely to use this approach (consciously and/or unconsciously), since words are our stock in trade. We can feel as though we have "mastered" pain by expressing its nuances in apt phrases. A poem (Amichai, 2016) contrasts our capacity to pin down our various types of suffering, as opposed to our less well-defined experiences of joy. It refers to "the blurriness of joy and the precision of pain" (p. 5). We can discriminate burning pain from sharp pain, but we have trouble finding precise words for different strains of joy. Perhaps we feel more urgency about communicating what hurts and exactly how it hurts, as though if we find the most accurate words we will get help.

I think it is true that having a nuanced vocabulary can change the structure of experience. Usually, this is an improvement. When a patient can distinguish fear from anxiety, for example, this signals more than just a better developed vocabulary. Having a different word for *fear* means that we can collect our fear experiences, try to discern patterns in them, and learn from what has diminished them in the past. Finely distinguished categories of experience can make us more intelligible to others and to ourselves. If someone asks me whether I am angry with them, and I am able to say actually I am frustrated, I have clarified myself.

Words leave a record. Unlike us, they don't die. The meaning this can carry is made abundantly clear by Paul Kalanithi's (2016) fierce determination to record his experience in the final stages of his illness (as discussed above). It is also amply illustrated by his family's (and his publisher's) absolute dedication to helping him finish his memoir. He didn't just want to leave his words as a legacy; he *needed* to. One of his dying wishes was that the manuscript be finished and published.

But Paul's feelings about the power of words shifted some over time. At first, he saw "language as an almost supernatural force, existing between people, bringing our brains, shielded in centimeter-thick skulls, into communion" (p. 39). But just a bit later, he complains of the "weightlessness" of words and longs for direct experiences to inform him. Sometimes, when a patient is reluctant to speak, rather than hear it as resistance to the treatment, I wonder if it is (or also is) resistance to squeezing complicated moments into the Procrustean beds of words. Sullivan's "syntaxic" (dictionary-definition) language can be understood by anyone fluent in that tongue, because it isn't burdened by quirky personal connotations. This makes it easy to comprehend but, possibly, devoid of its most interesting ambiguities. Common denominators simplify, which is their strength as well as their potential to reduce experience and mislead us. The speaker's experience, while vague, felt alive, constantly changing its shape. But put into ordinary words it becomes plain, in more than one sense.

Sometimes words subtly promote splitting. A patient says: "My mother was kind; my father was harsh." But, of course, that over-generalizes moment-to-moment experience. Words can also incline us toward our more rational, logical thinking and away from a full appreciation of the paradoxical, which, I believe, is so essential in treatment. Clinicians have to be capable of profound conviction about what we know is subjective. And, as we search for words, it can be hard to hold onto contradictory truths. Only a real poet has the skill to capture such truths in words, as in Samuel Beckett's (1955) naming of *The Unnamable*: "I can't go on. I'll go on" (p. 414).

For most of our history, analysts have relied on verbal "formulations." I am (once again) reminded of T. S. Eliot's (1943) great poem "East Coker," which could easily be seen as a description of the grave difficulty (for both treatment participants) of finding adequate words to convey some meaningful experiences. I am sure every clinician (and poet) can identify with Eliot's portrayal of struggling to find just the right words, failing differently with every try but nevertheless persisting.

But analysts have put great stock in finding words to express experience, outside treatment sessions as well as within them. For example, as noted above, H. S. Sullivan (1953) believed that "consensual validation" of experiences, gained through finding adequate (syntaxic) words to describe it, spares us from the potentially harmful effects of our "parataxic" (idiosyncratic) life circumstances. In what I see as a similar spirit, the vast "attachment" literature claims that if people are able to make a coherent narrative out of the story of their lives, even if their lives have been highly challenging, healthy development is possible. No doubt these theories have validity. But most of us find it hard to convey our most profound experiences into words. It feels as though we are reducing them to something more commonplace.

In his last year of life, Sam Shepard (2017) began the memoir that documents the final stages of his death from ALS. His three adult children and a friend helped as his illness forced him to write in longhand, then record, and, in his final days, dictate the last pages. Shepard's memoir reads like poetry, in that the words evoke felt experience. For example, he describes the feeling of having something (perhaps an insect) crawling up his ear and being unable to do anything about it. Shepard makes his terrible helplessness palpable when, toward the end, he remembers: "One year ago exactly more or less, he could walk with his head up. He could see through the air. He could wipe his own ass" (p. 79). The piling up of minute, matter-of-fact observations evoke stronger feelings (at least, in me) than would any piteous cry.

I think the impact of Shepard's words derives from the combination of describing precisely and evoking emotion powerfully. In a sense, they take advantage of one of the primary strengths of words—their ability to create specific images in the receptive mind. But, unlike some words, they also evoke strong feelings. Imagining mind and empathic heart are equally engaged. Reading Shepard, I am drawn to imagine what it would be like for me to be in his position. The line between him and me thins. At some point, I am not so much imagining as actually *experiencing* helplessness. With Shepard, I feel what it is like to know that, from now on, I will be separated from normal sensation, normal functioning, by an unbridgeable chasm. With him, I know (to some degree) what it is like to see the beautiful, various world from a distance I used to cross so effortlessly but will never cross again. How arbitrary it feels!

What if (like Shepard and Kalanithi) remaining yourself (for as long as possible) entails making observations that break your heart? What if your mind can't help searching for the meaning of the situation? What if it is natural to you to compare then and now, and what could have been with what is?

More recently, analysts have put more emphasis on lived experiences in treatment, rather than verbal formulations of insights. Words are still valued, but "enactments" breathe life into them. Perhaps I knew that my patient, Mary, could be dismissive, but when I feel the sting of it in an interplay in a session, I may "know" it much more profoundly. Before this event, I had words to describe Mary's contemptuous attitude, but now the same words convey deeply felt experience.

So words can help us jump the gap between self and other. When just right, they can convey and even evoke felt experience. They are like magic in their conjuring. But, like all magic, transformational words are the exception. Most words are pedestrian. They describe their bit of reality, plainly enough to make sense. We all know that few moments in treatment sessions sound like poetry. Our "interpretations" generally fall far short of that mark. If they capture any truth at all, we feel successful.

When treatment is caricatured, the clinician usually parrots some rephrased version of what the patient already said. For example, the patient describes a scene in which his mother didn't understand him, and the clinician says, "You feel misunderstood." Often, this is counted as a good moment by both participants. Unlike with his mother, the patient felt understood. There may be something reassuring in this, but there is no magic—only a bit of effort and average linguistic skills. Nothing was really conjured; nothing new happened; no one emerges transformed. Like most caricature, this portrayal of treatment has a kernel of truth, however exaggerated and over-generalized it may be.

But magic can be evil, as well as good. I am not just referring to genuine evil, when patients are gaslighted into believing something harmful about themselves or when the power of words is deliberately employed to seduce, silence, or overpower. I am suggesting something less sinister but (I believe) much more common. Words can actually cover over misunderstandings, promote false senses of alliance, and bury quirky individuality. Without any (conscious or even unconscious) ill intentions, they can paper over what is truly meant.

When my patient and I use the word *love*, do we mean the same thing? Might we be misled into thinking we understand each other better than we really do? Similarly, when using diagnostic terminology, clinicians may feel clearer than is good for us as well as our patients. Having readily available terms might prevent us from being as bewildered as we should be.

The suffering patient may be all too eager for the clinician's words to signal real understanding and helpfulness. But when the session ends, and the patient leaves feeling no better and faces unaltered dilemmas, it is easy to fall into self-blame or despair. The patient may embrace some version of "I am too broken to profit from treatment" or "I must be resisting." Often, this repeats experiences of choosing to continue to believe in a parent's love or power, rather than face the grim truth. Unfortunately, this can come at the expense of genuine self-understanding and compassion for oneself.

Suffering and emotional balance

It is consonant with my previous writing (Buechler, 2004, 2008, 2012, 2015, 2017) to suggest that the experience of suffering, like any other part of life, is shaped by the balance of other positive and negative emotions one simultaneously feels. That is, at least theoretically, profound curiosity has an impact on what might otherwise be purely painful. For example, a patient feeling shame might be encouraged to question the shame, to wonder at it, to play with thoughts about it, and to experiment with ideas about changing it. In a particularly striking poem, "When Death Comes," Mary Oliver (2010) sings the praises of curiosity to make even death bearable. Oliver expresses her wish to remain open to amazement and always ready to take the whole world into her arms. She hopes to be as faithful to this stance as though she were married to it.

To remain that curious and eager to embrace the unexpected makes life an adventure. Henry Krystal (1975) suggests that all of life can be experienced with wonder. While I think there are some experiences that are too profoundly painful to view that way, I do agree that a curious stance can often add a playful dimension.

Besides curiosity, we all know that hope can also alter suffering and that love carries us through many of life's trials. And we certainly can bear suffering more easily when we feel a sense of purpose and when our courage has been recruited. On the other hand, we know (from Freud) that powerful ambivalence complicates the sorrow of loss, and most of us know from (painful) experience that sorrow feels deeper when it is accompanied by regret.

In other words, suffering, like much else in life, changes with the (emotional) company it keeps. Just as painters recognize that red looks different against a background of blue than it does against a background of yellow, the pain of loss alters depending on whether or not it appears in a context of significant regrets.

Ann Burack-Weiss (2015), whose work I referenced above and in Chapters 2 and 3, wrote about life's difficulties by establishing a dialogue with well-known authors who have commented on the subject. Among others, she "talked back" to Nancy Mairs, who, in addition to life's usual difficulties, suffered from multiple sclerosis and depression and coped with her husband having cancer. Mairs makes clear that her anguish is greatly exacerbated by the painful shame dependency brought her. So, in addition to the inevitable sorrow, she bore intense humiliation.

> What I need—repetitively, interminably—is help performing even the most elementary tasks. I can't butter my own bread. Before long I may not even be able to use the toilet by myself. My dependency, in resembling that of a young child, makes me feel demeaned, diminished, humiliated. This is a horrible situation, one that wracks me with grief and fury for which no socially acceptable outlet exists.
>
> (p. 65)

But just as humiliation can exponentially augment sorrow, some positive feelings can diminish it or, at least, reframe it. For example, much of the world's culture has as a central theme love's ability to console. The poem "Dover Beach" by Matthew Arnold (2016) comes to mind. It sounds "[t]he eternal note of sadness" and reminds us of "the turbid ebb and flow of human misery . . ." (p. 14).

But then the poet asks for the *only* possible consolation: that he and his love would be true to one another. That is all there is, in a world made bleak by "ignorant armies" that "clash by night." The world seems "[t]o lie before us like a land of dreams, / So various, so beautiful, so new . . ." (p. 15).

The way the world seems in this beautiful picture only deepens our sadness once we apprehend the real dimensions of human suffering. What sorrow in dreams that will never be realized in a world of infinite unfulfilled promise! But love that is true creates its own *fulfilled* promise.

Aside from love, of the other positive feelings I think joy balances pain most effectively, but it is often overlooked, at least in the analytic literature. In fact, Robert Emde (Buechler, 2008) joked that there is very little *Freude* (German for *joy*) in Freud's psychoanalytic psychology. Why is that? I think joy is hard to put into words (which probably causes, as well as reflects, its neglect). Amichai (2016), the poet I referred to above, so beautifully captured this truth, when he referred to "the precision of pain and the blurriness of joy" (p. 5). As noted above, people can be precise about pain—this one is sharp, that one throbs. But we become global, almost speechless, in describing joy. Do we even have language for different kinds of joy? Are there different kinds?

And yet, joy is a significant aspect of our emotional lives and certainly plays a role in our capacity to bear suffering. Elsewhere (Buechler, 2008), I called joy the "universal antidote," in that it can counter all of the negative emotions. Joy can connect us to others, which helps us bear life's unavoidable sorrows. It bonds us, which mitigates life's inevitable loneliness. It can make us feel capable of soaring above the obstacles that anger us and the losses and limitations that sadden and depress us. Losing track in joy, we are less consumed by our fears and anxieties. Its lightness and affirmation eclipses shame, guilt, and regret.

What is joy? In my 2008 chapter on it, I wrote about it as a universal human experience. An emotion theorist defined it as:

> often accompanied by a sense of harmony and unity with the object of joy and, to some extent, with the world. Some people have reported that in ecstatic joy they tend to lose individual identity, as in the case of some mystical experiences associated with meditation.
>
> (Izard, 1977, p. 27)

My own (clinical and personal) experience corroborates this observation, but, I find, just as often joy accompanies a *sharpened* self-definition. For example, Erich Fromm (1976) wrote that "[j]oy, then, is what we experience in the process of growing nearer to the goal of becoming ourselves" (p. 106). So, joy can accompany blurring the outline of individual identity, as well as etching it in more clearly.

Is joy possible during times of intense suffering? That is, can our pain elicit a feeling of being connected to the rest of suffering humanity and, at the same time, acquaint us with our particular, personal way of bearing the human condition? Rilke's description of his own suffering comes to mind: "For you cannot be sure whether your heart did not also grow with it and whether this immense fatigue is not actually the heart growing and expanding" (Baer, 2005, p. 98).

Just a bit later, Rilke explains how he needs to work out the meaning of his suffering: "For everything I suffer is a task for myself, and so purely and exactly meant for my own work and ways of solving things that I am almost ashamed and have a bad conscience about involving the physician . . ." (p. 99).

How can we help someone access the emotions that would allow them to bear suffering well? As clinicians, I think we are better able to help people deal with blocks to bearing suffering well (like shame, guilt, anger, regret, and ambivalence) than we are at recruiting (or even understanding) feelings that would help.

In his preface to his wife's Holocaust memoir, Paul Ornstein (Ornstein & Goldman, 2004) writes that strong Zionistic ideals enabled her to bear her ordeal.

> This outlook gave us inner strength to withstand daily humiliations, even pain and hunger. In labor camps, such resiliency of spirit could be life saving-it was a bulletproof vest against the atrocities perpetrated against us. It helped us remember who we were, the pride we could feel in being Jewish, in being a link in countless generations of the people of the book, that had survival value under these circumstances. This gift our families transmitted to us made it possible for Anna to survive with the fullness of her love of life, her dreams and ambitions intact. Her stories, and the spirit they express, are testimonies to the importance of these values for the emotional survival of one Hungarian Jewish girl among many.
>
> (pp. 12–13)

Bearing suffering well: Conclusions and further speculations

In times of suffering, some turn to Nature and physical sensation for consolation. It is not a surprise to me that Rilke expressed this beautifully.

> The most divine consolation is without a doubt contained within the human itself. We would not know very well what to do with the consolations of a god. All that is necessary is for our eye to be a trace more seeing, for our ear to be more receptive, for the flavor of a fruit to enter us more completely, for us to be able to tolerate more scent, and, in touching and being touched, to be more present-minded and less oblivious—in order to receive from our most immediate experiences consolations that would be more convincing, more significant and truer than any suffering that can ever unsettle us.
>
> (Baer, 2005, p. 60)

What sustains some sufferers seems to me to involve an unbreakable attachment to their identity, a spiritual sense of purpose, some form of love, and, perhaps, an ability to escape the present moment in dreams of the future. I can relate each of these aspects to threads in the preceding chapters. I have already suggested that, regardless of the type of suffering, we can bear it better when we can, at least, retain our sense of self. Looking at the positive side of the identity issue, we have come across the idea that recognizing tell-tale signs of our unique selves can elicit joy (Buechler, 2008). Becoming more nearly ourselves was defined as a treatment goal by Fromm (1976). I would suggest that during any crisis a sense of remaining oneself, of meeting the challenge in our own, characteristic style, can be a saving grace. Frank Sinatra's song "I Did It My Way" rings with expansive pride and self-assertion.

Some forms of suffering may be most likely to challenge the capacity to feel we will remain ourselves. It seems clear that physical and mental disabilities can have that power, although, as we saw in Chapter 4, some people (like Miller, the man who lost both legs and one arm in an accident and went on to become a palliative care doctor) are able to retain and even enhance their identities during trying periods of their lives. But it seems probable that certain severe blows to self-esteem put this capacity to a test (Chapter 7). For some, an inability to settle into a career or a loss of a stable, predictable world also put identity into question (Chapter 5).

Victor Frankl's (1985) moving autobiographical Holocaust memoir makes the point that the human capacity to assign personal meaning to one's experience can never be taken away by any enemy. While I believe this to be true, I would suggest that the "enemies" most likely to call this ability into question are those that lie *within* us. For example, in states of depression, we may feel that our pain and, more generally, our lives have lost all meaning, and we are no longer recognizable to ourselves. Perhaps this is the greatest loss we can suffer.

We bring an already established psychic structure to the times we suffer. Orange (2010) emphasizes: "Each suffering person suffers in multiple contexts that give the current trouble layers of meaning . . ." (p. 110). While I am mindful of the dangers of any generalization, I wonder whether certain defensive proclivities exacerbate certain kinds of suffering. For example, in times of pervasive stress, when a crisis colors all our hours, is it harder to survive if we happen to be people who have never relied on compartmentalization? Or, if a traumatic event punctures normal life, can our survival depend on a capacity for thorough repression or dissociation? More generally, what allows us to go on living, in the midst of various kinds of suffering? Bromberg (1998) has written of the part dissociation can play in ongoing life. Is there a particular part that each defense can play, under certain circumstances, if it is already well-practiced? We have long known that two people who suffered a "similar" event may have starkly different outcomes. Is that (partly) because one happens to have honed defenses that are better suited for bearing that particular crisis?

I can only speculate about the part accustomed defenses play in our bearing suffering well, but my clinical and personal experience suggests that some defenses are especially likely to hinder our ability to cope with certain kinds of crises. For example, I think that obsessive preoccupation renders us unable to take needed five-minute "mini-vacations" from a threatening health-related issue. A patient who has not yet heard the results of a biopsy can think of nothing else, so she doesn't have a chance to become curious, or joyful, or engaged in any positive aspect of her life. In other situations that directly challenge self-esteem, over-reliance on dissociation and splitting may prevent the sufferer from having a sturdy enough sense of pride and identity to weather the crisis. Furthermore, I would speculate that the person who has always relied on projection may be especially vulnerable to helplessness. For such a person, the power to determine the effect of circumstances has always seemed to reside outside oneself.

On the other hand, perhaps sometimes denial may allow us to focus on non-traumatic aspects of our lives, and gain strength, during some forms of crisis. It seems likely to me that sublimations (like Fromm's concept of social character) allow us to want to do what society needs us to do, and so may make it easier to develop adaptation as a fundamental approach to life. This may make some problematic situations easier to bear.

Of course, defenses have many consequences, and no generalization about them will be true in all specific situations. But what I would suggest is that a capacity for using *all* the defensive maneuvers, rather than an *over-reliance on any one defense*, probably better equips us for the suffering life brings. I believe that all my speculations about the defenses and their impact on suffering are only hypotheses, but I find it intriguing to wonder how our psychic equipment affects our ability to cope with the sorrows and challenges of our particular lives. In the toughest moments of our lives, our signature coping styles may interact with the nature of the crisis in ways that affect our resilience.

I conclude with a statement by Paul Kalanithi (2016) as his life was ending. His self-reflection does not claim that joy can emerge from suffering but, rather, that it can exist side by side with it, with neither cancelled by the other. He and his wife, Lucy, had decided to have a child when they knew he didn't have long to live. Their daughter, Elizabeth Acadia (Cady), was born about nine months before Paul died. Paul wanted to leave Cady a message about herself, something she could reflect on when she was old enough. Here is the message he left for her.

> When you come to one of the many moments in life where you must give an account of yourself, provide a ledger of what you have been, and done, and meant to the world, do not, I pray, discount that you filled a dying man's days with a sated joy, a joy unknown to me in all my prior years, a joy that does not hunger for more and more, but rests satisfied. In this time, right now, that is an enormous thing.

(p. 199)

In an epilogue to Paul's book, his wife Lucy wrote that although her experiences during the last period of his life were "difficult—sometimes almost impossible—they have also been the most beautiful and profound of my life, requiring the daily act of holding life and death, joy and pain in balance and exploring new depths of gratitude and love" (p. 219).

References

Amichai, Y. (2016). Open closed open. In H. M. Seiden (Ed.), *The motive for metaphor* (pp. 4–7). London: Karnac.

Arnold, M. (2016). Dover beach. In H. M. Seiden (Ed.), *The motive for metaphor* (pp. 14–15). London: Karnac.

Baer, U. (2005). *The poet's guide to the wisdom of Rilke*. New York: Modern Library.

Becker, E. (1973). *The denial of death*. New York: Free Press.

Beckett, S. (1955). *The unnamable*. New York: Alfred A. Knopf.

Bishop, E. (2016). In the waiting room. In H. M. Seiden (Ed.), *The motive for metaphor* (pp. 22–25). London: Karnac.

Bromberg, P. (1998). *Standing in the spaces: Essays on clinical practice, trauma, and dissociation*. Hillsdale, NJ: Analytic Press.

Buechler, S. (2004). *Clinical values: Emotions that guide psychoanalytic treatment*. Hillsdale, NJ: Analytic Press.

Buechler, S. (2008). *Making a difference in patients' lives*. New York: Routledge.

Buechler, S. (2010). No pain, no gain? Suffering and the analysis of defense. *Contemporary Psychoanalysis, 46*, 334–354.

Buechler, S. (2012). *Still practicing: The heartaches and joys of a clinical career*. New York: Routledge.

Buechler, S. (2015). *Understanding and treating patients in clinical psychoanalysis: Lessons from literature*. New York: Routledge.

Buechler, S. (2017). *Psychoanalytic reflections: Training and practice*. New York: IPbooks.

Burack-Weiss, A. (2015). *The lioness in winter: Writing an old woman's life*. New York: Columbia University Press.

Casey, N. (Ed.) (2001). *Unholy ghost: Writers on depression*. New York: HarperCollins.

Dark, A. E. (1994). In the gloaming. In J. Updike & K. Kenison (Eds.), *The best American short stories of the century* (pp. 688–704). New York: Houghton Mifflin.

Didion, J. (2005). *The year of magical thinking*. New York: Alfred A. Knopf.

Douthat, R. (2017, 29 October). The misery filter. *New York Times Sunday Review*, p. 9.

Eliot, T. S. (1943). East coker. In *Four quartets* (pp. 23–32). New York: Harcourt, Inc.

Frankl, V. (1946). *Man's search for meaning*. New York: Simon and Schuster.

Fromm, E. (1976). *To have or to be?* (R. N. Anshen, Ed.). New York: Harper and Row.

Hilgers, L. (2017, 5 November). Let's open up about addiction and recovery. *New York Times Sunday Review*, p. 3.

Hollis, J. (1996). *Swamplands of the soul: New life in dismal places*. Toronto: Inner City Books.

Izard, C. (1977). *Human emotions*. New York: Plenum Press.

Jones, T. (1999). I want to live. In J. Updike & K. Keniston (Eds.), *The best American short stories of the century* (pp. 671–687). New York: Houghton Mifflin.

Kalanithi, P. (2016). *When breath becomes air*. New York: Random House.

Krystal, H. (1975). Affect tolerance. *Annual of Psychoanalysis*, *3*, 179–217.

May, R. (1953). *Man's search for himself*. New York: W. W. Norton & Company, Inc.

Mukherjee, B. (1992). The management of grief. In J. C. Oates (Ed.), *The Oxford book of American short stories* (pp. 697–713). New York: Oxford University Press.

Munro, A. (1991). Mrs. Cross and Mrs. Kidd. In *The moons of Jupiter* (pp. 160–181). New York: Vintage.

Oliver, M. (2010). When death comes. In K. Young (Ed.), *The art of losing: Poems of grief and healing* (p. 269). New York: Bloomsbury.

Orange, D. (2010). *Thinking for clinicians: Philosophical resources for contemporary psychoanalysis and the humanistic psychotherapies*. New York: Routledge.

Orange, D. (2016). *Nourishing the inner life of clinicians and humanitarians: The ethical turn in psychoanalysis*. New York: Routledge.

Ornstein, A., & Goldman, S. (2004). *My mother's eyes: Holocaust memories of a young girl*. Cincinnati, OH: Emmis Books.

Shepard, S. (2017). *Spy of the first person*. New York: Alfred A. Knopf.

Sullivan, H. S. (1953). *The interpersonal theory of psychiatry*. New York: W. W. Norton.

Winnicott, D. W. (1971). *Playing and reality*. London: Tavistock.

Chapter 10

Training

How do we nurture the capacity to inspire health? In this chapter, I describe some of the roadblocks, confusions, and misconceptions that can make this process even more difficult than it is inherently. I offer some suggestions that I think might have better results. But first, I want to tell something of my own training experience. I will then use it to explore, in more general terms, the trajectory of the developing clinician's capacity to be of genuine help to patients struggling with life's greatest challenges. In addition to my personal experience, I am also relying on what I have heard from candidates and graduates in my many years of supervising at several pre- and post-doctoral institutes.

My experience of training

Trained by students of Erich Fromm, H. S. Sullivan, and Frieda Fromm-Reichmann, I frequently look to them for guidance. Often, I find inspiration in their passionate dedication to facilitating their patients' progress toward healthier, richer lives. I discussed the contributions of each in Chapter 5. Taken together, these three analysts contributed greatly to the foundation of Interpersonal psychoanalysis. While they used different words, I think there was some significant overlap in their messages about healthy functioning. In this section, I explore how I believe the legacy of each of these Interpersonal analysts has affected my own professional development.

My personal H. S. Sullivan

Sullivan was my hero during my graduate school days and beyond. Looking back, I think his work provided a singular voice of hope. While others exhorted, Sullivan inspired through his profound dedication to his patients' welfare. I was struggling to find some way of bearing the bleak conditions and searing tragedies in inpatient facilities. I worked in New York State and Veterans' Administration hospitals. The walls were dingy, the professional staff mainly burnt out, the patients in varying states of mind. Some, recently released from military service in Vietnam, were not psychotic but were intensely angry. Many had lost their spirits, in addition to limbs or other body parts. In one hospital, the average stay was 20 years. Many patients had not taken their medication in years. They found creative ways to dispose of it, some feeding it to the cats that roved the hospital grounds.

I was unprepared for these jobs, in many senses. I knew very little theory about psychological treatment, psychosis, or any related field. The hospital environment was unfamiliar. I had little standing as a professional and no confidence as an "authority." I was young, emotionally intense, and highly impressionable. I looked around for mentors but found only nurses, social workers, psychologists, and psychiatrists who were counting the hours until they could leave work. Most of my graduate-school teachers had never been inside a mental hospital. I felt they frowned on the work I was doing, as though I had put myself in a compromising position by "dirtying my hands" with a lowly inpatient job.

Sullivan was a beacon in this bleak picture. I started to read his work early in my career and quickly arranged a tutorial to study his thinking in depth. Here was someone who believed even patients in chronic wards were "more simply human than otherwise!" Here was someone who thought he could actually help them! Sullivan's utter conviction that one could become an "expert" in interpersonal relations and help patients move toward healthier living inspired me.

Sullivan (1953) provided several versions of his idea, which he called the "one genus postulate." In *The Interpersonal Theory of Psychiatry*, he said:

> I have become occupied with the science, not of individual differences, but of human identities, or parallels, one might say. In other words, I try to study the degrees and patterns of things which I assume to be ubiquitously human.
>
> (p. 33)

The more memorable version states that, "everyone is much more simply human than otherwise . . ." (p. 32). I think he is saying something important in this postulate.

As I look back about half a century later, I think there were several aspects of Sullivan's perspective that heartened me. A product of mid-century America, Sullivan espoused a fundamentally "can do" philosophy. The one genus postulate, in itself, inspired me in its humanistic intention and hopefulness. The ranting patient in front of me in the day room of the State hospital who frightened me was a human being, more like than unlike other people I knew. He had been an infant and had a history. He was born needing contact with other people, however he acted toward them now. Perhaps if I treated him with these beliefs in mind, I could reach him.

Many experiences reinforced the interpersonal perspective for me. For example, one patient wouldn't speak to me but played the song "For Once in My Life" every time I walked on the ward. However strange and limited it was, we had a relationship. Sullivan's thinking communicated respect, for my patients and for the work I was trying to do. I was very young and idealistic. I needed a sense that what I was doing was worthwhile. Beyond that, I think it told me that I could use what I *did* know (about myself and others) to begin to understand my "simply human" patients. They were not a foreign species. It began to feel both possible, and worthwhile, to stretch to try to reach them emotionally.

Much later in my career, I took further steps to become more of an "expert" in interpersonal relations from a Sullivanian perspective. I entered training at the William Alanson White Institute in New York and chose as my training analyst and supervisors faculty who, themselves, had been trained by Sullivan and Fromm. I was very eager to develop competence and confidence that I had a viable way to work with my patients. I deliberately chose to train with people who identified as "Interpersonalists" and sought to develop a definable style of working in that tradition. For me, this meant that I was taught what Levenson might call an algorithm of treatment. It included frame setting as a first phase of the work. I include in frame setting trying to be as clear as possible about both participants' expectations. The next phase consists of taking a rather extensive history. It lays the groundwork for later understandings.

While each treatment and each history is different, we usually try to find out about the patient's life experiences at home, at school, and, later, work, and with friends and later partners. I usually start a history by asking about "the situation you were born into." This is just as much a statement as a question. We were all born into an environment, an interpersonal, social, geographic, temporal context, which will affect our experience growing up. The bulk of the treatment is called the detailed inquiry. In it, Sullivan emphasizes staying in touch with even minute shifts in the patient's level of anxiety. I would broaden that to include staying in touch with shifts in my own anxiety, and shifts in intensity of all the fundamental emotions in each participant. Fundamental emotions include curiosity, joy, sadness, disgust, anger, fear, shame, guilt, and contempt. During the detailed inquiry, interpersonal patterns get clarified. My way of talking about this is to try to understand what recurs in the patient's interpersonal life. I hope to inspire the patient's curiosity about him or herself. I believe that a great deal of treatment really occurs outside the session, as the patient notices reactions, interactions, and feelings that might have gone unnoticed previously. As I have written many times, I believe that it is principally life experience that cures people, but treatment can make more life experience possible. My hope is that the way we live the session together, and the enhanced self-awareness and appreciation of emotional nuance, will facilitate more life outside the session. This way of working can make the treatment a true collaboration. Each participant has a crucial role. Neither can function without the other. But, perhaps just as important, *each can conceivably fulfill their function, with effort.*

My training emphasized the importance of a termination phase, with effort put into looking back over the work we have done, noting what has helped, what has not, and what we each feel is still to be accomplished, possibly through experiences other than treatment. From these ideas and my own experience, clinical and otherwise, I have developed the belief that, mainly, it is life experience that has the power to cure. Nothing we can do in 45 minutes a few times a week has as much impact. Of course, we become part of the patient's life experience. Equally important is that, as already noted, treatment can help make more life experience possible. But I will wager that if you think back in your own life, you will see that life experience is what changed you most.

What does working this way do for the patient and the clinician emotionally? I think it can greatly contribute to both participants' confidence that the treatment can improve the patient's life experience. Having a relatively clear sense of the goals and phases of the work helped me feel like more of an "expert" and, I think, fortified me and enabled me to communicate to the patient that our work had purpose, direction, and a good chance for a life-enhancing outcome. (For some of the drawbacks of this approach, see Chapter 5.) Initially laying the groundwork with history-taking and careful inquiry gives the treatment pair something to do while the transference develops. No one is born knowing how to be a patient (or a clinician). It can be a relief to have a job to do. Even the neophyte clinician can feel relatively competent at taking a history. Once that groundwork is laid, it is possible to make multi-dimensional interpretations. That is, if something comes up in three domains—the history, the treatment relationship, and the patient's outside interpersonal life—it literally feels substantial. For example, a patient of mine needed to minimize his feelings, most especially distress. We developed a language for it: that whatever happened was "no big deal." Going over his history together helped us see this pattern. I think seeing it in all three realms made it feel substantial to both of us. The phrase "no big deal" lives on in the patient's memory (and my own) long after the treatment has ended. Phrases like that help the patient (and me) create a relationship, in that any intimate relationship has a special language, words or phrases that have a particular meaning to us. These phrases often operate like magnets, drawing momentary experiences to them and helping create a sense of coherence. Thus, when the patient's father asked him to make a major sacrifice for the family, and he felt compelled to deny what it would cost him, I said to him, "What your father is asking is no big deal," and he knew exactly what I meant. It was a moment of closeness for both of us. I believe it had much more meaning because of all the work that we had done in exploring his history. I hope that, in the years to come, the phrase helps him notice some moments that he might have missed and feel more whole, more coherent to himself.

For clinicians, having done thousands of histories helps us have a kind of base point. When something seems to me glaringly absent, I am more likely to notice it. I pay special attention to what seems to recur in the patient's interpersonal life. Over time, we will try to understand this more fully. I usually do a two-session consult to allow both me and the patient some time away from each other to think about whether we want to work together. Once we decide to try, in one of the next sessions, I usually ask the patient to start working on a timeline at home. In my training, I was taught to explain why this is important and to ask the patient to take a piece of paper and write down dates of events that had an impact on them, with a few words explaining what happened. If the Mets winning a game had an impact, write it down. We will go over each event and fill in more details about that period of their life. If, for example, as happened with a patient, she left out a brother from her history, I should notice this and, perhaps, comment on it. It takes tact to feel out what to ask about and what to leave alone for the moment.

The inspiring story and clinical legacy of Frieda Fromm-Reichmann

As a model of absolute dedication, and what I would later describe as clinical values (Buechler, 2004), no one had more influence on me than Frieda Fromm-Reichmann (who was always called, simply, Frieda). Although I never met her, her impact on my own analyst, and my teachers and supervisors, was unmistakable. In what follows, I describe some of the values I think her legend conveyed. (For further discussion of her work, see Chapter 5.)

In my training, no one epitomized the power of determined dedication more than the much-fabled Frieda. Perhaps more than anyone else, she was held up to us as an example of what sheer conviction, stamina, and perseverance can do. Frieda Fromm-Reichmann verbalized her strong beliefs about what constituted emotional health and enacted them in her work with patients. I believe the strength of these convictions greatly contributed to her therapeutic effectiveness.

How did she become such a powerful presence? For the biographical data in this section, I am relying on Gail Hornstein's (2000) excellent book. A German Jew, Frieda was born to Adolf and Klara Reichmann on October 23, 1889, about ten months after her parents' marriage. From early in her life, she used her talent for understanding emotional nuances to help soothe hurt feelings in those around her. Hornstein suggests that Frieda's parents needed her to succeed to make up for their own failures. From a very young age, she became a confidante for each of her parents, trying to reconcile each of them to the foibles of the other.

The academic, moral, and behavioral expectations for Frieda and her two younger sisters were very high, but Frieda mostly rose to the challenge. Adolf wanted Frieda, his oldest daughter, to go to medical school, and, over her mother's objections, she did.

Frieda began her medical training in 1908, the first year women were admitted to Königsberg's university, the Albertina. Some of the professors were openly antagonistic to teaching women, putting Frieda, among others, through humiliating trials. Frieda responded with a determination to excel in all her courses and she succeeded. Encounters with patients, in which she could intuit her own talent for reaching even the most disturbed, convinced her to go into psychiatry. But in 1914, the war interrupted Frieda's plans for further study. She was offered a job at a Königsberg neurological clinic, which was hastily formed to deal with the huge number of brain-injured veterans. When she was ordered to leave the hospital because the Russian army had surrounded Königsberg, Frieda refused, unwilling to allow anything to interfere with her care of the soldiers. After the war, she moved to Frankfort to study neurology with Kurt Goldstein. Frieda clearly absorbed Goldstein's ideology, most especially his emphasis on experimenting with ways to help patients and sometimes courageously taking risks. After two years, Frieda returned to Königsberg and studied the methods of "psychotherapy," as they were then understood, under Johannes Heinrich Schulz. Discovering Freud's writings, Frieda determined to train at Karl Abraham's institute in Berlin. During this period, Frieda was deeply affected by becoming friends with Georg Groddeck, whose methods were original, if not orthodox. He believed in using any method that brought out the patient's self-healing capacities. Frieda was unstinting in her lifelong gratitude for the chance to learn from him. In particular, she felt encouraged in her belief that part of her responsibility was to offer her patients hope. Frieda's humanistic approach was also shaped by her study of the writings of Sándor Ferenczi.

Frieda's approach embodied her irrepressible hope, determination, hard work, and strong belief in the patient's inherent self-curing powers. She integrated these attitudes with the values she learned from her Judaic background. Eventually, she moved to Heidelberg to start her own sanitarium.

A year after her father died in an elevator accident, Frieda began an affair with Erich Fromm, who had been her patient, and eventually they married. But their relationship was full of conflict. After a short time, Erich, who was diagnosed with tuberculosis, left for treatment for this condition, and Frieda and Erich never lived together again.

In 1933, realizing she was in terrible danger from the Nazis, Frieda escaped to Strasbourg, forced to leave behind most of her possessions except a few things that she was able to salvage. But, sensing she was still in danger, she fled, first to Palestine, and then to the United States in 1935, where she got a job at Chestnut Lodge in Rockville, Maryland, and started a new life. Chestnut Lodge was a mental hospital that specialized in the psychoanalysis of psychotic patients. In this phase of her life, Frieda was totally dedicated to her career. She had a cottage on the grounds of the hospital and made little separation between her personal and professional activities.

Frieda supported many of her relatives during the war, including her mother, who had resisted leaving Germany, and consequently missed the chance to come to the United States and was stranded in London. While her immediate family survived, more than 100 of Frieda's relatives were killed by the Nazis. During these years, Frieda worked tirelessly, perhaps partially out of survivor's guilt, certainly out of a need for money, and, clearly, out of a passionate desire to be of help to her patients.

Once at the Lodge, Frieda was able to enlist others, including Harry Stack Sullivan, in her efforts to save colleagues, friends, and their families from the Nazis. Sullivan became one of her closest friends and taught a four-year seminar at Chestnut Lodge. Both clinicians were extraordinarily able to reach even the most disturbed patients. Focusing on the interpersonal nature of treatment, they became intensely interested in each other's ideas. Frieda paid homage to Freud's groundbreaking discoveries, but her treatment style differed from Freud's in significant ways including, of course, the question of the analyst's neutrality.

In 1950, Frieda published her major work, *Principles of Intensive Psychotherapy* (1950). Colleagues agree that she saw treatment as a mutual adventure, urged her patients to guide the process, and had an unshakable belief in psychotherapy.

Time after time, she refused to give up on her patients, going to extraordinary lengths to reach them. As may be expected, she couldn't reach them all, which led to disappointments for both participants. But, like Ferenczi, she worked tirelessly and suffered greatly on their behalf. Hornstein suggests that her extreme dedication may have shortened her own life. But, in addition to the patients she reached, she also had a significant impact on a whole generation of young clinicians.

Frieda Fromm-Reichmann's sense of purpose

What is the legacy that Frieda left for future generations of clinicians? Surely, part of it is her embodiment of certain attitudes toward life in general and treatment in particular. For example, even her detractors saw her clinical work and writing as expressing an abiding sense of purpose. As I understand it, having a strong sense of purpose requires that the analyst embrace several seemingly contradictory truths (Buechler, 2004). Clinical work occurs in a particular time and place but also, in a sense, outside time. It is based on a profound acceptance of patients as they are now and a powerful need for change to occur. It attempts to know the ultimately unknowable unconscious. It is an interpersonal process where two equal human beings play very different roles that can, at times, feel hierarchical. The analyst is paid as an "expert" in a process that, by definition, is largely ineffable.

Training is the process whereby clinicians learn to hold these seemingly contradictory truths simultaneously. Hopefully, at the same time, they are learning to embody a sense of purpose and inspire it in their patients.

The need to experience our work as having purpose is embedded in a set of fundamental clinical values that clinicians absorb from our professional culture. This sense of purpose includes an expectation that the work will be meaningful. The clinician's sense of purpose is most often expressed in what we privilege. That is, our attitude of purposefulness shows itself in a focus that looks for meaning and both embraces and eradicates time. For me, Frieda embodied the strengths these attitudes can inspire, as well as their personal costs and, perhaps especially for the young clinician in training, the ever-present danger of overestimating what treatment can provide.

The inspiring legacy of Erich Fromm

As I discussed in Chapter 5, Erich Fromm epitomizes the strengths and potential pitfalls of fervently championing one's personal vision of health. Here I will mention some aspects of Fromm's writing that I think had the most profound effect on my own development.[1]

1 In health, we experience life directly. We feel our feelings, rather than *look at* our feelings from the outside. We are in our lives, rather than ego-invested and worried about our image. This eliminates the problem of anxiety. "If a person has really woken up—if a person has really seen the reality of his Self, has thrown away most of his Ego, then indeed there is no need to compensate for anxiety any more, because there isn't any" (Fromm, 2009, p. 19).

2 Another statement is that we are healthy to the degree that our life-oriented passions (passion for love, interest in the world, in people, in nature, in reality, pleasure in thinking, and artistic interest) prevail against "the archaic passions: intense destructiveness, intense fixation to the mother, and extreme narcissism" (pp. 42–43).

3 In what I see as a very significant departure from other theories, Fromm advocates *creating* a conflict between the patient's childlike, irrational passions and his or her more adult rational strivings. The picture he paints is of the analyst stirring this conflict, rather than aiming to resolve already existing conflicts. In this context, health is a state in which the adult aspect of the patient holds sway. Fromm sees other approaches as inadequate if they address only the child or only the adult. In treatment, we fan the flames of this conflict with vivid, evocative images and experiences in the session. As Fromm put it, we "help the patient be unhappy rather than to encourage him" (p. 51). Since suffering is a part of life, Fromm sees the direction of health as moving toward inhabiting it, rather than avoiding it. Elsewhere (Buechler, 2010), I have written about three attitudes toward suffering that I think significantly affect the clinician's work. Fromm's attitude about suffering clearly distinguishes him from those who see the suffering, itself, as the problem. For Fromm, the problem is not so much the suffering itself as the ways we try to avoid it.

4 It is important to Fromm that we have a vision of how our lives could be. Human beings need a dream to augment our passionate pursuit of health.

5 *The way the analyst focuses is an expression of values, intentions, and feelings.* Reading Rainer Funk's (2009) paper "Direct Meeting," I was struck by his description of how much Fromm expressed in his way of establishing eye contact. In Funk's words: "His gaze corresponded to his way of being interested in my inner life, my soul" (p. 61). This reminded me of an experience of my own. As a candidate, I volunteered to present a case to Alberta Szalita in an all-day conference at W. A. White Institute. The day was unforgettable and formative for me. The unwavering intensity of her focus on me was palpable. I felt as though her eyes reached into my innermost being and saw into me as one can see into clear water, to its very depths.

6 *The importance of attempting to "heighten the immediate reality and concreteness of the situation" as the patient talks about an experience.* Reading an article by David E. Schecter (2009) felt truly resonant with my own perspective. He describes some of Fromm's methods for connecting the patient with immediate experience in words that recall to me some of the advice I have so frequently given supervisees. I can't count the number of times I have told them that it doesn't have much impact to develop a fine, abstract theory about the patient, with the patient. Experience is what changes people.

7 *The centrality of the analyst's courage.* Ruth M. Lesser (2009) described Fromm as expressing how much courage it takes to be an analyst. This has been a central theme in my own writing.

8 *The importance of embracing the paradox that human beings express our-selves in characteristic patterns, and nothing human is alien to us all, but we are also very much individuals.* In much of Fromm's work, I now see the effort to recognize patterns that recur in human beings, but also acknowledge each person's unique individuality. Holding the tension between these view-points has always challenged me in teaching the course on diagnosis at W. A. White Institute.

9 Fromm's emphasis on values directly influenced my own writing, especially in my book *Clinical Values* (Buechler, 2004). His attitude of cherishing truth deeply affected me. I have often asked supervisees to voice "inconvenient truths" and become "radical truth tellers."

10 My belief that clinicians should aim for *relatively non-narcissistic* invest-ments in our patients now seems to me not unlike Fromm's (2009) way of expressing "central relatedness." In his words:"Then I do not think about myself, then my Ego does not stand in my way" (p. 18).

11 I love Fromm's (2009) way of trying to make sure he doesn't promise patients more than he can deliver. In his words: "When you come to me, I will be completely open to you, and I shall respond with all the chords in myself which are touched by the chords in yourself. That is all we can promise, and that is a promise we can keep" (pp. 26–27).

12 My thinking about the role of empathy in treatment has evolved a great deal over time. I think it has circled closer to Fromm's. I love what Harold Davis (2009) wrote about Fromm: "His directness was a means of being in touch with a person without physically touching; the essence of empathy" (p. 87).

Fromm's passionate promotion of passion in treatment directly affected my work. His privileging of the power of human feeling has always very much appealed to me. His thinking about hope, his open promotion of biophilia, his distaste for cliché, canned interpretations, and sentiment, his compassionate humanism, his willingness to take positions and stand up for what he believed in, his champion-ing of freedom, have moved me all my adult life.

Helping clinicians develop as therapeutic instruments

In their earliest years, clinicians in training may experience conflicting injunc-tions. For example, their patients may clamor for direct advice about how to conduct their lives, but teachers, supervisors, and others warn against giving concrete advice. Or patients may want help getting their defenses to operate more smoothly, while faculty define progress as a decreasing reliance on those defenses. Or patients want treatment to focus on getting "past" mourning a loss, while supervisors encourage supervisees to help their patients better tolerate being in mourning.

Other conflicts are particularly common in analytic training. The supervisee is coached to foster the patient's increased self-reflection, while patients are invested in changing the behavior of others in their lives. Often, patients are impatient with insight as a goal, wanting their lives to feel different. They want more success, in love and work, and not just better understanding of what tends to recur. Many want to feel less angry, less anxious, less sorrow, less envy, fear, shame, guilt, loneliness, and other painful emotions. They want more fulfilling lives *now*. But supervisees are encouraged to help their patients privilege long-term over short-term change.

As we might predict, there are many ways of coping with these competing pulls. Some try to please supervisors when they are in supervision and patients when they are doing treatment. I think it is worth asking just what is learned under these circumstances. I would suggest that the results may include some very negative feelings about one's professional integrity.

Of course, some are less eager to please both their supervisors and their patients. They may not feel much conflict, or they may find the opposing pulls challenging in a positive sense.

Some view treatment as the application of techniques and so may not "tune in" to any of these issues. Interestingly, I don't think this attitude is a product of any one theoretical orientation. While it is easiest to imagine more behavioral or cognitive theories as lending themselves to this attitude, I don't believe it is limited to their adherents. Analytic candidates can also hunger for techniques that can be applied in a relatively unvarying approach.

But I think most early career clinicians do experience some conflict. Their patients ask them how to meet a partner, what to say to the boss, how much to conform to their parents' demands, how to discipline their children, whether to "compromise" more with their partners, how to find a balance of their priorities in their daily lives, and so on. Faculty make it clear that:

1   We don't really know how to answer these questions.
2   Even if we did, we shouldn't "gratify" patients' desires for answers. Patients would then keep expecting to be gratified, whenever questions arise in their lives.
3   Supplying answers won't help patients find their own paths, become more self-reliant, and develop greater self-confidence.
4   The clinician operates to help the patient get in touch with the obstacles that block finding their own answers. Supplying answers won't serve that purpose.
5   The clinician who "indulges" patients with advice is suffering from an unanalyzed neurotic problem. He or she may be "grandiose" and think of doing treatment as their chance to be a savior. Or, they might have a masochistic streak that fosters submitting to bullying patients' demands. Possibly, they may be over-identifying with the patients' sense of entitlement to answers or sense of urgency. The budding clinician might be too vulnerable to patients' depictions of their situation as a crisis that warrants waving aside the usual rules and roles.

I am sure that readers can think of other objections to direct advice-giving that faculty frequently cite. Each of these might be valid to some degree in some situations. And yet, with great regularity, patients demand advice, direction, concrete help coping with the challenges life presents to us all. No one stays a stranger to aging, mourning, uncertainty, and all the other aspects of life considered in this book. In preparing clinicians to field these questions, I think we can do better than advocating no advising, all the while knowing the pressures on young clinicians to keep patients in treatment, for therapeutic, educational, and financial reasons. The long-term results of this conflict can include the clinician's sense of fraudulence, ineffectiveness, and insufficient integrity. Regardless of whether the clinician gives advice and fails to mention it in supervision, or tries to convince the patient not to want the advice, the clinician often doesn't emerge with a sense of professional competence.

Asking for concrete advice is just one example of patients' wishes when faced with serious challenges. The aging, or mourning, or deeply confused person, the profoundly lonely or spiritually lost person, the human being facing hardship, may yearn for comfort in any of a number of forms. Perhaps they hope the clinician will share experiences of facing similar difficulties. Or maybe they hope for a bit of wisdom or an inspiring story. Or perhaps what would be most precious is space, an hour to pour out feelings without concern for their impact on anyone else. Or maybe what is most wanted is sympathy, perhaps even more than empathy. The great yearning may be a desire for a sense of being "in it" together.

But even if patients hope for these responses, the clinician may not feel it is best to satisfy these wishes. The question I am raising in this chapter is, how do we educate clinicians to become better able to face patients' demands/requests/ pleas/desires? One answer is already clear. We do not help them if we foster a feeling that they have to keep their "gratifications" of their patients a secret from their supervisors and others in positions of authority. I think that is obvious. But, in a more positive sense, how can we best prepare the clinician for a career that is bound to include many moments of facing these requests?

In order to feel competent, the beginning clinician often yearns for "techniques," for theories that direct choices in sessions. Early in a clinical career (and later on, as well), the task can seem bewildering. We are faced with countless choices every moment about whether, when, and how to respond. Nothing really prepares us for many of our interchanges with patients. And yet, a lot can be at stake. A patient can really be on the verge of committing suicide. A child can be, or seem to be, on the edge of lifelong addiction. Our response (whether silent or verbalized) can feel as though it might have long-lasting consequences. Naturally, like any other human beings, we would like to know what we are doing. We may even feel as though we have made an implicit promise that we will know just by agreeing to "treat" someone. This makes it very tempting to believe in a series of "techniques," rules to follow faithfully. Much like any other belief system, they may seem to provide a path toward salvation.

Let me emphasize that I am not just referring to the more obvious systems of "techniques," such as behavioral or cognitive behavioral methods. Any set of rules has the same allure and inherent pitfall, from my point of view. Whether we are taught, as I was, a series of procedures, such as history-taking followed by "detailed inquiry," or analysis of transference/defense/working through, or living out and repairing empathic failures, all give structure and direction to an inherently confusing task. Even the injunction to make unconscious conscious, or to confront dissociation, or reduce anxiety, or "resolve" Oedipal issues has a similar objective. Each of these prescriptions reduces the chaos of the lived moment. Perhaps more accurately, each places the moment in a setting that defines its meaning within a preordained theoretical framework. Some believe that where id was ego shall be, while others define treatment's goals as enhanced self-knowledge, self-confidence, self-esteem, or some other good result. All of these and other goals can operate like a compass, orienting the clinician and funneling his or her moment-by-moment perceptions in a certain direction. If, for example, my patient tells me she was disappointed in me last session, I can hear her as expressing negative transferential feelings. This places the moment into a conceptual framework. Depending on my training and many other factors, I can perceive the moment as having a meaning that implicitly confirms my professional worldview. I may have the comforting feeling that I am on a well-traveled road. Analytic explorers before me have charted the path, and I have only to study the maps they provided and follow along. Suddenly, a moment that could have unhinged me, that might have thrown me down a rabbit hole, has acquired direction. It is this, and not that.

Lest this sound as though I am suggesting we abandon all efforts to teach a theory of technique, let me make clear that:

1   Enough of a sense of comfort, competence, and security is obviously necessary for the clinician to function.
2   No clinical perception is possible without some pre-existing conceptual framework, whether or not it has been consciously formulated.
3   Some concepts that provide guidance, such as the idea of the frame and its restrictions, are absolutely necessary.

But the education that I am advocating is an education about the human condition. Anything less is not adequate to the task. This is made much more difficult by our compartmentalizing educational system, especially in my own country (USA) at least, as I have experienced it.

However, I don't want to join the many grumblers about our "trade school" mentality, however much I may sympathize with them. I tend to feel we each take an over-determined position about the best preparation for a clinical career. Our attitude is shaped by our own characters, our defensive proclivities, as well as our personal, professional, and cultural experiences. If, in my (professional and wider) culture, with my (childhood and adult) experiences, in my (personal and therapeutic) setting, I ascribe to a particular way of working, it must serve my needs in many ways.

What is especially ironic and potentially highly significant about this is that, for each clinician with each patient, *our way of negotiating with our theoretical heritage plays out, in front of the patient, some of the very same issues that the patient faces in their own life*. That is, just as the patient, facing aging, mourning, uncertainty, hardship, and other human situations, must continually find and re-find a position regarding adaptation, emotional intensity, and verbal formulation, so must the clinician. Every minute of every session is an opportunity to live these issues out loud.

A patient tells me how painfully disappointed she was in her partner's holiday gift. It is (at least partially) within her conscious awareness that she is wondering how much to adapt to his gift-giving smoothly, making no fuss. Should she prioritize a harmonious moment or the expression of what she is feeling? If she does choose to tell him about her disappointment, should she wait until she can speak calmly, without any intense emotion in her voice? Is it most important that she tell him (and herself) in words, or are there other, equally effective ways to communicate her feelings?

The same questions can be asked about the patient's choices in the session *talking about* this incident. How does she understand her role in the session and what "adaptation" to it would require of her? For example, in order to fulfill this role, is she required to be curious about her own expectations of her partner and the part they played in the interchange? Does she feel she is *supposed to* tell the story at a particular emotional pitch? Does everything significant need to be formulated in words, or can some aspects be expressed in tone, innuendo, or even silence? In every walk of life, we meet challenges about how much to adapt, how to bear intense feelings, and how much to formulate experience into words. These questions are with us as we grow up, as we age, as patients on our analyst's couch, and as analysts listening to our patients.

The fact that the same issues face analysts and our patients adds to the complexity (but, also, to the opportunities) inherent in sessions. Every moment can be seen as a dance, in which two people adapt to each other to a degree, express their emotions to a degree, and formulate their experiences in words to a degree. In fact, any interchange between people can be viewed through this lens, but, unlike most interactions, treatment is a form of relating that looks at itself (at least it should, from my point of view).

I would like to examine the very mundane situation created when my patient expresses her disappointment about her husband's holiday gift. I am leaving out all the details about our personal histories and the history of the treatment relationship. While this myriad of details is all relevant to understanding what happens in the session, here I am just using the moment to stand in for an infinite variety of implicit questions that occur in sessions. In describing her husband's gift and her own reaction, I think my patient is indirectly asking me whether or not her response is warranted. Should she have been more satisfied with the piece of jewelry he chose for her, even though it is not her style and she suspects he had the salesperson pick it out?

In other words, in her marriage, how much should she choose to harmonize with her husband, smoothly fitting in with his hopes for her response? Should she take what (at least on the surface) looks like the easier road and heartily thank him? Should she tell herself that she is lucky she has a husband who bothers to get her a gift at all and say thank you to him and, in a sense, to life? Should she put the moment in perspective, reminding herself of the millions who go to bed hungry, remembering her own mother, for whom gifts of any kind were a rarity? Or should she tell herself that she has worked very hard, in her treatment and elsewhere, to feel entitled to a voice, so she should give that voice this chance to be heard?

Even if my patient decides to voice her disappointment, there is still the question of the intensity that is "warranted." Is it a sign of progress if she tries to find a modulated, careful way to express herself, waiting until she can master anguished cries of pain? Should we count ourselves successful in our work together if she can temper her feelings by silently telling herself something like: "What I feel is really not just about this gift. It stems from much of my experience as a child. It would not be fair to take it all out on my husband."

Further, should we see it as progress if she can formulate her feelings into words, for herself, for her husband if she chooses to tell him, and for us in the session? Can we consider it a victory for our work if she can call her feeling "disappointment," rather than something less specific, like "I didn't like it" or "I wasn't happy?"

We can ask the same questions as we look at what transpires in the session. Does my patient try to adapt to what she thinks I expect? For example, does she couch her story with something like: "I know my own issues played a part in how this felt?" In other words, in the telling, how much does the patient adapt to me and the analytic culture and values I represent? How much does she try to fit herself into the mold of "good patient?" And if she feels as disappointed with my "gifts" to her as she is with her husband's, if she feels *they* were not chosen for her, with her in mind, does she say anything about that? That is, just as she feels the jewelry might have been selected by the salesperson, does she also feel that I give her generic psychotherapeutic help that has not been crafted specifically for her? Even if she chooses to let herself say something about this, does she try to sound "reasonable," stifling the intensity of a hurt cry? Does she wait until she can formulate words that are well-considered and considerate, with feelings tucked into phrases that make grammatical sentences?

We can add to the complexity of the moment by thinking about how much the *patient* is giving *me* a hand-crafted gift that has me in mind. That is, in how she tells me the story, is she thoughtfully fitting in with her recipient's style? In other words, is she carefully telling me her story in a manner that conforms with the way she knows I like to hear stories, adapting to my needs, keeping emotions at intensity levels that she knows are bearable for me, formulating thoughts clearly enough for me to grasp, pitching the story so it is interesting but not too threatening for me to hear? Has she (mostly unconsciously, of course) timed and articulated her story in a way that she has learned appeals to me, evokes my most empathic responses?

It is also quite possible that my patient could tell her story in a way that is perfectly attuned to what I am *least* able to hear. As she herself would say, not all gifts are well-intentioned. She might privilege not harmonizing with me, or, at least, she might privilege other goals more, like asserting her freedom to speak as she pleases. She might express herself with an unapologetic intensity of affect that announces that heights of feeling are fine with her. Or she could feel fine about intense anger and less fine about heightened sorrow or anxiety, for example. She could use any words that come to her, indirectly telling me that formulating words to communicate experiences accurately may be my goal more than it is hers. For example, she might simply say, "His gift was awful," and leave it at that. If I followed up with questions that imply it would be good for us to find more exact words for her experience, she might counter with, "It was just awful. Don't you understand?"

The same complexity attends my response. If my patient were to say, "It was just awful," *do I adapt* to her? If I am frustrated, do I allow myself to express it and, if so, how intensely? Do I try to formulate my experience in words that are exact enough to be likely to be clear to her? Or do I blurt out something like, "That's not enough!" In other words, in my response, *how do I live out my attitudes about mutual adaptation, emotional intensity of expression, and verbal formulation of experience?*

I think it is obvious that, aside from the personal experiences that have helped to make each of us who we are, societal values about marriage, relationships between men and women, and many other mores affect my patient's behavior and my own. Have we been brought up in the same culture and in the same era? Where she comes from, do people try harder to harmonize than where I come from? What did our culture, era, and personal experiences teach each of us about expressing emotional intensity, about formulating experience to communicate it to others, about getting along with other people, about being a wife, and so on? There is an endless array of factors that affect my patient and me in this moment. And, then, there is our impact on each other. Am I different from usual with this patient? Have I decided that I had better help her express her feelings fully, regardless of the effect it may have (on her husband, on me, at work, and so on)? On a less global level, within this session, did she communicate to me that she is feeling very fragile, and have I "decided" (mostly outside my awareness) to avoid confronting her, but just to try to "feel into" what it is like to be her?

Most importantly, for this chapter, what can best prepare me for this clinical exchange? Are there theories that give me guidance? Which ones? What aspects of who I am and what I have learned do I draw on in the moment? More specifically, what can help me use my inner responses to therapeutic effect? Let's say I, personally, would want to be "gracious" about such a gift, if I were in her place. Though I may well believe that I should respond neutrally, without my personal values coloring my response, as her analyst and not as her judge or an expert on social etiquette, my inner response is bound to have an impact, in my opinion. If my own, inner response closely matches hers, fewer questions may immediately come to mind. In fact, if our cultural and personal experiences, character styles, and other factors similarly incline us in situations such as this, I might not even *notice* how she responded to her husband. To use an exaggerated example, if both my patient and I came from a culture that expected wives to do everything possible to make their husbands comfortable, and my patient told me that she had simply said "thank you" for the gift, I think I would be unlikely to ask anything further. I might not even notice that she sounded sorrowful, or that I, myself, was holding back a tear. Her behavior would be so ordinary that, probably, neither of us would see it at all. While I am describing an extreme, I think patients and analysts are members of cultures that blind us, to varying degrees, to the rules we have always lived by, and we carry these blind spots into sessions as we carry them everywhere else. In that sense, neutrality can't exist.

Before I address how our education can prepare us to deal with clinical exchanges, I want to express my own astonishment at the complexity of the therapeutic task. I am outlining just a few of the issues inherent in one, ordinary, relatively uncomplicated clinical interchange. I have not brought in the many layers of my more specific knowledge of this patient's life history, as well as my own, that I think affect how we live this moment together. In my experience, sessions usually include many moments that are much more complicated. They stir echoes of all the lived experience my patient and I have had with each other. They ring of our previous mutual accommodations. They hearken back to interchanges about what each of us feels about our own "rules" set, partly, by my profession and adhered to, in my own fashion, by me. As I have suggested in other chapters in this book, much of treatment centers on issues such as aging, illness, loss, grave uncertainty, spiritual vacuums, and other inherently difficult human challenges that are bound to be hard to face for both participants in a session. In treatment, we are talking to another person about the life events that we, ourselves, have faced or may face in our own lives. What can prepare us for these encounters, every hour, every day, over the span of a clinical career?

I have written extensively about training (Buechler, 2008, 2009, 2012, 2017) and broken it down to the cognitive, emotional, and interpersonal elements. I have emphasized that not only is it important for the clinician to be self-aware in general, but it is especially significant to be aware of one's defensive proclivities, as these can result in blind spots. Most often when countertransference is discussed, reference is made to feelings, attitudes, cultural and personal experiences that lean the clinician in a certain direction or resonate with his or her past. Of course, self-awareness about anything that may bias us is extremely important. But, in my view, it is even more significant to be aware of defensive patterns that may make it impossible to focus on what is happening, within ourselves as well as interpersonally. For this purpose, nothing can substitute for one's own analysis.

What I want to add here is an appreciation of the strengths and limitations of theory as a guide to clinical process and the study of theory as preparation for a career doing treatment. In my judgment, theories help us prioritize some material over other material and, in so doing, may well make clinical work less daunting.

Studying theory may quell some of the anxiety and potential sense of fraudulence of working "by the seat of one's pants." As I wrote in 2004 (Chapter 9), each theoretical orientation probably provides a somewhat different ballast for the clinician. Briefly, Erich Fromm can facilitate a passionate sense of purpose, while H. S. Sullivan can help us become better, more secure participant/observers. With Kohut, we may gain greater appreciation for how hard it is to keep self-esteem afloat and greater empathy for the desperate measures of the permanently insecure. Each analytic pioneer offers us a prism, which may narrow the field of vision in some ways, but also clarifies it and makes us feel grounded.

I would not want to work without my "internal chorus" of internalized voices, of those who have taught me in one way or another. I am most especially indebted to the supervisors, analysts, and teachers who helped me develop an analytic identity and the confidence to hone a personally resonant style.

We also need to be acquainted with theoretical contributions to technique and, most importantly, to the concepts of the frame, boundaries, and the strengths and limitations of the therapeutic alliance. We would, quite literally, be lost without them. Every clinician I have ever taught (in whatever format) has wanted more help with these basics, no matter how well-trained and experienced they were. We all, always, have these needs, whether or not we have the courage to give them voice.

But my point in this chapter is that none of this is enough to help patients face the issues referred to in the other chapters of this book. Perhaps nothing can really prepare us. Perhaps even the thought of being "prepared" is wrong-headed. And yet, in order to be of any help to anybody, the clinician does need to feel some measure of security and competence.

So how do we prepare the young clinician to help patients face the challenges of aging, the sorrows of loss, the uncertainties of child-rearing, the profound regrets of opportunities squandered, lives forever stalled, vast unexplored landscapes? Do we just throw up our hands and say, "Their own life experience will have to teach them?"

No. I know I would not have accepted this answer when I started doing clinical work in my early 20s. I knew well enough that I was profoundly unprepared. I felt acutely enough that it might not be wise to show anyone in authority just how ill-equipped I was. But I deeply wanted to be better equipped. And I would not have simply gone away empty-handed if someone had said, "Wait until you are older. Then you will understand." I had patients to see every hour, and I couldn't tell them to wait until I was older.

In much of my more recent writing (Buechler, 2015, 2017), I have suggested learning about human character patterns from great fiction writers, like Tolstoy, Dostoevsky, Munro, and many others. They understood character so well they could embody it with mere words. And I think we can learn most about emotional challenges from great poets, like Eliot, Dickenson, Wilbur, and many others. In short, for an education about the human condition, I would go to those who made an art form out of it. We can also turn to music, sculpture, painting, and the other arts that express human feeling. No one has chronicled aging better than Rembrandt, in my opinion.

But our "training" institutions, our professional organizations, and the clatter of our daily lives make it less and less possible to get our "degrees" from these sources. Licensing boards have their standards, as they must. Even if they were to grant a Ph.D. in human suffering, the graduate would find it hard to get a job. Many prospective employers would not be impressed and would need to see credentials that can be put on Medicare forms. Furthermore, the graduate him- or herself might well feel lacking in essential skills. Once fully acquainted with life's most painful junctures, will the new clinician immerse themself in their patients' (at least seemingly) more mundane concerns?

A "training" program in helping people cope would be (inherently) subjective and might never end. Who could really prove themselves proficient? But, as I look back on my own education, I wish that I had learned more about life and less about abstract ideas that made a name for someone or, even, created a school but won't come to mind when my next patient gets a fatal diagnosis.

I am not trying to disparage theory. Personally, I have enjoyed it immensely and still study it. But there are countless clinical exchanges where it is not of much help. Looking back, I think the teachers that helped me most were those who lived out loud. That is, I was helped to get the feel of a self-reflective process by those who self-reflected all the time in the way they spoke to me. When a teacher could say, "No, what I just said was not what I mean," or "Let me try again. I wasn't concentrating," I learned a way of being. I learned a kind of isomorphic integrity from those who demonstrated it.

This "living out loud" is one useful tool, but not nearly enough. I don't know how we can "teach" or, perhaps, inspire courage, but I do know that it takes courage to live and to help others live. Elsewhere (Buechler, 2012), I have expressed my strong feelings about some of the ways I think we undercut the development of this courage. For one thing, if we essentially pit candidates against themselves by "teaching" them to control (the overt expression of) helpfulness, I think the most powerful effect of this is to discourage the cherishing of truth that is so essential to the clinician. Candidates are incentivized to lie, either to their supervisors or themselves or both, about natural impulses. Or, just as harmfully, they may actually deaden their wishes to be of help to the suffering human beings who come to them for treatment. I think this can "neutralize" the centered courage doing treatment depends on. That is, to be a courageous clinician requires firm resolve. Only if the clinician can approach the task with every fiber of her being can this purposeful determination be achieved. It takes all we have, all the humanity, all the compassion, all the intelligence, all the gutsy, stubborn grit. A candidate who has to hide natural feelings or who is taught they are "anti-analytic" or "countertransferential" (in a negative sense) or "pathological" (in any sense) is like a house divided.

As I see it, we undercut the development of tensile strength in the clinician when we shame him or her for being interested in helping, less engaged in learning theory than in learning about concrete situations in sessions, motivated to feel competent (which is often seen as obsessively controlling), self-sacrificing (which is often seen as masochistic), or unusually intuitive (which is often seen as grandiose or, worse, self-delusional). What I think we all have to live with is that, of course, each of these assumptions could have some truth in specific situations. But they shouldn't be assumed to be true. And, even if they have some value at times, they are never the whole story.

How do we teach people to care within a frame, help analytically, make a living without apologizing for profiting, bear the limits (and the extent) of our influence, face the sea of suffering inherent in being human without flinching (too much), and address it without (too much) reliance on our own, personal (potentially blinding) defensive maneuvers? I suppose that comfort with the contradictory is important. Here are some of the contradictions I have found clinically helpful to inhabit, out loud, in supervision *and* treatment.

1   *Post-postmodern subjectivity/objectivity*. At one and the same time, clinicians need the humility to know that we do not have any ultimate answers about how to live life, and yet we will be implored to give answers that amount to judgments about this. Patients often become adept at asking these questions in indirect enough ways to soothe the clinician's concerns about being directive. So they listen for what we question and where our focus stays, rather than directly asking whether we think they should marry Joe. Do we ask how old Joe is? Whether he has been married before? Are we more silent than usual in this session? Do we get distracted? Look distressed at the end? Forget to end on time? Patients are interpreting us at the same time as we are interpreting them. There is no way to be absolutely neutral, because our focus is inevitably selective, although we are often not conscious of some of the factors that are shaping it. And yet it is true that we owe our patients a value-free space within which to find their own answers.

2   *Our own ambivalence about being concretely helpful*. Most of the time, patients come into treatment wanting help with something that is going wrong in their lives. They don't want a better theory about how they got into their dilemma; they want help getting out of their dilemma, or they want the dilemma itself to go away. But, as I have already suggested above, many training programs communicate negative valuation of direct helpfulness and, perhaps more destructively, of supervisees' desire to help. It is seen as a defect. I am afraid that there are partially hidden prejudices that play a role in these attitudes: old prejudices against women, especially women who are mothers and women who are social workers. Those in these categories are not "intellectuals" according to these prejudices. Pathologically masochistic or narcissistic, they are deluded into believing they can (and should) save the world. This "helpfulness" stands in the way of a more long-term, analytically oriented solution. But I think it is our job to be helpful *and* thoughtful, not one or the other. That this can be hard to do does not make it wrong to try.

3   *We are entrepreneurs whose livelihood depends on caring.* I don't think most patients stay in treatment unless they feel cared about in some basic way. It is often the practitioner who feels uncomfortable with the business end of the transaction, because it seems contradictory to charge a fee for it. As I have already indicated (above), it is part of our job to live with this, among other seemingly contradictory truths. Our own discomfort with this often shows itself in anger when patients cancel sessions or don't pay on time, forcing us to directly engage with them about the practicalities. We blame the patient, because we are uncomfortable having to confront these issues squarely. If only they would be "good," we could avoid facing these aspects of our profession. Perhaps some of the discomfort comes from perceived similarities to the "oldest" profession. In any case, anger at the patient for "making" us deal with the business aspect of the work just makes these issues harder to address in treatment.

4   *We are humanistic diagnosticians.* Insurance forms require us to compartmentalize, in many senses (putting people into cubby holes, but also occupying one ourselves, in the sense that while writing the form we look through one lens and in sessions we look through another). We value and, hopefully, recognize the unique individuality of each person, and yet we are paid as experts in pattern recognition. That is, part of what we contribute to the treatment dialogue is our familiarity with what paranoia sounds like, what obsessive language says, what it is like to be in a room with someone who defends themselves narcissistically, how it feels to be the object of borderline rage, and so on. We have to see the unique and the recurrent at one and the same time.

5   *We are, ourselves, defensive, imperfect perceivers, who must rely on our perceptions.* Who among us doesn't engage in obsessive power struggles at times? Who is free from denial, repression, dissociation? Yet we have to believe in what we are seeing, feeling, and doing. We are lost without our (imperfect) instruments, which are ourselves. In Sullivan's language, we are participant observers, flawed, and yet he chose to call us "experts." Just what makes us experts? I believe it is, in part, our ability to recognize patterns. The pediatrician has seen the measles many times so is unusually quick to label it. Similarly, the clinician can spot projection with alacrity, even though he or she is not immune to its use.

6   *Like any other creative process, treatment requires an ability to express something as it is being formulated, not afterwards.* That is, the poet discovers the poem as he or she writes it. Similarly, the analyst discovers the interpretation as he or she speaks it. This is the only way the process can be truly alive, and fulfill its creative potential. But it can be very frightening to speak before we know what we will say. We could say so many "wrong" things, or so we may feel. We are not supposed to use the patient to serve our own needs (except when this also serves the treatment's needs and the patient's needs—a distinction that requires us to constantly make exquisite,

moment-by-moment judgment calls). We may well feel we should not evoke traumatizing (or re-traumatizing) anxiety, shame, and other painful feelings. We have to live with an awareness of these prohibitions while sharing thoughts spontaneously enough to keep the process alive. We have to think, and speak, on our feet, not knowing precisely where we are going, though being held responsible for progress and, as with all the other helping professions, for doing no harm. I think this takes supreme confidence in our own mainly non-hostile motivations (otherwise we wouldn't feel comfortable voicing spontaneous thoughts). It takes a firm belief that the unconscious knows the way, that is, that our own and the patient's unconscious processes will lead to good results eventually, if given reign.

How do we train people to live in a world of contradictions? I am clearer about how *not* to do this than I am about how to do it. Of course, part of this teaching is through living with contradictions ourselves and being transparent about our own struggles with them. And adequate humility is a requirement for supervisors, teachers, and all those involved in "training." Fortunately, there is much about the learning process that is conducive to humility, such as the fact that we, ourselves, are often extremely overwhelmed and bewildered while "conducting" treatments and supervisions. It can also be a source of humility to realize how much analytic "experts" don't agree about, including such basics as the goals of treatment, the most effective "therapeutic action," and so on. But, as we know, nothing guarantees that we develop adequate humility. In fact, I think it is often the case that, out of our own insecurities about trying to "pass" as experts, we adopt a superior tone. It can be very hard to maintain over the course of our careers that we feel we have something valuable to give in treatment and analytic educational processes, when we know the limitations, subjectivity, defensive aspects of our own perceptions of everything and everyone.

From my point of view, this question asks how we can nurture centered, passionate commitment to a helpful *and* reflective treatment process. How do we "educate" people to love the truth for itself, and not as a means to any end? How do we "train" clinicians to value honest self-reflection more than looking good to oneself, one's patients, supervisors, colleagues, and so on?

The only way I know runs counter to a good deal of the current analytic and wider culture. In our field and outside it, we have learned to be highly suspicious of certainties of all kinds. On a superficial level, it isn't "cool." On a deeper level, our certainties have led us into genuine trouble when, for example, we have stigmatized and pathologized people for their "unhealthy" or supposedly less than fully mature sexuality. By now, hopefully, we have embraced the attitude that all perceptions are subjective, that culture and era dictate our values, often more than we know at the time. All of this seems to me undoubtedly beneficial and true. And yet, I also feel that the fully committed clinician needs absolutes. Some unquestioned beliefs center us, drive us forward, empower us to keep going despite countless difficulties. I am persuaded that clinicians need to hang on to some personally resonant articles of faith.

Because they must be personally resonant, I can only know what some of those articles of faith are for me and not for anyone else. Perhaps the most important is the unquestionable belief that treatment can alter life, can enrich a life, and that it *is* possible to change the past by understanding it differently. I learned this most unforgettably as a patient in my own analysis. When a patient or anyone else asks me what good treatment can do, I don't need to think on the spot. I very much believe in the idea, expressed so beautifully by Victor Frankl (1946/1985), that the one human capacity that can never be taken from us is the power to give our own meanings to our life experiences. I carry within me Erich Fromm's essential message that our most fundamental choice is whether or not to choose life. I am reminded of a meaningful essay by David Brooks (2016). Brooks asks what can make young people tough enough to navigate today's world. I discussed his reflections in the introduction to this book. Briefly, Brooks believes that all of us would be fragile without a clear sense of the purpose of our lives. To become tough, we need clarity about the role we want to play in society and the commitments we want to make to specific others. For Brooks, fragility, a seemingly psychological problem, really has a philosophical answer. The resilience of the truly tough is rooted in absolute beliefs, dedication to missions, and fervent love.

So how can we help beginning clinicians develop sustaining beliefs, sufficient confidence and resolve, and an inquiring, open mind? I will make a few suggestions, but this is a question I have yet to fully answer for myself.

1   I think clinicians bring to training an (often non-conscious) assumption that their competence is demonstrated by the ability to make sense of the information about the patient. In case presentations, we reward coherence. We all like a good story, with a clean, logically connected narrative that arcs toward "progress." Implicitly, we communicate that the more adept clinician can get the treatment to unfold in this fashion and then tell a neat story about it. This does not foster comfort with the paradoxical, messy realities of life experience in general and clinical experience in particular. It is the rare beginner who can withstand the pull to make sense. No matter how much praise we may heap on the narrator of a nifty case presentation, the clinician knows that their real experience was far less measured. This does not enhance confidence at all. In fact, what I think it often breeds is the feeling of having to cover up a vague inferiority that can never be overcome, because it is too imperfectly understood. Even to formulate a question, such as "Why doesn't anything make sense to me?" would be extremely challenging and probably quite threatening to the questioner and the questioned.

2   Perhaps out of related anxieties, we tend to teach "techniques" that promise to help the clinician feel skilled. Teachers, as well as their mentees, are afraid of being or seeming fraudulent. Since our expertise is so nebulous in some ways, we are all eager to pin it down. We are questioned by patients, not to mention insurance companies, about just how we will be of help. We need to have a ready answer, as do those who invest time, effort, and money into

becoming more "trained." Partially as a result of this, we don't tend to provide courses in humanism, in life's fundamental challenges, in the wisdom of the poets, philosophical treatises on the human condition, or any of the subjects that might awaken greater awareness of the significant issues that will be raised throughout clinicians' careers and that have formed the subject matter of this book. Naturally, particularly early on, clinicians want to know what to say, what to do, how to become "legitimate," how to qualify. This makes it nearly impossible to take the time to ponder one's personal approach to life's most painful passages.

3   Related to that is the need, in institutes and other training facilities, to promote their "brand," often at the expense of profoundly curious inquiry into other ways of thinking and working. I have written extensively about institutional politics and their deleterious effects (Buechler, 2009, 2012) and will not repeat those arguments here. But it seems to me that whenever agreement and loyalty are equated, the freedom to question is curtailed, and "education" becomes a form of indoctrination.

4   Without awareness, too often we teach in binary terms. Keeping the "frame" is seen as necessarily inimical to spontaneity, just as wanting to help is regarded as antithetical to analyzing. Once again, this fosters inner conflict in supervisees and a fundamental lack of self-confidence. Fractured by competing goals, the clinician can't formulate a centered approach.

5   Along a similar line, and perhaps most significantly, we teach clinicians that the personal should be kept separate from the professional. It is, indeed, crucial that we communicate that the clinician should not impose his or her religious, political, or any other belief systems on patients. Without question, this is absolutely essential. But, to me, it is equally true that (as already noted above, and in much of my previous work) our values play inevitable roles in our focus in sessions and so many other choices. Beyond that, I think it is also necessary to bring our personally meaningful tenets to our work with our patients. My passion about life is essential to my clinical work. I can't sustain commitment without believing in what I am doing with my whole heart. Some might say we can believe in a value-free inquiry or in promoting self-reflection. There certainly is value in these ideas. I can only say that, for me, this would not be enough. I need to feel I am fighting for some things and against others. As I have written elsewhere (Buechler, 2004), when I am treating a depressed patient, I need to feel I am fighting on the side of life. And this is not just true when the patient is depressed. When I wrote about searching for a "passionate neutrality" (Buechler, 1999), I was referring to a dilemma inherent in our work. We can *never* "resolve" the dilemma of being necessarily neutral, in some senses, and necessarily full-throated advocates of a point of view about the human condition, in other senses. We have to live with this. As is often true, my point has been best expressed in a poem. The poet Gerald Stern (2016) gave me words for what I most need, in his poem "I Remember Galileo."

I remember Galileo describing the mind
as a piece of paper blown around by the wind,
and I loved the sight of it sticking to a tree,
or jumping into the back seat of a car,
and for years I watched paper leap through my cities;
but yesterday I saw the mind was a squirrel caught crossing
Route 80 between the wheels of a giant truck,
dancing back and forth like a thin leaf,
or a frightened string, for only two seconds living
on the white concrete before he got away,
his life shortened by all that terror, his head
jerking, his yellow teeth ground down to dust.
It was the speed of the squirrel and his lowness to the ground,
his great purpose, and the alertness of his dancing,
that showed me the difference between him and paper.
Paper will do in theory, when there is time
to sit back in a metal chair and study shadows;
but for this life I need a squirrel,
his clawed feet spread, his whole soul quivering,
the loud noise shaking him from head to tail.
O philosophical mind, O mind of paper, I need a squirrel
finishing his wild dash across the highway,
rushing up his green, ungoverned hillside.

(p. 115)

Note

1 Some of these ideas were presented at the International Erich Fromm Research Conference, Berlin, June 27, 2014.

References

Brooks, D. (2016, 30 August). Making modern toughness. *New York Times*, p. A21.

Buechler, S. (1999). Searching for a passionate neutrality. *Contemporary Psychoanalysis*, *35*, 213–227.

Buechler, S. (2004). *Clinical values: Emotions that guide psychoanalytic treatment.* Hillsdale, NJ: Analytic Press.

Buechler, S. (2008). *Making a difference in patients' lives.* New York: Routledge.

Buechler, S. (2009) (Ed.). Special issue on the ideal psychoanalytic institute. *Contemporary Psychoanalysis, 45*.

Buechler, S. (2010). No pain, no gain? Suffering and the analysis of defense. *Contemporary Psychoanalysis, 46*, 334–354.

Buechler, S. (2012). *Still practicing: The heartaches and joys of a clinical career.* New York: Routledge.

Buechler, S. (2015). *Understanding and treating patients in clinical psychoanalysis: Lessons from literature*. New York: Routledge.

Buechler, S. (2017). *Psychoanalytic reflections: Training and practice*. New York: IPbooks.

Davis, H. (2009). Directness in therapy. In R. Funk (Ed.), *The clinical Erich Fromm* (pp. 85–91). Amsterdam: Rodopi.

Frankl, V. (1946/1985). *Man's search for meaning*. New York: Simon and Schuster.

Fromm, E. (2009). Being *centrally* related to the patient. In R. Funk (Ed.), *The clinical Erich Fromm* (pp. 7–39). Amsterdam: Rodopi.

Fromm-Reichmann, F. (1950). *Principles of intensive psychotherapy*. Chicago: University of Chicago Press.

Funk, R. (2009). Direct meeting. In R. Funk (Ed.), *The clinical Erich Fromm* (pp. 59–70). Amsterdam: Rodopi.

Hornstein, G. A. (2000). *To redeem one person is to redeem the world: The life of Frieda Fromm-Reichmann*. New York: Free Press.

Lesser, R. M. (2009). There is nothing polite in anybody's unconscious. In R. Funk (Ed.), *The clinical Erich Fromm* (pp. 91–101). Amsterdam: Rodopi.

Schecter, D. (2009). Awakening the patient. In R. Funk (Ed.), *The clinical Erich Fromm* (pp. 73–79). Amsterdam: Rodopi.

Stern, G. (2016). I remember Galileo. In H. M. Seiden (Ed.), *The motive for metaphor* (p. 115). London: Karnac.

Sullivan, H. S. (1953). *The interpersonal theory of psychiatry*. New York: W. W. Norton.

Index

abstinence 24, 28–29, 98
abuse victims, and the unharmed self 154
adaptation 4–5, 6–9, 44; and aging 50,
    51–57; author's perspective on 13–15;
    decathecting life 57–58; as an issue in
    training 197, 199; to values of society
    170; as a way to avoid anxiety 7–8; *see
    also* adjustment
addiction 26, 167
adjustment 76–77, 161, 170; *see also*
    adaptation
adolescence, and identity 54, 117
advice-giving 194–195
Agee, James 39–41
aging 8, 50; attempts to conceal 64–65;
    and decathecting life 57–58; emotional
    coping patterns 67; fighting or adapting
    to 50, 51–57; focus on past, present or
    future 58–60; and identity 54–55, 56,
    171; and loss 55; "mind over matter"
    65–67; relationship to customs 61–62;
    and shame 62–65, 168; in short fiction
    67–68; and treatment 50, 67–70
Alexander, F. 14, 30, 99
Alexie, Sherman 37–38
alienation 109
aloneness: avoidance of 26; capacity for
    18, 25; difference from loneliness 20,
    29; non-anxious 24; nurturing capacity
    for in treatment 25–30; pathologizing
    of 20–25; and relationship 17–20;
    valorizing of 21; *see also* loneliness;
    solitude
ALS (amyotrophic lateral sclerosis;
    motor neurone disease) 171; *see also*
    Shepard, Sam
Altman, N. 97
Amichai, Y. 179

analysts: annoyance in 13–15; articles of
    faith 205–206; and burnout 105, 142,
    161; "clinical values" 69; courage of
    192; as entrepreneurs 204; as "experts"
    10, 186, 187, 204; as "good introject"
    26; as humanistic diagnosticians 204;
    and humility 136; individual treatment
    style 27, 115–116; integrity of 27, 30,
    68–69, 93; and joy 131; and loneliness
    22; and love 81–82; provision of
    holding environment for patients 25;
    relationship to work 115, 129–131;
    self-disclosure and psychological
    accessibility 23–24, 141, 146;
    separation of personal and professional
    207; superego functioning of 141;
    "vacations" from suffering 80–81;
    yearning for "techniques" 195–196,
    206–207; *see also* supervision; training
"analytic attitude" 79
Arnold, Matthew 179
Art of Loving, The (Fromm) 20, 144
atonement 156–159, 161, 162
attachment theory 25
Auden, W. H. 38–39, 77

"bad objects" 26–27
Baer, U. 21, 43, 75, 103, 111–112, 116,
    121, 129, 180
"Bartleby the Scrivener" (Melville)
    122–123
Baudelaire, C. 128
Bayley, John 38
Becker, E. 166
Beckett, Samuel 85, 176
"Being Centrally Related to the Patient"
    (Fromm) 110
Beland, Hermann 154–155, 156

Benchley, Robert 122
Bergmann, Martin 59
Bialosky, Jill 43
Bion, W. R. 92
"biophilia" 27
Bishop, Elizabeth 58–59, 173
"Blackwater Woods" (Oliver) 47–48
Bloom, Harold 81, 88, 143, 147
Bollas, Christopher 84, 129
Bowlby, J. 25
Breuer, J. 75
Bromberg, P. 23, 85, 181
Brook, Peter 157
Brooks, David 2, 3, 127, 206
Bruner, Margaret E. 153, 154
Buckley, S. 20
Buddhism 76
Burack-Weiss, Ann 52, 54, 58, 64–65, 65–66, 170–171, 178

Campbell, Joseph 57, 79
cancer 169, 170, 172
Carlyle, Thomas 128
Carver, Raymond 82–83
Casey, Nell 86–87, 167
certainty 99; see also conviction; uncertainty
Chestnut Lodge 190
children: need for parents' attention 135; see also attachment theory
"chum" 30
Civilization and Its Discontents (Freud) 121
Clinical Values (Buechler) 160–161, 193
"clinical values" 69, 161, 189, 191
clinicians see analysts
Coltart, Nina 22
Coming into the End Zone (Grumbach) 66
compassion 47; impact on shame and guilt 140–141
computers, and work 118
concentration camp survivors 66; see also Holocaust
confession 141
conflicts, in training 193–195
"consensual validation" 87
consumerism 119
contradictions, in supervision and treatment 203–205
contrast, role of in treatment 10
conviction 92, 93–95, 99; balancing with curiosity 100–102; blessing and curse of 111–113; and Fromm 93–94, 108–111;

and Fromm-Reichmann 104–108; potential for misuse 103–104
"correctional emotional experience" 14, 30, 99
countertransference 14, 80, 131, 138, 142, 200
courage, of analysts 192
craftsmen, medieval 118
creativity, and solitude 21
curiosity 92, 94, 95, 98; balancing with conviction 100–102; and resilience 79–80; and suffering 178; and work 128–129
customs, and aging 61–62

Dark, Alice Elliott 174
Davis, Harold 20, 193
Day of Atonement (Yom Kippur) 159
death: acceptance of 53–54; and aging 50; fighting 34–37; palliative care 73–74; refusal to register loss 37–41; resistance to 8, 51, 52; from shame 139; see also mourning
Death Be Not Proud (Gunther) 34–37
Death in the Family, A. (Agee) 39–41
"Death of Ivan Ilych, The" (Tolstoy) 57–58, 162–163
decathecting life 57–58
defensive patterns: and avoidance of pain 74, 75; refusal to register death 37–41; and suffering 173, 182
Denial of Death, The (Becker) 166
dependency 66–67
depression: and emotional intensity 86–87; and shame 167
desensitization 59
desire, entering sessions with/without 92
"Detail" (Grennan) 78
Dickinson, Emily 11–12, 77, 83–84, 112
Didion, Joan 38, 173
"Dilettante, The" (Mann) 124–126
"Direct Meeting" (Funk) 192
discrete emotion theory 76
dissociation 110; early experiences of 23; refusal to register death 37–41
Donley, C. 20
Douthat, Ross 166–167
"Dover Beach" (Arnold) 179
downsizing 52, 170–171
Dream (Brook) 157
Drowned and the Saved, The (Levi) 153
durability 105

"East Coker" (Eliot) 88, 176
Elegy for Iris (Bayley) 38
Eliot, T. S. 59, 62–63, 88, 129, 176
embarrassment 139
Emde, Robert 179
Emerson, Ralph Waldo 53–54
emotion theory 34, 44, 54, 60, 79,
    128–129, 161, 179
emotional balance, and suffering 178–180
emotional intensity 4–6, 9–10; and aging
    50; aiming to decrease in mourning
    43–46; as an issue in training 197, 199;
    author's perspective on 13–15; and
    decathecting life 57–58; fear of 85–86;
    and resilience 85–87
emotional strength 2
emotions: and aging 67; as
    communications to ourselves 44;
    "correctional emotional experience"
    14, 30, 99; hierarchical beliefs about
    150–151; modulation of by concurrent
    emotions 34, 44
empathy 107–108, 193
enactments 23, 99, 177
equipment for living 55, 93, 103, 120, 168
Erikson, E. 60, 117
Erlich, H. Shmuel 154–155, 156
Erlich-Ginor, Mira 154–155, 156
Escape from Freedom *(Fromm)* 120
Essays after Eighty (Hall) 63–64, 66
"even hovering" 99, 163
exceptions 136, 138, 152–153
eye contact 192

"Factors Leading to Patient's Change in
    Analytic Treatment" (Fromm) 110
Fairbairn, W. R. D. 23
"fake it 'til you make it" approach to
    resilience 73, 76, 78
Farber, Leslie 142
Fasting Girl (Stacey) 144
Fed with Tears-Poisoned with Milk
    (Erlich, Erlich-Ginor and Beland)
    154–155, 156
Feeling it Enough (Buechler) 163
Ferenczi, Sándor 190, 191
Ferro, Antonino 129
Fisher, M. F. K. 64–65
Fitzhenry, R. I. 124, 128
"fixedness" 94–95
focus: shift in 78–79; in treatment session 15
forgetting, and forgiving 150

forgiving 149–150; arguments against as
    inherently healthy 154–156; arguments
    for as inherently healthy 150–154;
    author's odyssey 159–163; in the
    clinical context 156–159, 163–164;
    forgiving life 85, 182; and resilience
    84; terms and conditions 150; for whose
    benefit 150
formal authority 95–96
"found wanting" 63–64
Frankel, Esther 135, 140–141, 144,
    146–147, 158, 159
Frankl, Victor 66, 181, 206
freedom, and aging 61–62
Freud, Anna 29, 99, 163
Freud, S. 75, 85, 128, 136, 137, 138, 152;
    on melancholia 46; on mourning 33–34,
    36, 45, 46; on work 121
Freudian analysis, attitudes to solitude in 22
Friedman, Thomas L. 95–96
Fromm, Erich 6–7, 20, 27, 76–77, 89,
    97, 112, 123, 129, 142, 144, 147, 159,
    160–161, 170, 181, 182, 190, 201,
    206; on alienation 109; and conviction
    93–94, 108–111; definition of treatment
    10–11; influence on author's training
    191–193; and moral authority 96; and
    self-realization 117–118, 119 120; on
    social character 120–121, 122, 182
Fromm-Reichmann, Frieda 25–26,
    27–28, 29, 112, 158; and conviction
    104–108; influence on author's training
    189–191
Frost, R. 116–117
"Funeral Blues" (Auden) 39
Funk, Rainer 118, 119, 192
future, the, and aging 59–60

Galen 128
Garson, Barbara 118
generativity, and aging 60
Gilligan, James 137
Going Sane: Maps of Happiness
    (Phillips) 101
Goldstein, Kurt 189–190
"good objects" 26–27, 30
*Greatness and Limitations of Freud's
    Thought* (Fromm) 108
Green, André 80
Green, Hannah 27–28
Greenberg, J. R. 23, 27–28, 105–108, 158
Grennan, Eamon 78

grief *see* mourning; suffering
"Grief Calls Us to the Things of This World" (Alexie) 37–38
Groddeck, Georg 190
"Grudge and the Hysteric" (Khan) 150
Grumbach, Doris 66
guilt 136; absence of, and shame 137–138; *versus* shame 138–143; working with 144–147
Gunther, Francis 34–37
Gunther, John 34–37

Hall, Donald 63–64, 66
Handbook of Interpersonal Psychoanalysis (Schlesinger) 22
happiness, inner and outer 125
Hass, Robert 12
hatred 136, 156
health: assumptions about 20; conceptions of 3; implicit assumptions about in relational theory 22–24
Henry V (Shakespeare) 151
Heresy of Self-Love, The (Zweig) 143
"Heroic Simile" (Hass) 12
Hilgers, Laura 167
Hirsch, Edward 11–12, 88
history-taking 101–102, 187, 188
Hitler, Adolf 7
Hoffman, Eva 84, 130
Hoffman, I. Z. 30, 92
holding environment, analysts' provision of for patients 25
Hollis, J. 170
"hollow" people 77, 170
Holocaust 84, 180, 181, 190; responses to 154–155, 156
homosexuality 6, 76, 96, 110
hope: Emily Dickinson's poem on 11–12; inspiration of 105–106; and suffering 170, 178
Hope and Dread in Psychoanalysis (Mitchell) 100
Hornstein, Gail 158, 189, 191
Horwitz, A. V. 45
"House at the End of the World, The" (Mooallem) 73–74, 163
Howe, Marie 42–43, 46–48
Hubbard, Elburt 119
human functioning, immutable laws in 7
humiliation 136; and shame 136, 138; and violence 137, 138
Humiliation (Koestenbaum) 138

humility 66, 107, 135–138, 146
humor, and aging 66
hysteria 94, 98, 142

I Never Promised You a Rose Garden (Greenberg) 27–28, 105–108
"I want to Live" (Jones) 172–173
identity: and adolescence 54, 117; and aging 54–55, 56, 171; and suffering 171–174, 181; and work 117
"In the Gloaming" (Dark) 174
"In the Waiting Room" (Bishop) 173
individual character 120; *see also* social character
individual responsibility 155
inner world, and aging 59
institutional "brands" 207
integrity 117, 118; of analysts 27, 30, 68–69, 93
"internal chorus" 7, 81, 110, 141–142, 201
Interpersonal psychoanalysis 22, 23, 24, 25, 76, 100, 112, 155, 185, 187
Interpersonal Theory of Psychiatry, The (Sullivan) 186
invisibility, and aging 58
Izard, C. 62, 179

James, Henry 51–52
James, William 15
Jewish tradition: mysticism 135; Passover Seder 152–153; Yom Kippur (Day of Atonement) 159
Jones, Thom 172–173
Joseph, J. 61
joy: and analysts 131; and suffering 179–180, 181
Joyce, James 88

Kalanithi, Paul 170, 175, 182–183
Keats, John 112
Kendall, Tim 117
Kenyon, Jane 64
Khan, Masud 150
kindness, importance of in treatment 141
King Lear (Shakespeare) 41, 81, 82, 123, 127, 142–143, 147, 151
Knight, G. Wilson 81, 147
knowing, and love in psychoanalysis 81–82
Koestenbaum, W. 138
Kreuzer-Haustein, Ursula 155
Krystal, Henry 178

Lazare, Aaron 136
"'Lear' Universe, The" (Knight) 147
Lerner, M. 55–56
Lesser, Ruth M. 192
"Let Me Not to the Marriage of True
    Minds" (Shakespeare) 19
Letters to a Young Poet (Rilke) 17, 18
Levenson, Edgar 23, 78, 100, 187
Levi, Primo 153
Levine, Philip 127
life: forgiveness of 85, 152; loving anyway
    19, 149; object constancy towards 19
life force of patients, belief in 107
Lindsay-Abaire, D. 77
Lioness in Winter, The (Burack-Weiss) 54
"Little Selves" (Lerner) 55–56
logical positivism 2, 3, 93, 98
loneliness 22; and analysts 22; in company
    of another 12; definition 20; difference
    from aloneness 20, 29; optimum level
    of in treatment 25; *see also* aloneness;
    solitude
loss: and aging 55; of memory 58, 84,
    172, 173; practicing of 58–59; *see also*
    mourning
Loss of Sadness, The (Horwitz &
    Wakefield) 45
love: and analysts 81–82; Davis's
    definition 20; Fromm's definition 20;
    and knowing in psychoanalysis 81–82;
    meanings of 177; and suffering 179,
    181, 182–183; Sullivan's definition
    20; therapeutic power of 147; *see also*
    relationship
Love in the Time of Cholera (Marquez) 38
"Love Song of J. Alfred Prufrock, The"
    (Eliot) 62–63

Maccoby, Michael 111, 119–120
Mairs, Nancy 58, 178
Making a Difference in Patients' Lives
    (Buechler) 161
"Management of Grief, The" (Mukherjee)
    44, 169–170
Mann, Thomas 124–126
Marcus, P. 117, 129
"marketing character" 77, 170
Marquez, G. G. 38
materialism 119
May, Rollo 45, 76, 77, 97, 170
"me-you" patterns 94
melancholia 46

Melville, H. 122–123
memory: entering sessions with/without
    92; healing power of remembering 84;
    loss of 58, 84, 172, 173
Merchant of Venice, The (Shakespeare)
    151–152
"Middle Years, The" (James) 51–52
Midsummer Night's Dream, A
    (Shakespeare) 157
Miller, B. J. 73–74, 75–76, 78, 80, 163, 181
Mills, C. Wright 118, 128
Milton, J. 144
"mind over matter" 65–67
"Misery Filter, The" (Douthat) 166–167
Mitchell, Stephen, A. 96, 100
modeling, in treatment 141–142, 144–145
Mohacsy, I. 25
"moments of being" 88
Mooallem, Jan 73–74, 163
moral authority 95–98
mother figure: and the capacity for solitude
    18; *see also* attachment theory
mourning 5, 33; adaptation to loss 33;
    clinical approach 46–48; decreasing
    intensity of 43–46; dwelling on details
    41–43; fighting death 33–37; refusal to
    register loss 37–41; and regret 33–34;
    "work" of 34, 43, 45
"Mourning and Melancholia" (Freud) 36
Moyers, Bill 79
"Mrs. Cross and Mrs. Kidd" (Munro) 67, 172
Mukherjee, Bharati 44, 169–170
Munro, Alice 67, 172
Murdoch, Iris 38
"Musée des Beaux Arts" (Auden) 38–39
*My Mother's Eyes: Holocaust Memories of
    a Young Girl* (Ornstein) 84, 180
Mystery of Things, The (Bollas) 84
myth, functions of 57

narcissism 94, 98, 126, 127, 144, 146; and
    countertransference 142; and exceptions
    152; *see also* "Dilettante, The" (Mann)
Nature, and suffering 180
"negative capability" 112
neutrality 2, 5–6, 23–24, 28–29, 93, 98;
    author's odyssey 159–163; "even
    hovering" 99, 163
"now moments" 88

object constancy 19
object relational theory 23

objectivity: post-postmodern subjectivity/
   objectivity 203
observation 101, 102–103
obsession 94, 98, 127
Oedipus 19, 149, 196
Oliver, Mary 47–48, 178
On Being Human (Funk) 118
"On Love" (Phillips) 81
"One Art" (Bishop) 58–59
one genus postulate 109, 186
open-mindedness 94
Orange, Donna 97, 167, 173, 181
Ornstein, Anna 84
Ornstein, Paul 180
"other-directedness" 77, 170
others, avoidance of 26
outliers 122

Paradise Lost (Milton) 144
paranoia 29, 94, 95, 98
parents, children's need for attention from 135
past, the, and aging 58–59
Pathways to Bliss (Campbell) 57
patients: analysts' provision of holding
   environment for 25; belief in life force
   of 107; clinicians' "education" of 1–2;
   usefulness of "analytical attitude" for 79
pattern recognition 56
Penfield, Wilder 35
persecutory anxiety 26
perseverance 106–107
Phillips, Adam 3, 74, 81, 98, 101, 129
phobic way of coping 127
"Plea for Tolerance" (Bruner) 153, 154
"poetic crossing" 88
poetry, transformative power of 11
post-Freudian analysis, attitudes to
   solitude in 22
post-postmodern subjectivity/objectivity 203
pride 139; and self-love 143–144; working
   with 144–147
Principles of Intensive Psychotherapy
   (Fromm-Reichmann) 27, 105, 190
prisoner of war survivors 25–26
"pro-adaptation" clinicians 9–10
projection 56
projective identification 108
psychoanalysis: knowing and love in
   81–82; *see also* analysts; treatment
*Psychoanalysis and Psychotherapy:
   Selected Papers* (Fromm-Reichmann)
   27, 105

Psychoanalysis and Religion (Fromm) 6–7
puppet show 99
purpose, sense of 146, 206; and aging
   57–58; and capacity for aloneness
   26; of Fromm-Reichmann 191; and
   generativity 60; in living 2; and
   suffering 178, 181

Queen for a Day 166

"Rabbit Hole" (Lindsay-Abaire) 77
Rank, Otto 124
reframing 78
regression 23, 102
regret 33–34, 52
Reik, Theodor 12
relational theory 25; implicit assumptions
   about health in 22–24
relationship: and aloneness 17–20;
   avoidance of 26; capacity for 24;
   nurturing capacity for in treatment
   25–30; valorizing of 20–25; *see also* love
religion, and forgiveness 151
"Remember Galileo" (Stern) 207–208
remembering, healing power of 84
repression 110
resilience 2, 3, 73–74, 161, 206; cognitive
   sources of 78–79; and emotional
   intensity 85–87; emotional sources
   of 79–81; "fake it 'til you make it"
   approach 73, 76, 78; and healthy
   suffering 74–77; interpersonal sources
   of 81–84; resistances to 84–85; and
   verbal formulation 87–90
"response biases" 3
retirement 70
Richard III (Shakespeare) 137
Rilke, R. M. 17, 18, 21, 30, 43–44, 75, 103,
   111–112, 116, 118, 121, 123, 129, 180
*Ritual and Spontaneity in the
   Psychoanalytical Process* (Hoffman)
   92, 130
Rosenbaum, Ron 151, 157

Sacred Therapy (Frankel) 140, 146–147
Safer, Jeanne 150, 151, 154, 156, 157, 158
Sane Society, The (Fromm) 118
Schachtel, E. 128
Schafer, R. 79
Schecter, David E. 140, 192
schizoid ways of coping 94, 98, 127
Schlesinger, G. 22

Schoen, S. 96
Schulz, Johannes Heinrich 190
"Searching for a Passionate Neutrality"
    (Buechler) 160
secondary gains 104
secure attachment 25, 29
Seiden, M. 112–113
self, sense of 54, 181
self-esteem 67, 146
self-love 56; and capacity for aloneness
    26; and love for the other 20; and pride
    143–144
self-recognition 54
self-respect 146
self-sufficiency 67
self-worth 140
sexuality: and aging 58; homosexuality 6,
    76, 96, 110
Shakespeare, W. 19, 26, 41, 81, 82, 123,
    127, 137, 142–143, 147, 151–152, 157
Shakespeare through the Ages (Bloom) 81
shame 136; and absence of guilt 137–138;
    and aging 62–65, 168; death from 139;
    versus guilt 138–143; and humiliation
    136, 138; and suffering 166, 167;
    and violence 137, 138; working with
    144–147
Shepard, Sam 171, 176–177
shift in focus 78–79
significant material, availability of
    102–103
silence 89–90
Sinatra, Frank 56, 181
Singer, E. 24, 100, 115
Slochower, Joyce 22–24, 100–101
"Small, Good Thing, A" (Carver) 82–83
social character 120–121, 122, 182
Social Character in a Mexican Village
    (Fromm & Maccoby) 111
solitary confinement 25–26
solitude: capacity for 24; definition 20;
    pathologizing of 20–25; and relationship
    17–18; see also aloneness; loneliness
Solitude: A Return to the Self (Storr) 21
"Some Character Types Met with in
    Psychoanalytical Work" (Freud) 152
spontaneity, and ritual 92, 130
"spots of time" 88
Spy of the First Person (Shepard) 171,
    176–177
Stacey, Michelle 144
Stern, Donnel 23, 88, 97, 134

Stern, Gerald 207–208
Stevens, Wallace 112
Still Practicing (Buechler) 161
Storr, Anthony 21, 22
Stringer, Lee 86–87
structural change 141
subjectivity: awareness of 100–102; post-
    postmodern subjectivity/objectivity 203
sublimation 120–121, 122, 182
suffering 166–169, 180–183; attitudes
    to adaptation to 168, 169–171; and
    compassion 47; connection with
    other sufferers 82–83; and emotional
    balance 168, 178–180; healthy
    74–77; and identity 171–174, 181; as
    an inevitability to be accepted 9, 45, 75,
    168; as a pain to be quickly reduced 9,
    45, 74, 75, 168; and shame 166, 167;
    as a source of personal identity 9, 45,
    75, 168; "vacations" from 80–81, 182;
    verbal formulation 169, 174–178
Sullivan, H. S. 6, 7–8, 10, 11, 20, 23, 30,
    55, 56, 76, 87, 93, 94, 96, 101, 102,
    103, 112, 123, 137, 141, 142, 144, 156,
    170, 176, 190, 201, 204; influence on
    author's training 185–189; one genus
    postulate 109, 186; potential for misuse
    of conviction 103–104; on sublimation
    120–121, 122
supervision 81; and conflicts in training
    193–195; contradictions in 203–205;
    see also analysts
Swamplands of the Soul: New Life in
    Dismal Places (Hollis) 170
Szalita, Alberta 192

Taylor, Richard 45, 144
"techniques," analysts' yearning for
    195–196, 206–207
technology: and parents' attention to
    children 135; and work 118
Tempest, The (Shakespeare) 151, 152
termination phase 187–188
"Terminus" (Emerson) 53–54
theory, and training 200–201, 202
Thomas, D. 8, 51, 52
Tillich, Paul 20
Tolstoy, L. 57–58, 162–163
training 6; author's experience of 185–193;
    cognitive, emotional, and interpersonal
    elements 200; conflicts in 193–195;
    helping clinicians develop as therapeutic

instruments 193–208; and institutional "brands" 207; and theory 200–201, 202; *see also* analysts
transference 29, 78, 131, 188, 196
treatment: and aging 50, 67–70; contradictions in 203–205; empathy in 107–108, 193; as an expert-client relationship 10; goals of 109; and humility 135–138; importance of kindness in 141; modeling in 141–142, 144–145; and mourning 46–48; mutative factor in 23, 30
truth, allegiance to 106
Truth and Reconciliation Commission 155
Tutu, Desmond M. 155
"Two Tramps in Mud Time" (Frost) 116–117

uncertainty 92–93, 95, 99, 112–113; *see also* conviction
unharmed self 154
Unholy Ghost (Casey) 86–87, 167
United States, culture of 112, 119–120, 154, 167, 186
"Unknown Citizens" (Auden) 77
Unnamable, The (Beckett) 176

"vacations" from suffering 80–81, 182
Vaillant, G. 60
Valentine, Jean 43
values, clinical 69, 161, 189, 191
Vendler, H. 12
verbal formulation 4–5, 10–13; and aging 50; author's perspective on 13–15; costs of 89–90; downside of 13; as an issue in training 197, 199; and mourning 47–48; and resilience 87–90; and suffering 174–178
Vietnam War veterans 185–186
Virtue Ethics (Taylor) 45

Wake, N. 76
Wakefield, J. C. 45

"Warning" (Joseph) 61
"What I Do Not Like in Contemporary Society" (Fromm) 118
"What the Living Do" (Howe) 42–43, 46–48
"What Work Is" (Levine) 127
What's Normal? (Donley & Buckley) 20
When Breath Becomes Air (Kalanithi) 170, 175, 182–183
"When Death Comes" (Oliver) 178
"When in Disgrace with Fortune and Men's Eyes" (Shakespeare) 82
"When You Are Old" (Yeats) 52–53
Whitman, Walt 59
Wilbur, Richard 139
William Alanson White Institute 187, 193
Winnicott, D. W. 18, 24, 25, 26, 29, 30, 81, 129, 137, 174
Winter's Tale, The (Shakespeare) 151
Wolstein, Benjamin 23, 24, 97
women, and aging 64–65
Woolf, Virginia 88
words: costs of 89–90; and suffering 174–178; transformative power of 11–12, 88; *see also* verbal formulation
Wordsworth, W. 88
work 115–116; analyst's relationship to 115, 129–131; as a calling 123–124; psychic functions of 116–129; as self-realization 116–120; as social adaptation 120–123; as source of self-respect 124–126; as source of structure 127; as therapeutic 127–129

Year of Magical Thinking, The (Didion) 38, 173
Yeats, W.B. 52–53
Yom Kippur (Day of Atonement) 159
young adults 127, 206

Zen Hospice Guest House 73–74
Zimmer, Heinrich 79
Zweig, Paul 143, 144